STUDY GUIDE

Social Psychology

STUDY GUIDE

Fred Whitford
Montana State University

Social Psychology

Fifth Edition

Sharon S. Brehm
Ohio University

Saul M. Kassin
Williams College

Steven Fein
Williams College

HOUGHTON MIFFLIN COMPANY   **BOSTON**   **NEW YORK**

Senior Sponsoring Editor: Kerry T. Baruth
Associate Editor: Sara Wise
Editorial Assistant: Nirmal Trivedi
Project Editor: Angma Jhala
Executive Marketing Manager: Ros Kane
Senior Manufacturing Coordinator: Priscilla Bailey

Printed in the U.S.A.

ISBN: 0-618-12981-2

23456789-POO-05 04 03 02

Contents

PART II   SOCIAL INFLUENCE

PART III   SOCIAL INTERACTION

PART IV   APPLYING SOCIAL PSYCHOLOGY

To the Student

Students often ask us for ideas or tips about how best to study for their social psychology quizzes or exams. Some worry that because there are so many important concepts and findings reported in the textbook, and because the field of social psychology covers such a diverse set of topics, there is no way they can learn them all. They worry that they will confuse concepts that seem similar but have subtle, yet important, differences. They want to know not only on *what* they should focus, but also *how* they should study. We emphasize to these students the importance of doing three things: (1) try to organize the material so that you understand "the big picture" and can see which details are most important toward this end; (2) take an active approach to learning in which you test yourself, put concepts into your own words, etc.; and (3) always ask yourself *why* – *why* this theory predicts what it does, *why* this study found what it did and not something else, *why* this principle is thought to tie together the theory and research so well, and so on.

We have designed this *Study Guide* with these three goals in mind. The material in this guide is designed to help you organize the material and identify the details that are most important in shaping "the big picture," to give you opportunities to take an active approach in your studying by providing various exercises, and to offer explanations for the practice questions that emphasize *why* the answers are correct – and why others are *not* correct.

This *Study Guide* is designed to accompany *Social Psychology*, Fifth Edition, by Sharon Brehm, Saul Kassin, and Steven Fein. If followed properly, the materials and exercises found in this guide will not only increase your mastery of the concepts, ideas, and facts found in the textbook, but also enhance your ability to "show what you know" on exams covering material from the textbook.

For every chapter in your textbook, there is a corresponding chapter in the *Study Guide*. Each of these chapters is divided into four major sections: Learning Objectives, Major Concepts: The Big Picture, Key Term Exercise, and a Practice Quiz which itself is divided into Multiple-Choice Questions (along with answers to these questions and explanations for why the correct answers are correct and why the alternative answers are not) and Essay Questions (along with sample essays). These sections are designed to enhance your comprehension of the material in the textbook – each in a different way.

LEARNING OBJECTIVES: GUIDELINES FOR STUDY

The Learning Objectives section that begins each *Study Guide* chapter provides you with an explicit and thorough list of the most important ideas and points of each textbook chapter. A student who masters a chapter's Learning Objectives can be confident that he or she has a thorough understanding of the most important material in the textbook chapter. These Learning Objectives provide you with a detailed road map that points toward command of the material. Keep them in mind as you study the chapters.

Note that page numbers locating the relevant material in the textbook are included next to each objective. Ideally, these objectives should be read *after* you have read the corresponding textbook chapter once, but *before* you read the chapter a second time. The use of these Learning Objectives as a guide for studying will help you organize your studying and make the most of your time.

MAJOR CONCEPTS: THE BIG PICTURE

The learning of complex material is best enhanced not by focusing on details but by understanding how those details fit into the general principles. So, where the Learning Objectives provide you with the important details of the corresponding textbook chapter, the Major Concepts section of each *Study Guide* chapter is provided to help you see where these details fit in "the big picture" of the textbook chapter. For each chapter, therefore, we have provided a summary of the basic issues and principles that organize the chapter. You should know these issues and principles well as they will help you put the more specific details in context, thus improving both your overall understanding of these details and your chances of recalling them successfully when tested later.

KEY TERM EXERCISE: THE CONCEPTS YOU SHOULD KNOW

The Learning Objectives and the Major Concepts sections of each *Study Guide* chapter are designed to help you learn and study the material. The Key Term Exercise and the Practice Quiz are designed to show you, in part, how well you know your stuff. By actually doing these exercises, rather than reading and rereading the material, you will not only improve your comprehension and ability to recall the material but also receive feedback that indicates what you need to spend more time studying. In short, you will use your time more efficiently and wisely.

A clear understanding of the key terms from each chapter is essential. If the authors of the textbook think that these terms are important enough to be highlighted in **bold** and defined in the margins of the textbook and in the glossary, then it's a good bet that your instructor will expect you to know them. The Key Term Exercise in each *Study Guide* chapter is designed to help you study these terms and concepts, and to provide you with a way to test your understanding of them. All of the key terms highlighted in bold in the corresponding textbook chapter are included in the Key Term Exercise.

The Key Term Exercise can be done in one of several different ways, depending on your ambition and the kinds of tests your instructor gives. The simplest way is to treat it like a matching test. That is, try to match each term from the exercise to its textbook definition. But a more complete way of doing the exercise – the method that should promote the deepest understanding – is to take each of the key terms and concepts listed first in the exercise and define them *in your own words*. Challenging yourself to explain these terms in your own words is an excellent way to study, allowing you to find out how well you *really* know them. Once you have defined these terms in your own words, try to match each one to the textbook definitions that are provided. Note how your own definitions compare to the textbook definitions. Are they very similar? Or do these comparisons reveal that you were a bit confused about the meaning of some of these terms? Yet another way to do this exercise is a compromise between the other two ways. That is, define as many terms as you can, and simply try to match the rest of the terms with the corresponding textbook definitions.

PRACTICE QUIZ

The best test of your knowledge of the chapter is to take the Practice Quiz. The Practice Quiz is designed to give you experience with the kinds of questions that are likely to appear on an exam. Thus, we have included multiple-choice questions as well as essay questions in each Practice Quiz. Some of the multiple-choice questions concern factual or conceptual information stated in the textbook; others ask you to *apply* the theories, concepts, and research findings to some practical problem or situation. The multiple-choice questions and the essay questions pose a diverse set of challenges, sometimes asking you to differentiate one concept from another, sometimes asking you to distinguish the predictions of one theory from another, and sometimes asking you to apply your knowledge of social psychological research to predict how people would respond in particular situations. Thus, these questions require a fine-tuned understanding of ideas, terms, and facts in social psychology.

This *Study Guide* is rather unusual in that it not only gives the correct answers to the multiple-choice questions contained in the Practice Quiz, but it also *explains* these answers. That is, in the answer section, we repeat the question (so you won't have to flip pages back and forth constantly), identify the correct answer, and explain *why* that response is the best way to answer the question. In addition, we also explain why the other choices are incorrect, with special attention to alternative responses that *seem* to be appropriate answers but in actuality are not. Because we knew these explanations would be included, we did not hesitate to make many of these questions rather challenging; that is, we often included several possible answers to a question that appear to be plausible. By reading our explanations as to why one response is correct and the others are incorrect, you will have a much more comprehensive understanding of the material.

This *Study Guide* is also somewhat unusual in that it provides brief sample essays to illustrate how to answer the essay questions. We do not want you to consider these sample essays as the *only* way to answer the essay questions; rather, they are included to provide you with examples of good answers. For even more practice writing short essays concerning the material in the chapter, you may wish to return to the Learning Objectives at the start of each *Study Guide* chapter and treat them as essay questions.

If you achieve all of the Learning Objectives, understand the Major Concepts, and perform well in the Key Term Exercises and Practice Quizzes, you can be confident that you have a solid command of the material in the textbook. Remember, however, that learning the material in this guide is not a substitute for a careful reading of the textbook or thorough preparation for an exam. The *Study Guide* cannot begin to cover the breadth of concepts, theories, and research findings discussed in the textbook. But it will prepare you well for the kinds of questions you're likely to encounter on a test. That, in turn, should help you master this course in social psychology.

I would like to thank Steven Fein and Steven Spencer for their substantial contributions to earlier editions of this *Study Guide*.

Fred Whitford
Montana State University

1

Introduction

LEARNING OBJECTIVES: GUIDELINES FOR STUDY

You should be able to do each of the following by the conclusion of Chapter 1.

1. Define social psychology. Identify the kinds of questions that social psychologists try to answer. (*pp. 5-8*)

2. Explain how social psychology differs from sociology and other fields of psychology. Explain how social psychological findings may be distinguished from common sense. (*pp. 8-11*)

3. Describe the early origins of social psychology and the state of the field up until 1950. Identify when the field of social psychology became a separate field of study, who the founders are considered to be, and the incident that inspired interest in and shaped the field of social psychology. Explain the contributions made by Allport, Sherif, and Lewin. (*pp. 11-15*)

4. Describe the state of social psychology from the 1960s to the mid-1970s, and from the mid-70s to the 1990s. Explain what it means to characterize social psychology as "pluralistic." (*pp. 15-17*)

5. Distinguish between social psychological perspectives that emphasize "hot" versus "cold" approaches to understanding human behavior. Define social cognition. Summarize the increasing effort in social psychology to develop an international and multicultural perspective. (*pp. 17-19*)

6. Explain how social psychology incorporates biological, evolutionary, and sociocultural perspectives of human behavior. Describe the role of new technologies such as, PET and fMRI, on social behavior. (*p. 19*)

MAJOR CONCEPTS: THE BIG PICTURE

Below are three basic issues or principles that organize Chapter 1. You should know these issues and principles well.

1. Social psychology is the scientific study of the way individuals think, feel, and behave in regard to other people and how individuals' thoughts, feelings, and behaviors are affected by other people. Social psychology often emphasizes the power of the situation in affecting people. Social psychology can be distinguished from other disciplines, including sociology, clinical psychology, personality psychology, and cognitive psychology, however, social psychology overlaps with each of these disciplines as well. Social psychology may at first appear to be common sense, but common sense often makes contradictory claims and many of the findings in social psychology would not be predicted by common sense.

1

2. Social Psychology has a relatively brief history. Early social psychology began in the late 1800s with research by Triplett on how the presence of others affects performance, and the field took root as several textbooks were written on social psychology in the early 1900s. From the 1930s to 1950s the field grew quickly as it tried to understand the horrors of World War II and Nazi Germany. Kurt Lewin was a particularly important figure who fled Nazi Germany for the United States during this period. The 1960s and early 1970s saw a rise in confidence and expansion of the field, but also a time of questioning and debate. The late 1970s to the 1990s saw the birth of a new subfield, social cognition, and greater international and cultural perspectives in social psychology.

3. As we begin a new century it appears that there will be several important new emphases in social psychology. The integration of emotion, motivation, and cognition, biological and evolutionary perspectives, sociocultural perspectives, and new technologies are all likely to shape the field in the near future.

KEY TERM EXERCISE: THE CONCEPTS YOU SHOULD KNOW

Below are all of the key terms that appear in **boldface** in Chapter 1. To help you better understand these concepts, rather than just memorize them, write a definition for each term in your own words. After doing so, look at the next section where you'll find a list of definitions from the textbook for each of the key terms presented in random order. For each of your definitions, find the corresponding textbook definition. Note how your definitions compare with those from the textbook.

Key Terms

1. social psychology

2. cross-cultural research

3. interactionist perspective

4. behavioral genetics

5. evolutionary psychology

6. social cognition

7. multicultural research

8. social neuroscience

Textbook Definitions

a. The study of how people perceive, remember, and interpret information about themselves and others.

b. A subfield of psychology that uses the principles of evolution to understand human social behavior.

c. The scientific study of how individuals think, feel, and behave in regard to other people and how individuals' thoughts, feelings, and behaviors are affected by other people.

d. Research designed to compare and contrast people of different cultures.

e. A subfield of psychology that examines the role of genetic factors on behavior.

f. Research designed to examine racial and ethnic groups within cultures.

g. An emphasis on how both an individual's personality and environmental characteristics influence behavior.

h. The study of the relationship between neural and social processes.

ANSWERS FOR KEY TERM EXERCISE

Each of the key terms listed below is followed by the letter of the textbook definition that matches it.

1. social psychology   **c**   5. evolutionary psychology   **b**
2. cross-cultural research   **d**   6. social cognition   **a**
3. interactionist perspective   **g**   7. multicultural research   **f**
4. behavioral genetics   **e**   8. social neuroscience   **h**

PRACTICE QUIZ: TEST YOUR KNOWLEDGE OF THE CHAPTER

Multiple-Choice Questions

1. Kurt and Ernest both study human behavior. Kurt is a social psychologist, and Ernest is a journalist. Based on the definition of social psychology, one can assume that an important difference between Kurt and Ernest is likely to be that

   a. Kurt uses statistics, whereas Ernest does not.
   b. Kurt uses the scientific method to study people, whereas Ernest does not.
   c. Kurt studies various groups of people, whereas Ernest studies various individuals.
   d. Kurt is interested in how people behave toward each other, whereas Ernest is interested in people's attitudes toward each other.

2. Betty is a psychologist who specializes in neuroscience. Betty studies the effects that drinking alcohol has on the brain. Carmen is a social psychologist, and also is interested in the effects of alcohol. Compared to Betty, Carmen is *more* likely to

   a. apply the principles of the scientific method in her research on alcohol.
   b. examine the effects of alcohol from an applied research perspective.
   c. conduct experiments on the effects of alcohol.
   d. focus on the effects of alcohol on social behavior.

3.   One major difference between social psychologists and sociologists is that social psychologists tend to focus on _____ while sociologists tend to focus on _____.

   a.   prejudice; culture
   b.   aggression; violence
   c.   the individual level; the group level
   d.   social cognition; political attitudes

4.   Social psychology started to become established as a distinct field of study

   a.   in the late seventeenth century.
   b.   in the late eighteenth century and early nineteenth century.
   c.   in the late nineteenth century and early twentieth century.
   d.   in the mid-1950s.

5.   Which of the following is *least* consistent with the ideas of Kurt Lewin?

   a.   Behavior is a function of the person and the environment.
   b.   Social psychologists should concentrate on basic research rather than on applied research, which represents the "selling out" of social psychology.
   c.   Social psychologists should integrate research from personality psychology into their own theories and research.
   d.   The behavior of different people may vary even if they are placed in the exact same social situation.

6.   Personality psychologists are generally *more* interested than social psychologists in

   a.   how people think, feel, and behave.
   b.   understanding the underlying causes of behavior.
   c.   the scientific approach to psychology.
   d.   differences between individuals that are stable across situations.

7.   Susan's research emphasizes cognition. Much of her research focuses on how people's thoughts affect their behavior. Susan's research may be said to be

   a.   a "cold" approach.
   b.   a meta-analysis.
   c.   an interactionist approach.
   d.   high in external validity.

8.   Constantine and Mahboud are interested in social cognition. Therefore, they should be most inclined to conduct a study in which

   a.   personality factors are combined with social factors.
   b.   people's interpretations of information about other people are examined.
   c.   the level of analysis is the social group, rather than the individual.
   d.   an applied, rather than a basic, approach is taken.

9. The German immigrant who made a major contribution to the development of social psychology by helping to establish principles like "behavior is a function of the interaction between the person and the environment" was

   a. Allport.
   b. Dollard.
   c. Bandura.
   d. Lewin.

10. In the 1960s and early 1970s social psychology experienced a period of

   a. expansion and debate.
   b. introspection and stagnation.
   c. pluralism and development.
   d. foundation and reform.

11. Asch, Festinger, and Heider were three influential theorists of the 1950s that developed basic theories about

   a. attraction and aggression.
   b. attitudes and person perception.
   c. the self and health.
   d. helping and business.

12. A study illustrating the power of the situation to affect people's perceptions of who won a debate (Fein et al., 2001) found that people's perceptions were more affected by _____ what was said than by _____ what was said.

   a. the content of; other people's reactions to
   b. other people's reactions to; the content of
   c. the emotional tone of; the elegance of
   d. the humor of; the persuasiveness of

13. Leroy is a social psychologist and Barney is a clinical psychologist. If they both study aggression Leroy is *more* likely than Barney to

   a. examine the situational determinants of aggression in an experiment.
   b. develop therapeutic techniques to control people's aggression.
   c. develop theories about what leads people to be aggressive.
   d. develop a questionnaire to measure which people are most likely to be aggressive.

14. Many of the strong disagreements that occurred during the period of "Confidence and Crisis" were a reaction to the predominant use of

   a. archival methods.
   b. unobtrusive measures.
   c. the interactionist perspective.
   d. laboratory experiments.

15. Of the following individuals, the one who is credited as being one of the founders of social psychology is

    a. Norman Triplett.
    b. Kenneth Gergen.
    c. David Sears.
    d. Harry Triandis.

16. Velma is a cognitive psychologist and Valerie is a social psychologist. Velma is *less* likely than Valerie to be interested in

    a. reasoning about risky decisions.
    b. how quickly people can learn new tasks.
    c. the thinking required to solve a problem.
    d. how social interactions affect memory for people.

17. Which one of the following is *not* a characteristic of social psychology?

    a. A broad perspective
    b. A focus on the individual
    c. The frequent use of experiment methodology
    d. A focus on observation of behaviors

18. Unlike common sense, social psychological theories are

    a. always accurate.
    b. put to the test.
    c. based on educated guesses.
    d. always hard to anticipate.

19. Each of the following is true about the current period of pluralism in social psychology *except* that

    a. laboratory experiments have been discontinued and replaced by unobtrusive studies that take advantage of archival or correlational techniques.
    b. there are important variations in the aspects of human behavior being emphasized.
    c. the "socialness" of social psychology has increased owing to the influence of European social psychologists.
    d. cross-cultural research is being conducted more extensively than in previous periods.

20. As social psychology approaches the new century, all of the following are likely to be emphasized *except*

    a. biological and evolutionary perspectives.
    b. new technologies.
    c. the separation of emotion, motivation, and cognition.
    d. sociocultural perspectives.

Essay Questions

1. Provide a definition of social psychology and note how it is different from other similar fields.

2. Describe three periods in the history of social psychology and note two major characteristics of each period.

3. Explain two major differences between common sense understandings and social psychological theories.

ANSWERS TO THE PRACTICE QUIZ

Multiple-Choice Questions: Correct Answers and Explanations

1. Kurt and Ernest both study human behavior. Kurt is a social psychologist, and Ernest is a journalist. Based on the definition of social psychology, one can assume that an important difference between Kurt and Ernest is likely to be that

   b. Kurt uses the scientific method to study people, whereas Ernest does not. Social psychology is the *scientific* study of the way individuals think, feel, desire, and act in social situations. Social psychologists, therefore, apply the scientific method of systematic observation, description, and measurement in their research; journalists, in contrast, can and do use other methods. Journalists, like social psychologists, often use statistics in their work. The level of analysis for social psychologists typically is the individual, not the group. Social psychologists are interested in people's attitudes as well as their behaviors.

2. Betty is a psychologist who specializes in neuroscience. Betty studies the effects that drinking alcohol has on the brain. Carmen is a social psychologist, and also is interested in the effects of alcohol. Compared to Betty, Carmen is *more* likely to

   d. **focus on the effects of alcohol on social behavior.** An important distinction between social psychology and other subdisciplines within psychology is social psychology's focus on social behavior and social situations. But someone specializing in neuroscience should be no less likely than a social psychologist to apply the scientific method of systematic observation, description, and measurement in her research; to take an applied research perspective by attempting to increase the understanding of naturally occurring events and to find solutions to practical problems; and to conduct experiments.

3. One major difference between social psychologists and sociologists is that social psychologists tend to focus on _____ while sociologists tend to focus on _____.

   c. **the individual level; the group level.** This distinction is one important way that social psychologists and sociologists tend to differ. Both social psychologists and sociologists are likely to study prejudice, culture, aggression, violence, and political attitudes. They will tend to focus on different aspects of these topics, but both groups of social scientists study them. Social cognition is a subfield of social psychology in which how people perceive, remember, and interpret information about themselves and others is studied.

4. Social psychology started to become established as a distinct field of study

   c. **in the late nineteenth century and early twentieth century.** The first research article in social psychology (by Triplett) was published at the end of the nineteenth century, and the field began to be a distinct discipline with the publication of the first three textbooks in social psychology, from 1908 to 1924.

5. Which of the following is *least* consistent with the ideas of Kurt Lewin?

   b. **Social psychologists should concentrate on basic research rather than on applied research, which represents the "selling out" of social psychology.** Lewin showed a persistent interest in the application of social psychology, such as in his research on how to promote more economical and nutritious eating habits, so Lewin would not have warned against applied research. Lewin proposed that behavior is a function of the person and the environment. By emphasizing both the person and the environment, Lewin advocated what today is known as the *interactionist perspective*, which combines personality psychology and social psychology. Lewin proposed that even if people are placed in the exact same social situation, their behavior will vary to the extent that they perceive and interpret the situation differently.

6. Personality psychologists are generally *more* interested than social psychologists in

   d. **differences between individuals that are stable across situations.** Personality psychologists are usually quite interested in studying differences between individuals that are stable across situations. Although some social psychologists might be interested in some individual differences, they are usually less interested in this problem than personality psychologists. Both personality and social psychologists are interested in how people think, feel, and behave; understanding the underlying causes of behavior; and the scientific approach to psychology.

7. Susan's research emphasizes cognition. Much of her research focuses on how people's thoughts affect their behavior. Susan's research may be said to be

    a. a "cold" approach. Approaches that emphasize cognition – focusing on how thoughts affect people's feelings, attitudes, and behaviors – are often characterized as "cold" approaches, to be contrasted with "hot" approaches that emphasize emotion and motivation as determinants of thoughts and actions. A meta-analysis does not characterize an approach to social psychology; rather, it is a set of statistical procedures used to review literature by combining the quantitative results from multiple studies. Interactionist approaches combine personality and social psychology; this is not especially typical of approaches that emphasize cognition. External validity is the degree to which one can be reasonably confident that the same results would be obtained for other people and in other situations; there is no reason to assume that studies that emphasize cognition should be particularly high on this dimension.

8. Constantine and Mahboud are interested in social cognition. Therefore, they should be most inclined to conduct a study in which

    b. people's interpretations of information about other people are examined. Social cognition is the study of how people perceive, remember, and interpret information about themselves and others. Social cognition research is no more likely than other forms of research within social psychology to combine personality factors with social factors, or to take an applied (research whose goal is to increase the understanding of naturally occurring events or to find solutions to practical problems), rather than a basic (research whose goal is to increase the understanding of human behavior, often by testing hypotheses based on a theory), approach. The level of analysis of most research within social psychology, including social cognition, is the individual rather than the group.

9. The German immigrant who made a major contribution to the development of social psychology by helping to establish principles like "behavior is a function of the interaction between the person and the environment" was

    d. Lewin. Kurt Lewin was the psychologist who made this classic statement. He was a very important figure in social psychology who fled Nazi Germany and came to the United States in the 1930s. Allport was another important psychologist from the early 1900s whose works included a seminal book on *The Nature of Prejudice*. Bandura and Dollard were two influential theorists who made important contributions to the study of aggression.

10. In the 1960s and early 1970s social psychology experienced a period of

    a. expansion and debate. This is the period that the book called "Confidence and Crisis." During this time there was a lot of new research and an expansion of research into new topic areas. However, this was also a time of intense discussion and debate about the use of experiments in the field. Although there was some introspection during this period it was not a period of stagnation. Pluralism emerged on a larger scale after this period, so although it was a period of development, pluralism and development does not seem to be the best answer. Finally, this period is probably best characterized as a period of building on the foundation rather than the foundational period, so although there were some reform movements during this period, foundation and reform is probably not the best answer either.

11.   Asch, Festinger, and Heider were three influential theorists of the 1950s that developed basic theories about

   b.   **attitudes and person perception.** In the 1950s Festinger developed his theory of cognitive dissonance and social comparison theory, both of which are important for understanding attitudes. Asch and Heider each developed theories that were seminal in our understanding of person perception. Heider's balance theory has some relevance to attraction, but none of these theorists did extensive research on aggression. Festinger's social comparison theory has some important insight for the understanding of the self, but none of the theorists studied or theorized about health. Finally, none of these theorists did research on helping or business.

12.   A study illustrating the power of the situation to affect people's perceptions of who won a debate (Fein et al., 1998) found that people's perceptions were more affected by _____ what was said than by _____ what was said.

   b.   **other people's reactions to; the content of** In this study Fein and his colleagues found that an audience's reaction to a debate had much more influence on people's evaluation of who won the debate than what the debaters actually said in the debate. Emotional tone, humor, and persuasiveness were not systematically evaluated in this study.

13.   Leroy is a social psychologist and Barney is a clinical psychologist. If they both study aggression Leroy is *more* likely than Barney to

   a.   **examine the situational determinants of aggression in an experiment.** Social psychologists are often interested in the situational determinants of behavior. They are more likely to be interested in this aspect of a topic than clinical psychologists. Clinical psychologists are more likely to develop therapeutic techniques to control people's aggression than social psychologists. Both groups of psychologists might be interested in developing theories about what leads people to be aggressive, and developing a questionnaire to measure which people are most likely to be aggressive.

14.   Many of the strong disagreements that occurred during the period of "Confidence and Crisis" were a reaction to the predominant use of

   d.   **laboratory experiments.** The dominant research method in social psychology up to the period of "Confidence and Crisis" was the laboratory experiment. Many people questioned the ethics and validity of this research strategy. Archival research, which involves the use of existing records of human behavior, has never been a predominant research strategy in social psychology. Unobtrusive measures, involving assessments of behavior that do not interfere with a subject's spontaneous and natural reactions, were not used predominantly during this period; their use can help researchers avoid some of the criticisms raised at the time about laboratory experiments. Finally, the interactionist perspective, which combines personality and social psychology, was neither predominant at the time nor seen as a controversial practice.

15.   Of the following individuals, the one who is credited as being one of the founders of social psychology is

   a.   **Norman Triplett.** Triplett published the first research article in social psychology at the end of the nineteenth century. The work of the other three social psychologists has been much more recent, extending from the 1970s through the present. Gergen played an important role in the 1961-1975 period of "Confidence and Crisis" by arguing that the theories being tested in the social psychology laboratory were historically and culturally limited. In 1986 Sears argued for the advantages of moving beyond convenience samples in social psychological research and including subjects from a variety of backgrounds. And Triandis's work is cited as an example of the increase in work on multiculturalism in Chapter 1.

16. Velma is a cognitive psychologist and Valerie is a social psychologist. Velma is *less* likely than Valerie to be interested in

   d. how social interactions affect memory for people. The investigation of reasoning about risky decisions, how quickly people can learn new tasks, and the thinking required to solve a problem are all topics that a cognitive psychologist might be interested in. How social interactions affect memory for people, however, is a topic that social psychologists are more likely to investigate. In particular, this topic is more likely to be studied by a psychologist interested in social cognition – the study of how people perceive, remember, and interpret information about themselves and others.

17. Which one of the following is *not* a characteristic of social psychology?

   d. A focus on observation of behaviors. Social psychologists sometimes study topics by observing behaviors, but this is not a focus or a characteristic of social psychology per se. Conversely, a broad perspective, a focus on the individual, and the frequent use of experiment methodology are all characteristics of social psychology.

18. Unlike common sense, social psychological theories are

   b. put to the test. Because social psychology is a scientific study, its theories are tested. Common sense ideas on the other hand are often contradictory and taken at face value without being tested. Social psychological theories are not always correct, sometimes they are proven wrong. And although social psychological findings are often hard to anticipate they are not always so. Finally, social psychological theories are often based on educated guesses, but common sense ideas often are as well.

19. Each of the following is true about the current period of pluralism in social psychology *except* that

   a. laboratory experiments have been discontinued and replaced by unobtrusive studies that take advantage of archival or correlational techniques. Laboratory experiments continue to be used in social psychology; other approaches, however, are used as well. Each of the other statements is true.

20. As social psychology approaches the new century, all of the following are likely to be emphasized *except*

   c. the separation of emotion, motivation, and cognition. It seems that as we approach the new century the integration rather than the separation of emotion, motivation, and cognition is likely to be emphasized. Biological and evolutionary perspectives, new technologies, and sociocultural perspectives are all topics that are likely to see extensive research scrutiny in the next century as well.

Answers to Essay Questions: Sample Essays

1.   Provide a definition of social psychology and note how it is different from other similar fields.

Social psychology can be defined as the scientific study of how individuals think, feel, and behave in regard to other people and how individuals' thoughts, feelings, and behaviors are affected by other people. Social psychology is different from sociology in that it focuses on the individual level rather than the group level of analysis. Social psychology is different from clinical psychology in that it is primarily concerned with the typical ways that people think, feel, and behave and is less concerned with people who have psychological difficulties and disorders. Social psychology is different from personality psychology in that it is less concerned with individual differences between people that are consistent across situations. Finally, social psychology is different from cognitive psychology in that it is more concerned with how thinking, learning, remembering, and reasoning are relevant to social behavior.

2.   Describe three periods in the history of social psychology and note two major characteristics of each period.

Early social psychology began in the late 1800s. This period had two defining characteristics – the beginning of research, with a study by Triplett on how the presence of others affects performance, and the defining of the field, as several textbooks were written on social psychology in the early 1900s. From the 1930s to 1950s the field grew quickly as it tried to understand the horrors of World War II and Nazi Germany. Kurt Lewin was a particularly important figure who fled Nazi Germany for the United States during this time. This period can be characterized as a period with foundational theories and groundbreaking experiments. The 1960s and early 1970s saw a rise in confidence and expansion of the field, but was also a time of questioning and debate. This period can thus best be characterized as a time of expansion and debate. The late 1970s to the 1990s saw the birth of a new subfield, social cognition, and greater international and cultural perspectives in social psychology. This period can be seen as a time of pluralism and redefinition.

3.   Explain two major differences between common sense understandings and social psychological theories.

Many people think the findings of social psychology are just common sense, but social psychology differs from common sense in two important ways. First, social psychology, unlike common sense, puts its ideas to the test. This scientific approach is the chief difference between social psychology and common sense. Second, common sense is often contradictory and thus can appear to explain everything. For example, common sense suggests that birds of a feather flock together and that opposites attract. So if people are attracted to similar others common sense appears to be true and if people are attracted to dissimilar others common sense also appears to be true. It is no wonder that social psychological findings appear to be common sense at times, whatever occurs could be predicted by one version of common sense in this example. By contrast social psychological theories should make non-contradictory predictions.

2

Doing Social Psychology Research

LEARNING OBJECTIVES: GUIDELINES FOR STUDY

You should be able to do each of the following by the conclusion of Chapter 2.

1. Explain the utility of learning about research methods in social psychology. Describe the process of generating ideas in social psychology, searching the relevant literature, and developing hypotheses. Distinguish between a hypothesis and a theory, and between applied and basic research. *(pp. 24-28)*

2. Explain how operational definitions are used to test conceptual variables. Summarize self-report and observational research practices, including advantages and disadvantages of each. Define construct validity and interrater reliability. *(pp. 28-33)*

3. Explain the usefulness of archival studies and surveys. Define random sampling, and explain its importance. *(pp. 33-35)*

4. Contrast correlational research with descriptive research. Define the correlation coefficient, and explain what it means to say that two variables are negatively correlated, positively correlated, or uncorrelated. Differentiate concurrent and prospective correlations. Summarize the advantages and an important disadvantage of correlational research. *(pp. 35-38)*

5. Explain the importance of control and random assignment in experimental research. Differentiate random sampling from random assignment, and laboratory experiments from field experiments. *(pp. 38-40)*

6. Define the following terms associated with experimental research: independent variable, dependent variable, subject variable, main effect, and interaction. *(pp. 40-43)*

7. Explain the importance of statistical significance, internal validity, and external validity. Describe how the external validity of a study is affected by mundane realism, experimental realism, deception, and the use of confederates. Define meta-analysis. *(pp. 43-46)*

8. Discuss the function of ethics in social psychological research. Describe the roles of institutional review boards, informed consent, and debriefing in protecting the welfare of human participants. Summarize the competing points of view about the role of values in science. *(pp. 46-49)*

MAJOR CONCEPTS: THE BIG PICTURE

Following are five basic issues or principles that organize Chapter 2. You should know these issues and principles well.

1. Learning about social psychology research methods should enable you to better understand the material presented in the textbook, as well as to improve your reasoning about real-life events.

2. The research process in social psychology begins with coming up with ideas, asking questions about one's social world, and searching the relevant literature to determine what research has already been done on these issues. Social psychologists develop testable hypotheses and theories. An important aspect of social psychological hypotheses and theories is that they can be put to the test and eventually improved upon. Social psychologists test their hypotheses and theories both in basic and applied settings.

3. A challenging part of the research process is developing specific definitions and measurements of social psychological variables. Researchers typically begin with rather vague, abstract conceptualizations of the variables of interest and eventually make them more concrete and specific. Researchers may measure variables using self-report or observational techniques; each of these approaches has its strengths and potential weaknesses.

4. Social psychological researchers use descriptive, correlational, experimental, and meta-analytic methods to test their ideas. The goal of descriptive research is to describe people and their behavior. Correlational research examines the association between variables. Experimental research examines the cause-and-effect relationship between variables. Researchers analyze the results of their research and evaluate the research in terms of internal and external validity. Meta-analysis involves using statistical techniques to combine the results of a number of other studies that have already been conducted.

5. Ethical issues must always be considered when research is conducted. In social psychology, the use of deception can be of particular ethical concern. Through institutional review boards, informed consent, and debriefing, social psychologists try to ensure the welfare of their research participants. The issue of values is also important in social psychological research. There are differences of opinion about whether social psychological research – like other research – can or even should be value free.

KEY TERM EXERCISE: THE CONCEPTS YOU SHOULD KNOW

Below are all of the key terms that appear in **boldface** in Chapter 2. To help you better understand these concepts, rather than just memorize them, write a definition for each term in your own words. After doing so, look at the next section where you'll find a list of definitions from the textbook for each of the key terms presented in random order. For each of your definitions, find the corresponding textbook definition. Note how your definitions compare with those from the textbook.

Key Terms

1. internal validity

2. theory

3. debriefing

4. experimental realism

5. correlational research

6. dependent variables

7. mundane realism

8. interrater reliability

9. meta-analysis

10. hypothesis

11. experiment

12. random sampling

13. basic research

14. experimenter expectancy effects

15. random assignment

16. subject variables

17. deception

18. external validity

19. correlation coefficient

20. informed consent

21. independent variables

22. construct validity

23. applied research

24. confederates

25. operational definition

26. main effect

27. interaction

Textbook Definitions

a. Variables that characterize pre-existing differences among the participants in a study.
b. The extent to which the measures used in a study measure the variables they were designed to measure and the manipulations in an experiment manipulate the variables they were designed to manipulate.
c. A set of statistical procedures used to review a body of evidence by combining the results of individual studies to measure the overall reliability and strength of particular effects.

d.   A testable prediction about the conditions under which an event will occur.

e.   An organized set of principles used to explain observed phenomena.

f.   Research whose goal is to increase the understanding of human behavior, often by testing hypotheses based on a theory.

g.   Research whose goal is to enlarge the understanding of naturally occurring events and to find solutions to practical problems.

h.   A statistical measure of the strength and direction of the association between two variables. The correlation coefficient can range from -1.0 to +1.0.

i.   A form of research that can demonstrate causal relationships because (1) the experimenter has control over the events that occur and (2) the participants are randomly assigned to conditions.

j.   In an experiment, the factors experimenters manipulate to see if they affect the dependent variables.

k.   In an experiment, the factors experimenters measure to see if they are affected by the independent variables.

l.   The degree to which there can be reasonable certainty that the independent variables in an experiment caused the effects obtained on the dependent variables.

m.   The effects produced when an experimenter's expectations about the results of an experiment affect his or her behavior toward a participant and thereby influence the participant's responses.

n.   Accomplices of an experimenter who, in dealing with the real participants in an experiment, act as if they also are participants.

o.   A method of selecting participants for a study so that everyone in a population has an equal chance of being in the study.

p.   A method of assigning participants to the various conditions of an experiment so that each participant in the experiment has an equal chance of being in any of the conditions.

q.   The degree to which the experimental situation resembles places and events that exist in the real world.

r.   The degree to which experimental procedures are involving to participants and lead them to behave naturally and spontaneously.

s.   Research methods that provide false information to participants.

t.   The degree to which different observers agree on their observations.

u.   An individual's deliberate, voluntary decision to participate in research, based on the researcher's description of what will be required during such participation.

v.   A disclosure, made to participants after research procedures are completed, in which the researcher explains the purpose of the research, attempts to resolve any negative feelings, and emphasizes the scientific contribution made by participants' participation.

w.   Research designed to measure the association between variables that are not manipulated by the researcher.

x.   The degree to which one can be reasonably confident that the same results would be obtained for other people and in other situations.

y.   The specific procedures for manipulating or measuring a conceptual variable.

z.   A statistical term indicating the overall effect that an independent variable has on the dependent variable, ignoring all other independent variables.

aa.   A statistical term indicating that the effect that an independent variable has on the dependent variable is different as a function of another independent variable.

ANSWERS FOR KEY TERM EXERCISE

Each of the key terms listed below is followed by the letter of the textbook definition that matches it.

1.	internal validity	l	15.	random assignment	p
2.	theory	e	16.	subject variables	a
3.	debriefing	v	17.	deception	s
4.	experimental realism	r	18.	external validity	x
5.	correlational research	w	19.	correlation coefficient	h
6.	dependent variables	k	20.	informed consent	u
7.	mundane realism	q	21.	independent variables	j
8.	interrater reliability	t	22.	construct validity	b
9.	meta-analysis	c	23.	applied research	g
10.	hypothesis	d	24.	confederates	n
11.	experiment	i	25.	operational definition	y
12.	random sampling	o	26.	main effect	z
13.	basic research	f	27.	interaction	aa
14.	experimenter expectancy effects	m			

PRACTICE QUIZ: TEST YOUR KNOWLEDGE OF THE CHAPTER

Multiple-Choice Questions

1. Hannah developed an explicit, testable prediction about what kind of advertising campaign would be most effective in selling a particular product. Specifically, she predicted that a campaign that makes an emotional appeal would be more effective than one that focuses more on appeals to logic. She tested her prediction in an experiment that compared both types of appeals. Hannah's prediction is an example of

   a. archival research.
   b. a hypothesis.
   c. a meta-analysis.
   d. survey research.

2. Which of the following studies is probably *highest* in experimental realism?

   a. Participants sit in a waiting room and are observed secretly using hidden video cameras while they wait for the experimenter to call them in to begin the study.
   b. Participants try to memorize a long list of words either alone or in the presence of other participants.
   c. Participants try to make judgments about each other's personalities based on small clues about each other, with the incentive that the participants whose judgments are most accurate will win $50.
   d. Participants from several different countries are selected through random sampling to participate in this study, in which they receive a questionnaire asking them their opinions about a variety of global economic and health issues.

3. Drew conducted an experiment to examine the effects of uncomfortably loud noise on the likelihood that people will aggress against each other. He manipulated the amount of noise in the room, and he measured the number of times that the participants looked at each other in threatening, aggressive ways. After reporting the results of his experiment, some researchers criticized Drew's measure of aggression as having poor construct validity. This criticism suggests that

    a. the operational definition of aggression that Drew used was flawed.
    b. the results of the study are not statistically significant.
    c. the independent variable was poorly designed.
    d. Drew did not use random assignment in his measure of aggression.

4. Some researchers conducted an experiment to examine the effects of noise and test difficulty on students' test performance. The researchers manipulated how much noise was present in a room (either a little or a lot) and how difficult the test was (either easy or very difficult). The researchers analyzed the results of their experiment and found that the manipulation of noise had little effect on test performance when the test was easy, but that it had a strong effect when the test was difficult – students did much worse on the difficult test if the room was noisy than if it was quiet. This pattern of results suggests that

    a. there was an interaction between the two independent variables.
    b. there was a main effect for the variable of noise.
    c. the correlation between noise and test difficulty was positive.
    d. the manipulation of noise was strong in external validity.

5. Alan wanted to test his hypothesis that people are more likely to vote in presidential elections when the economy of the country is bad rather than good. He decided to conduct archival studies to test this. Which of the following is the kind of archival study that Alan would be *most* likely to do?

    a. Randomly assign some participants to conditions so that some read information indicating strongly that the economy of the country is strong, and others read information indicating that the economy is weak and vulnerable. Next, give participants a chance to register to vote for an election.
    b. Look at existing records to determine the strength of the country's economy at different points in time and at other records to record the percentage of the eligible population who voted in presidential elections.
    c. Collect a number of published studies on the topic and calculate statistically how strong the effects are.
    d. Randomly sample the population of registered voters and distribute a survey that asks them to describe their feelings about the economy, and then ask them if they voted in the last election.

6. Angelia recruits participants for an experiment on crowding. She randomly assigns some participants to a small room and other participants to a large room. Through random assignment, Angelia hopes to ensure that

    a. differences that appear between conditions cannot be attributed to differences in the personal characteristics of the participants in the two conditions.
    b. the study is high in external validity.
    c. she will have a representative sample and not have to resort to using a convenience sample.
    d. the welfare of the participants will be protected.

7. Some researchers investigated the relationship between smoking and the likelihood of dying of cancer. The researchers found that as the amount one smoked increased, the likelihood of dying of cancer increased as well. Similarly, as the amount of smoking decreased, the likelihood of dying of cancer decreased as well. Which of the following correlation coefficients is *most* likely to reflect this relationship between amount of smoking and the likelihood of dying of cancer?

    a. A correlation coefficient of −.30
    b. A correlation coefficient of +.30
    c. A correlation coefficient of −10.00
    d. A correlation coefficient of +100.00

8. Some researchers measured the amount of television a number of boys watched when they were five years old, and then measured how creative they were when they were fifteen years old. They found that the boys who were relatively high in amount of television watching at age five tended to be relatively low in creativity at age fifteen, and that those who had watched the least amount of television at age five were the most creative at age fifteen. This is an example of

    a. a representative sample.
    b. an experiment with four independent variables.
    c. experimental realism.
    d. a prospective correlation.

9. Some researchers found a negative correlation between the number of fans attending hockey games and the number of fights that occurred during the games. Several other groups of researchers found the same negative correlation between these variables. This suggests that

    a. there is a very weak relationship between the number of fans attending hockey games and the number of fights that occur during the games.
    b. the presence of relatively large crowds causes hockey teams to play in a way that produces fewer fights.
    c. there is a greater chance that fights will occur during a hockey game at which relatively few fans are present than during a game at which many fans are present.
    d. fans are turned off by violence in hockey games and will stay away from games between teams that tend to fight a lot.

10. Surveys are much more likely to produce accurate results if

   a. the participants were randomly assigned to conditions.
   b. they are high in experimental realism.
   c. the participants were chosen using a random sample of the population.
   d. their design has strong internal validity.

11. Imagine two alien species: the Romulans and the Klingons. The Romulans were interested in developing a technique for use in extracting secrets from Klingon prisoners. The Romulans wanted to test Klingons' tolerance for pain under different conditions, so they gave some Klingons electric shocks after depriving them of sleep and gave other Klingons the same magnitude of shocks after letting them sleep as much as they wanted. They then measured the decibel level of the Klingons' screams. The independent variable in this experiment is

   a. the amount of pain the Klingons could tolerate.
   b. the intensity of shock voltage.
   c. whether or not the Klingons were deprived of sleep.
   d. the loudness of screams of the Klingons.

12. Min wants to assess people's attitudes about sex education in grade school. To do so, she mails a questionnaire to a large sample of individuals and asks the individuals to answer questions about their attitudes and then to mail the questionnaire back to her. Min's method of measurement is a(n)

   a. event-contingent method.
   b. archival record.
   c. self-report measure.
   d. behavioral observation.

13. Researchers found that the results of their study were statistically significant. Thus they concluded that

   a. the research is relatively high in internal validity.
   b. there is only a very small probability that the results occurred by chance.
   c. the results should generalize to different populations in different settings.
   d. the correlation found between the variables was positive and strong.

14. To study aggression, Neil randomly assigns participants to one of two movies. He makes the specially prepared movies equal in every way except aggressive content. The experimenters are kept uninformed about the hypotheses of the study. This study appears to have

   a. statistical significance.
   b. experimental realism.
   c. a representative sample.
   d. internal validity.

15. Margot hires some research assistants to help her conduct a laboratory experiment. She trains them so that they know exactly what to say or do with participants. However, she does not tell them what the hypotheses or predictions of the research are. By omitting this information, Margot hopes to protect the experiment from

    a. unethical practices.
    b. convenience sampling.
    c. experimenter expectancy effects.
    d. mundane realism.

16. One way to increase the chances that a study will be high in external validity is to use

    a. random assignment.
    b. random sampling.
    c. behavioral observations.
    d. self-report measures.

17. Elissa is interested in seeing what kinds of leaders have the most positive impact on the efficiency of groups of soldiers. She designs a series of experiments to examine this issue. Elissa is most likely to be interested in

    a. laboratory research.
    b. archival research.
    c. social cognition research.
    d. applied research.

18. Greta wants to know whether racially diverse work groups typically perform better or worse as a function of how task-oriented the group leader is. She searches the literature on this topic and finds a number of previously conducted studies that have investigated this issue. She determines that, rather than focusing on any single study, a more reliable and valid conclusion could be reached by examining these studies together and combining their results statistically. To reach such a conclusion, Greta should conduct

    a. a prospective correlational study.
    b. an analysis of the interrater reliability of the studies.
    c. a concurrent correlational study.
    d. a meta-analysis.

19. The use of deception in some studies highlights the need for researchers to

    a. conduct a thorough debriefing at the conclusion of each study.
    b. conduct research that is not influenced by their own values.
    c. use self-reports as well as behavioral observations whenever possible.
    d. create operational definitions of their variables that are high in external validity.

20.   At the start of his experiment, Conrad made sure to ask all participants whether they wanted to take part in the research. He also provided them with a great deal of information about what they could expect if they participated in the study. Conrad took these steps in order to

   a.   obtain informed consent.
   b.   increase the external validity of the experiment.
   c.   minimize experimenter expectancy effects.
   d.   create mundane realism.

Essay Questions

1.   Craig conducted a study in which he put some participants in very hot rooms and others in comfortably cool rooms, and then measured their levels of aggressiveness by observing their behavior. Craig found that those in the hot rooms were more aggressive than those in the cooler rooms. What further information would you need to determine whether this study was an experiment rather than a correlational study? What further information would you need to evaluate the external validity of this study?

2.   Describe the primary disadvantages in using self-report measures in social psychology research. Then discuss the role of interrater reliability in another type of measure used by social psychologists.

3.   Summarize three different positions that have been taken concerning the influence of values on science.

ANSWERS TO THE PRACTICE QUIZ

Multiple-Choice Questions: Correct Answers and Explanations

1. Hannah developed an explicit, testable prediction about what kind of advertising campaign would be most effective in selling a particular product. Specifically, she predicted that a campaign that makes an emotional appeal would be more effective than one that focuses more on appeals to logic. She tested her prediction in an experiment that compared both types of appeals. Hannah's prediction is an example of

    b. a hypothesis. A hypothesis is a testable prediction about the conditions under which an event will occur; Hannah developed such a prediction for her research. The other three answers are specific types of research, rather than a type of prediction, and there is nothing indicated in the question to suggest that Hannah conducted any one of these types of studies. Archival research involves examining existing records of past events and behaviors. A meta-analysis is a set of statistical procedures used to review a number of previously conducted studies. Survey research involves asking people to indicate their attitudes, beliefs, or behaviors.

2. Which of the following studies is probably *highest* in experimental realism?

    c. Participants try to make judgments about each other's personalities based on small clues about each other, with the incentive that the participants whose judgments are most accurate will win $50. Experimental realism is the degree to which experimental procedures are involving to participants and lead them to behave naturally and spontaneously. Trying to judge each other's personalities and winning money should be relatively involving to the participants and motivate them to take the tasks in the study seriously. In contrast, the study set in the waiting room should be very low in experimental realism, although it may be high in mundane realism (the degree to which the experimental situation resembles places and events that exist in the real world), since sitting in a waiting room might be a familiar, ordinary situation for the participants. Trying to memorize a long list of words is likely to be a rather dull task, neither very engaging nor interesting to the participants; therefore, the experimental realism is not likely to be very high. Surveys like the kind described in the final option do not have experimental realism.

3. Drew conducted an experiment to examine the effects of uncomfortably loud noise on the likelihood that people will aggress against each other. He manipulated the amount of noise in the room, and he measured the number of times that the participants looked at each other in threatening, aggressive ways. After reporting the results of his experiment, some researchers criticized Drew's measure of aggression as having poor construct validity. This criticism suggests that

    a. the operational definition of aggression that Drew used was flawed. In an experiment, a measure that is said to have poor construct validity does not correctly measure the conceptual variable it was designed to measure. In this case, the conceptual variable was "aggression," and the specific way that Drew measured aggression was his operational definition of aggression. Drew operationally defined aggression in his study as the number of times participants looked at each other in threatening or aggressive ways; this definition is likely to be flawed, as such looks are likely to be ambiguous and may have little to do with aggression. Thus, the measure has poor construct validity. Statistical significance refers to the likelihood that the results of a study could have occurred by chance; this question indicates nothing about whether the results were analyzed statistically to determine whether or not they were statistically significant. The independent variable is the variable that the experimenter manipulated. Drew manipulated the amount of noise in the laboratory room; the validity of this manipulation was not questioned. In an experiment, participants are assigned randomly to the different conditions of the independent variable(s); there is no random assignment of the dependent variable, which in this case was the measure of aggression.

4. Some researchers conducted an experiment to examine the effects of noise and test difficulty on students' test performance. The researchers manipulated how much noise was present in a room (either a little or a lot) and how difficult the test was (either easy or very difficult). The researchers analyzed the results of their experiment and found that the manipulation of noise had little effect on test performance when the test was easy, but that it had a strong effect when the test was difficult – students did much worse on the difficult test if the room was noisy than if it was quiet. This pattern of results suggests that

   a. **there was an interaction between the two independent variables.** There is said to be an interaction between two independent variables if the effect that one of the independent variables has on the dependent variable depends on the other independent variable. In this study, the effect that the manipulation of noise had on the students' test performance depended on the manipulation of test difficulty (the effect of noise was strong only if the test difficulty was high). A main effect is the effect of one independent variable without considering any other independent variables. In this study, there was no indication that either independent variable alone had a strong effect regardless of the other independent variable. A correlation is a measure of the association between two variables; the independent variables in this study were manipulated, not measured, and therefore there is no association to be measured. External validity refers to the degree to which one can be reasonably confident that the same results would be obtained for other people and in other situations. There is nothing indicated in this question that is relevant to the issue of external validity.

5. Alan wanted to test his hypothesis that people are more likely to vote in presidential elections when the economy of the country is bad rather than good. He decided to conduct archival studies to test this. Which of the following is the kind of archival study that Alan would be *most* likely to do?

   b. **Look at existing records to determine the strength of the country's economy at different points in time and at other records to record the percentage of the eligible population who voted in presidential elections.** Archival research involves examining existing records of past events and behaviors. Using existing records of economic indicators and voting patterns, Alan could test his hypothesis. The other three potential answers to this question describe kinds of research other than archival. Answer "a" describes an experiment, including random assignment to different conditions. Answer "c" describes a meta-analysis – statistical procedures used to review a number of previously conducted studies. The final option describes a survey rather than an archival study.

6. Angelia recruits participants for an experiment on crowding. She randomly assigns some participants to a small room and other participants to a large room. Through random assignment, Angelia hopes to ensure that

   a. **differences that appear between conditions cannot be attributed to differences in the personal characteristics of the participants in the two conditions.** Random assignment is an essential characteristic of an experiment. By randomly assigning participants to the different conditions, the participants assigned to one condition should not initially be different from those assigned to any other condition. External validity is the degree to which one can be reasonably confident that the same results would be obtained for other people and in other situations. The setting of the experiment and the type of sample used to obtain participants affect the external validity; random assignment cannot ensure high external validity. Random assignment also does not affect whether or not there is a representative sample, which is a sample of participants that reflects the characteristics of the population of interest; random sampling, in contrast, does affect whether a representative sample is likely to be obtained. The welfare of the participants is protected by following codes of ethics, including the use of informed consent and institutional review boards; random assignment by itself does not protect the welfare of human participants.

7. Some researchers investigated the relationship between smoking and the likelihood of dying of cancer. The researchers found that as the amount one smoked increased, the likelihood of dying of cancer increased as well. Similarly, as the amount of smoking decreased, the likelihood of dying of cancer decreased as well. Which of the following correlation coefficients is *most* likely to reflect this relationship between amount of smoking and the likelihood of dying of cancer?

   b. **A correlation coefficient of +.30** Correlation coefficients range from +1.0 to –1.0. A positive correlation indicates that as one variable increases, so does the other, and that as one variable decreases, so does the other. This is the kind of relationship that the researchers found between amount of smoking and likelihood of dying of cancer. A negative correlation indicates that as one variable increases, the other decreases. This is the opposite of what the researchers found. Because correlation coefficients range from +1.0 to –1.0, correlation coefficients of –10.00 and +100.00 are not possible.

8. Some researchers measured the amount of television a number of boys watched when they were five years old, and then measured how creative they were when they were fifteen years old. They found that the boys who were relatively high in amount of television watching at age five tended to be relatively low in creativity at age fifteen, and that those who had watched the least amount of television at age five were the most creative at age fifteen. This is an example of

   d. **a prospective correlation.** Prospective correlations are obtained at different times from the same individuals. A correlation is an association between two variables. These researchers examined the association between television viewing and creativity within the same individuals over time. There is no mention of the kind of sample used in this study, so there is no reason to assume that there was a representative sample, which is a sample of participants that reflects the characteristics of the population of interest. This study does not seem to have been an experiment; there was no random assignment to conditions, and the researchers did not control and manipulate any independent variables. Experimental realism is the degree to which experimental procedures are involving to participants and lead them to behave naturally and spontaneously; again, this study was not an experiment, and the description of the study does not give any details of the procedure that would allow one to evaluate it.

9. Some researchers found a negative correlation between the number of fans attending hockey games and the number of fights that occurred during the games. Several other groups of researchers found the same negative correlation between these variables. This suggests that

c. **there is a greater chance that fights will occur during a hockey game at which relatively few fans are present than during a game at which many fans are present.** A negative correlation indicates that as one variable (such as the number of fans attending a game) increases, the other variable (such as the number of fights in the game) decreases. Correlations can be used to make accurate predictions about the relationship between two variables. A negative correlation does not imply that the relationship is weak. Instead, the *magnitude* of the correlation coefficient, not the direction of the correlation (whether it is positive or negative), indicates the strength of the correlation – but the magnitude of the correlation coefficient is not indicated in this question. The other possible answers suggest that there is a causal relationship between the two variables, but one should never infer causality from a correlation.

10. Surveys are much more likely to produce accurate results if

c. **the participants were chosen using a random sample of the population.** Random sampling ensures that everyone in a population has an equal chance of being in a study. Surveys that use random sampling have a much better chance of truly representing the population, and, therefore, of producing accurate results. Randomly assigning participants to conditions is important for experiments, rather than surveys; in addition, surveys typically do not have different conditions to which participants are assigned. Experimental realism, the degree to which experimental procedures are involving to participants and lead them to behave naturally and spontaneously, is relevant for experiments, not surveys. Internal validity, which concerns how well an experiment establishes a causal relationship between the independent and dependent variables, is also relevant for experiments rather than surveys.

11. Imagine two alien species: the Romulans and the Klingons. The Romulans were interested in developing a technique for use in extracting secrets from Klingon prisoners. The Romulans wanted to test Klingons' tolerance for pain under different conditions so they gave some Klingons electric shocks after depriving them of sleep and gave other Klingons the same magnitude of shocks after letting them sleep as much as they wanted. They then measured the decibel level of the Klingons' screams. The independent variable in this experiment is

c. **whether or not the Klingons were deprived of sleep.** Independent variables are the factors manipulated in an experiment to see if they affect the dependent variable. The Romulans manipulated whether or not the Klingons were sleep deprived to see the effect of this manipulation on tolerance for pain. The amount of pain the Klingons could tolerate was the conceptual dependent variable, and the loudness of their screams was the operational definition of this conceptual dependent variable. The intensity of shock voltage was not varied in the study, so it was not an independent variable.

12. Min wants to assess people's attitudes about sex education in grade school. To do so, she mails a questionnaire to a large sample of individuals and asks the individuals to answer questions about their attitudes and then to mail the questionnaire back to her. Min's method of measurement is a(n)

c. **self-report measure.** A self-report measure is one in which people are asked to tell about their own thoughts, feelings, and actions. Despite some limitations, questionnaires and other self-report measures are widely used. An event-contingent method is a specific method of using self-report measures. With event-contingent self-reports, respondents report on a designated set of events as soon as possible after such an event has occurred. Because Min did not ask the respondents to report on specific events as soon as the events occurred, Min's study did not use an event-contingent method. Archival records are existing records of human behavior. This question does not suggest that Min consulted any such records. Behavioral observation involves the direct measurement of actions, in contrast to self-reports. Min did not observe her participants' behaviors or measure their actions.

13. Researchers found that the results of their study were statistically significant. Thus they can conclude that

   b. **there is only a very small probability that the results occurred by chance.** Statistical significance means that the odds that the results were obtained by chance alone are quite low (less than 5 out of 100). Internal validity refers to the degree to which there can be reasonable certainty that the independent variable in an experiment caused the effects obtained on the dependent variable. Although statistical significance indicates that the effects probably did not occur by chance, it does not indicate that the effects were necessarily caused by the independent variable itself; if, for example, the experiment did not contain the proper controls, there could be alternative explanations to account for the differences between conditions. Whether the results should generalize to different populations in different settings – in other words, whether the study is high in external validity – depends on the setting of the experiment and the sampling used; statistically significant results may not generalize to other settings or people if the study is low in external validity. There is no mention of whether the results of this study included any correlations; moreover, a negative correlation is just as likely as a positive correlation to be statistically significant.

14. To study aggression, Neil randomly assigns participants to one of two movies. He makes the specially prepared movies equal in every way except aggressive content. The experimenters are kept uninformed about the hypotheses of the study. This study appears to have

   d. **internal validity.** Internal validity is the degree to which there can be reasonable certainty that the independent variables in an experiment caused the effects obtained on the dependent variables. Neil's use of random assignment and the control he used to ensure that the only difference between the conditions was the manipulated independent variable gives this study a high degree of internal validity. Statistical significance means that the odds that the results were obtained by chance alone are quite low (less than 5 out of 100); but there is no mention made of the results in this example. Experimental realism is the degree to which experimental procedures are involving to participants and lead them to behave naturally and spontaneously; but in this example, there is no information given about how involving and real the procedures were for the participants. This question similarly offers no information about the sampling used, so there is no way to know whether a representative sample, which is a sample of participants that reflects the characteristics of the population of interest, was used.

15. Margot hires some research assistants to help her conduct a laboratory experiment. She trains them so that they know exactly what to say or do with participants. However, she does not tell them what the hypotheses or predictions of the research are. By omitting this information, Margot hopes to protect the experiment from

   c. **experimenter expectancy effects.** Experimenter expectancy effects refer to the influence of experimenters' expectations on participants' behavior. Margot tried to minimize the chances of these effects by keeping the research assistants unaware of the hypotheses and predictions so that they would be unlikely to have strong expectations that might influence their behavior toward the participants. Keeping the research assistants unaware of the hypotheses and predictions would not help protect the experiment from unethical practices; rather, the use of institutional review boards, informed consent, and debriefing are relevant to ethical considerations. Keeping the research assistants unaware of the hypotheses and predictions is irrelevant to the sampling procedure used (a convenience sample is a sample selected because the participants are readily available), and it is irrelevant to the mundane realism of the experiment (mundane realism is the degree to which the experimental situation resembles places and events that exist in the real world).

16.   One way to increase the chances that a study will be high in external validity is to use

  b.   random sampling. External validity is the degree to which one can be reasonably confident that the same results would be obtained for other people and in other situations. One way to increase this confidence is to have a sample of participants that is representative of the broader population. How can you get such a sample? One way is to use random sampling, in which every individual in a population has an equal chance of being in the study. Random assignment, in which all participants in an experiment have an equal chance of being assigned to any of the conditions, is essential for establishing cause-and-effect relationships in experiments but does not by itself increase external validity. Behavioral observations, which involve the direct measurement of actions, and self-reports, in which participants disclose their own thoughts, feelings, desires, and behavior, are two methods of measuring variables; neither method necessarily increases external validity.

17.   Elissa is interested in seeing what kinds of leaders have the most positive impact on the efficiency of groups of soldiers. She designs a series of experiments to examine this issue. Elissa is most likely to be interested in

  d.   applied research. The goal of applied research is to increase the understanding of naturally occurring events or to find solutions to practical problems; Elissa's interest in factors affecting the efficiency of groups of soldiers is consistent with this approach. Elissa may or may not be interested in laboratory research – experiments conducted in a controlled setting such as in a university lab; it is very possible (and rather likely) that she would instead conduct field research – real-world settings outside of the laboratory. In archival research, records of previous behavior rather than on-going actions are studied. There is no evidence that Elissa is interested in using such methods; she clearly is interested, however, in doing experiments. Social cognition is the study of how people perceive, remember, and interpret information about themselves and others; there is no evidence that Elissa is interested in these topics.

18.   Greta wants to know whether racially diverse work groups typically perform better or worse as a function of how task-oriented the group leader is. She searches the literature on this topic and finds a number of previously conducted studies that have investigated this issue. She determines that, rather than focusing on any single study, a more reliable and valid conclusion could be reached by examining these studies together and combining their results statistically. To reach such a conclusion, Greta should conduct

  d.   a meta-analysis. A meta-analysis is a set of statistical procedures used to review a body of evidence by combining the results of individual studies to measure the overall reliability and strength of particular effects. This is exactly what Greta is interested in doing. Prospective correlational studies involve taking measures at different times from the same individuals (such as having a group of individuals answer a set of questions on one day and then again five years later), and concurrent correlational studies involve taking measures of a number of individuals at a single point in time. Neither kind of correlational study involves combining the results of previously conducted studies. Interrater reliability refers to the degree to which different observers agree on their observations of the same behavior. Although interrater reliability may be relevant to some of the specific studies that Greta has discovered, it is not relevant to her general interest in combining the results of these studies.

19. The use of deception in some studies highlights the need for researchers to

   a. conduct a thorough debriefing at the conclusion of each study. A debriefing is the disclosure, made to participants after research procedures are completed, in which the researcher explains the purpose of the research, attempts to resolve any negative feelings, and emphasizes the scientific contribution made by their participation. Deceptions are revealed during the debriefing, and the researchers explain the purpose of using deception. Failure to "correct" these deceptions during debriefing would be unethical. Although some people believe that it is unethical or poor science to conduct research that is influenced by the researchers' own values, others believe that it is impossible to conduct value-free research, and still others believe that researchers should be encouraged to design their research according to their own values. While all are valid positions, there is no clear connection between the use of deception in studies and the role of values in research. Self-reports and behavioral observations are two ways of measuring variables; deception does not raise any issues concerning how best to measure variables. Operational definitions are the specific ways in which researchers manipulate or measure the variables they are studying, and external validity is the degree to which one can be reasonably confident that the same results would be obtained for other people and in other situations; the use of deception in studies is not relevant to these issues.

20. At the start of his experiment, Conrad made sure to ask all participants whether they wanted to take part in the research. He also provided them with a great deal of information about what they could expect if they participated in the study. Conrad took these steps in order to

   a. obtain informed consent. Informed consent is an individual's deliberate, voluntary decision to participate in research, based on the researcher's description of what will be required during such participation; Conrad's actions were taken in order to inform the participants and to obtain their informed consent. These actions would not increase the experiment's external validity, which is the degree to which one can be reasonably confident that the same results would be obtained for other people and in other situations. Experimenter expectancy effects refer to the influence of experimenters' expectations on participants' behavior; Conrad's actions would not minimize the effects of such expectations (if anything, his actions could increase these effects if his expectations influenced the way he told the participants what the study was about). Finally, Conrad's actions would not create mundane realism, which is the degree to which the experimental situation resembles places and events that exist in the real world.

Answers to Essay Questions: Sample Essays

1. Craig conducted a study in which he put some participants in very hot rooms and others in comfortably cool rooms, and then measured their levels of aggressiveness by observing their behavior. Craig found that those in the hot rooms were more aggressive than those in the cooler rooms. What further information would you need to determine whether this study was

an experiment rather than a correlational study? What further information would you need to evaluate the external validity of this study?

In order to determine whether the study was an experiment, one would need to know how much control the researcher had over the procedures and how the participants were assigned to the two conditions (i.e., to the hot versus comfortably cool rooms). This study would be an experiment if the researcher had control over the experimental procedures (i.e., if all those who participated in the study were treated in exactly the same manner except for the specific differences the experimenter wanted to create) and if the participants were assigned randomly to the two conditions. External validity is the degree to which one can be reasonably confident that the same results would be obtained for other people and in other situations. Both the participants in the study and the setting of the study have an impact on external validity, so one would need to know information about these two factors. To the extent that the sample of participants used in the study resembles a representative sample, which is a sample that reflects the characteristics of the population of interest, external validity should be higher than if the sample is a convenience sample, which is a sample selected because the participants are readily available. External validity may also be affected by the mundane realism and/or experimental realism of the study. There is a difference of opinion concerning the relative importance of these two types of realism. Mundane realism is the degree to which the experimental situation resembles places and events that exist in the real world, and experimental realism is the degree to which experimental procedures are involving to participants and lead them to behave naturally and spontaneously. To assess either form of realism in this study, one must know more both about the details of the procedure and about how the participants perceived the procedure. If the participants felt that the situation in which they found themselves resembled situations from their everyday lives, the study would be high in mundane realism; if the procedures were very involving to the participants and led them to behave spontaneously, the study would be high in experimental realism. If the study is high in both types of realism, external validity would be increased. If it is low in both, external validity would be decreased.

2. Describe the primary disadvantages in using self-report measures in social psychology research. Then discuss the role of interrater reliability in another type of measure used by social psychologists.

Self-reports are the most widely used measurement technique. In self-reports, participants disclose their own thoughts, feelings, desires, and behavior. Self-reports can give researchers direct access to an individual's beliefs and perceptions. But self-reports are not always accurate and can be misleading. Participants' concerns with looking good – both to themselves and to others – can bias their responses on self-report measures. The wording or ordering of questions can also affect their responses. For example, the way a question is structured, the "political correctness" of the terms used, and the available response alternatives can all affect participants' responses. In addition, participants may be unaware of some of their own desires or behaviors, or of the causes of their own actions, and thus give inaccurate responses. Interrater reliability is an important concern with observational measures. In contrast to self-reports, observational measures involve researchers observing people's actions. Interrater reliability refers to the level of agreement among multiple observers of the same behavior. The data collected using observational measures can be trusted to the extent that interrater reliability is high.

3.   Summarize three different positions that have been taken concerning the influence of values on science.

One position is that science should be value free. Adherents of this position argue that science should be totally objective and unbiased. A second position is that science cannot be value free and, thus, political advocacy is appropriate. That is, given that values always influence science, it would be irresponsible of researchers to try to ignore these influences. Instead, scientists should acknowledge the role of values in their work and use their research to help advocate for these values. A third position also acknowledges that science cannot be value free, but this position differs from the second position by advocating methods that try to reduce the biasing influence of these values. By adhering rigorously to the scientific method, scientists can attempt to free themselves of their preconceptions and weaken the influence of their values on their research as much as possible.

3

The Social Self

LEARNING OBJECTIVES: GUIDELINES FOR STUDY

You should be able to do each of the following by the conclusion of Chapter 3.

1. Explain the role of the self in focus of attention. (*p. 54*)

2. Identify which animals are capable of recognizing themselves, and the age when self-recognition occurs in humans. Explain the role of self-recognition and the role of others in the development of the self-concept. Distinguish between sources of the self-concept and components of the self-concept. (*pp. 54-55*)

3. Explain how introspection influences our explanations of our behaviors. Identify when it leads to faulty analysis of behavior and when it leads to accurate analysis of behavior. (*pp. 55-57*)

4. Describe self-perception theory, and explain how it can be used to understand emotion, behavior, and motivation. Define the overjustification effect, compare and contrast intrinsic and extrinsic motivation, and identify factors that can influence the effect of extrinsic factors on intrinsic motivation. (*pp. 57-60*)

5. Explain how people's social surroundings influence their spontaneous self-descriptions. Summarize social comparison theory, identifying when people tend to engage in social comparison and with whom they tend to compare themselves. Explain the two-factor theory of emotion. Identify situations in which social context does not influence interpretation of unclear emotional states. (*pp. 60-63*)

6. Identify the periods of life that are most likely to be recalled. Describe flashbulb memories. Explain how our self-concept influences our memories. (*pp. 63-65*)

7. Describe how our culture of origin can influence our self-concept. (*pp. 65-67*)

8. Define self-schemas, and explain how they can influence the way we perceive information. (*p. 67*)

9. Describe how self-esteem influences people's thoughts, feelings, and behaviors. Describe self-discrepancy theory and explain how the theory accounts for the general level of and changes in people's self-esteem. (*pp. 67-71*)

10. Describe how self-awareness influences feelings about the self. Identify the types of situations and the kinds of people associated with the greatest amount of self-focus. (*pp. 71-74*)

11. Describe the influences of gender, race and culture on our understanding of self. (*pp. 69-71*)

12. Explain the effects self-discrepancy theory on emotional states such as shame, guilt and anxiety. (*pp. 74-75*)

13. Explain ironic processes of self-control and their consequences. (*pp. 75-76*)

14. Identify four ways that people strive for self-enhancement and discuss the implications of self-enhancement for mental health and the perception of reality. (*pp. 76-83*)

15. Describe self-presentation. Compare and contrast strategic self-presentation and self-verification. (*pp. 83-86*)

16. Describe the differences between people who are high and low in self-monitoring. Explain how both of these strategies can be useful. (*pp. 86-88*)

MAJOR CONCEPTS: THE BIG PICTURE

Below are three basic issues or principles that organize Chapter 3. You should know these issues and principles well.

1. We have detailed and elaborate knowledge of ourselves – a self-concept. Gaining information about the self is more difficult than it might first appear, so although our self-impressions are not always reliable we gain information about the self from thinking about ourselves, watching ourselves, comparing ourselves to others, and assimilating to our culture. Once we gain information about the self, we organize our memories around these beliefs.

2. We evaluate ourselves; that is, we have a sense of self-esteem. We evaluate ourselves in comparison to how we think we ought to be and how we think we could ideally be. In addition, we vary in when and how much we evaluate ourselves. Some situations lead to and some people experience more self-evaluation than others. Yet, in general, we maintain a positive image of ourselves. We are able to think about most situations in ways that enhance our self-image.

3. We present an image of ourselves to others. We usually try to present ourselves so that others will perceive us in a favorable way, but we also want people to view us accurately.

KEY TERM EXERCISE: THE CONCEPTS YOU SHOULD KNOW

Below are all of the key terms that appear in **boldface** in Chapter 3. To help you better understand these concepts, rather than just memorize them, write a definition for each term in your own words. After doing so, look at the next section where you'll find a list of definitions from the textbook for each of the key terms presented in random order. For each of your definitions, find the corresponding textbook definition. Note how your definitions compare with those from the textbook.

Key Terms

1. overjustification effect

2. self-monitoring

3. downward social comparison

4.   self-presentation

5.   facial feedback hypothesis

6.   bask in reflected glory (BIRG)

7.   private self-consciousness

8.   self-esteem

9.   self-concept

10.   self-perception theory

11.   social comparison theory

12.   public self-consciousness

13.   two-factor theory of emotion

14.   self-awareness theory

15.   self-handicapping

16.   affective forecasting

17.   implicit egotism

Textbook Definitions

a.   Increasing self-esteem by associating with others who are successful.
b.   Defensive tendency to compare ourselves to others who are worse off than we are.
c.   The hypothesis that changes in facial expression can lead to corresponding changes in emotion.
d   The theory that people evaluate their own abilities and opinions by comparing themselves to others.
e.   Behaviors designed to sabotage one's performance in order to provide a subsequent excuse for failure.
f.   The tendency for intrinsic motivation to diminish for activities that have become associated with reward or other extrinsic factors.
g.   The theory that the experience of emotion is based on two factors: physiological arousal and a cognitive interpretation of that arousal.
h.   The theory that when internal cues are difficult to interpret, people gain self-insight by observing their own behavior.
i.   The tendency to change behavior in response to the self-presentation concerns of the situation.
j.   A personality characteristic of individuals who are introspective, often attending to their own inner states.
k.   The theory that self-focused attention leads people to notice self-discrepancies, thereby motivating either an escape from self-awareness or a change in behavior.
l.   An affective component of the self, consisting of a person's positive and negative self-evaluations.

m.   Strategies people use to shape what others think of them.
n.   A personality characteristic of individuals who focus on themselves as social objects, as seen by others.
o.   The sum total of an individual's beliefs about his or her own personal attributes.
p.   People's difficulty projecting forward and predicting how they would feel in response to future emotional events.
q.   A nonconscious and subtle form of self-enhancement.

ANSWERS FOR KEY TERM EXERCISE

Each of the key terms listed below is followed by the letter of the textbook definition that matches it.

1.   overjustification effect   f
2.   self-monitoring   i
3.   downward social comparison   b
4.   self-presentation   m
5.   facial feedback hypothesis   c
6.   bask in reflected glory (BIRG)   a
7.   private self-consciousness   j
8.   self-esteem   l
9.   self-concept   o
10. self-perception theory   h
11. social comparison theory   d
12. public self-consciousness   n
13. two-factor theory of emotion   g
14. self-awareness theory   k
15. self-handicapping   e
16. affective forecasting   p
17. implicit egotism   q

PRACTICE QUIZ: TEST YOUR KNOWLEDGE OF THE CHAPTER

Multiple-Choice Questions

1.   According to the two-factor theory of emotion, the experience of particular emotions requires both physiological arousal and

   a.   public self-consciousness.
   b.   downward comparison.
   c.   a cognitive interpretation.
   d.   autobiographical memory.

2.   Introspection can impair self-knowledge for behaviors that

   a.   consist of flashbulb memories.
   b.   result from facial feedback.
   c.   depend on social comparison.
   d.   are caused by affective factors.

3.   Herbert has a crush on Beth, but after thinking it over and weighing the pros and cons he decides to date Joan instead. Research by Wilson (1985) on the utility of introspection suggests that Herbert probably would

   a.   enjoy dating Beth more than Joan.
   b.   enjoy dating Joan more than Beth.
   c.   enjoy dating Beth in the short run but Joan in the long run.
   d.   enjoy dating Joan in the short run but Beth in the long run.

4. As a child, Pete played baseball because it was fun. Now that he is a professional, he receives $400,000 a year. Given his salary, he will probably experience

    a. social comparison jealousy.
    b. choking under pressure.
    c. an overjustification effect.
    d. self-handicapping.

5. Research by McGuire and his colleagues shows that when asked "Who are you?" people spontaneously rely on

    a. the hindsight bias.
    b. self-verification.
    c. distinguishing features.
    d. rewards for competence.

6. Elena spends a lot of time in introspection. She is very much "in touch" with her attitudes, values, and opinions. Elena is someone who is high in

    a. self-monitoring.
    b. self-handicapping.
    c. private self-consciousness.
    d. public self-consciousness.

7. Jennifer is preparing for an important interview. In order to appear upbeat but also to feel upbeat, she sits alone before the interview and smiles for a while. Jennifer is making use of the

    a. two-factor theory of emotion.
    b. self-reference effect.
    c. egocentric bias.
    d. facial feedback hypothesis.

8. People from western cultures tend to be more _____ than people from eastern cultures.

    a. interdependent
    b. compassionate
    c. shy
    d. individualistic

9. Monica thinks that she ought to spend more time with her family, but try as she may, she just can't seem to do it and also get her work done. Based on research by Higgins (1989) concerning the self-concept and self-guides one can predict that Monica is likely to feel

    a. disappointment.
    b. agitation.
    c. envy.
    d. shame.

10. The desire to have others perceive us as we perceive ourselves is called

    a. self-presentation.
    b. self-verification.
    c. self-consciousness.
    d. self-monitoring.

11. In their research on optimism and mental health Taylor and Brown (1988) argue that positive illusions about ourselves can

    a. be serious signs of mental disturbance.
    b. lead others to reject us.
    c. cause people to react violently in response to negative feedback.
    d. be adaptive in that they promote mental health.

12. People who drink alcohol often avoid the negative aspects of focusing on themselves and downplay the discrepancy between their real and ideal self-concepts. This process is called

    a. drunken self-inflation.
    b. self-monitoring.
    c. private self-awareness.
    d. self-handicapping.

13. James is a big fan of his college's football team. After the team wins the league championship, Jim wears his baseball cap with the college's logo for a week straight. Jim is probably

    a. high in self-esteem.
    b. a high self-monitor.
    c. making downward social comparisons.
    d. basking in reflected glory.

14. Jerry is a high school senior with slightly above-average grades. In order to feel good about his intellectual abilities, he selects a college with average-ability students. In doing so, Jerry makes it possible to engage in

    a. BIRGing.
    b. overjustification.
    c. downward social comparisons.
    d. drunken self-inflation.

15. During her job interview, Rachel goes out of her way to congratulate her prospective employers on their successful year and to agree with their strategies for the next fiscal year. Rachel's behavior is an example of

    a. the cocktail party phenomenon.
    b. the hindsight bias.
    c. ingratiation.
    d. basking in reflected glory.

16.   Preoccupied with their self-image, people who are high in self-monitoring go out of their way
       to learn about

   a.   their autobiographical memory.
   b.   self-verification strategies.
   c.   their self-discrepancies.
   d.   others with whom they'll interact.

Essay Questions

1.   Describe how the self-concept develops from the perception of one's own behavior and from
      comparisons with other people.

2.   Explain how the self improves and organizes our memories.

3.   Describe two ways in which people can enhance their self-image and cope with their faults
      and inadequacies. Explain how these self-enhancing biases can promote positive mental
      health.

ANSWERS TO THE PRACTICE QUIZ

Multiple-Choice Questions: Correct Answers and Explanations

1.   According to the two-factor theory of emotions, the experience of particular emotions re-
      quires both physiological arousal and

   c.   **a cognitive interpretation.** The two factors that the two-factor theory suggests are nec-
         essary and sufficient for an emotional response are physiological arousal and a cognitive
         label or a cognitive interpretation of the situation. Schachter emphasized in this model
         that we are particularly likely to look to others and their responses in the situation when
         forming a cognitive interpretation. Public self-consciousness, downward comparison,
         and autobiographical memory are not included in the two-factor theory.

2.   Introspection can impair self-knowledge for behaviors that

   d.   **are caused by affective factors.** Common sense tells us that introspection should lead to accurate self-knowledge, but Wilson's (1985) research suggests that introspection often leads to inaccurate self-knowledge. Millar and Tesser (1989) found this to be true primarily for self-beliefs that are affective in nature (e.g., romantic relationships). False feedback and social comparisons have not been shown to have an affect on introspection, and flashbulb memories are unrelated to the issue of introspection.

3.   Herbert has a crush on Beth, but after thinking it over and weighing the pros and cons he decides to date Joan instead. Research by Wilson (1985) on the utility of introspection suggests that Herbert probably would

   a.   **enjoy dating Beth more than Joan.** Wilson's research suggests that introspection often leads to inaccurate self-knowledge. This research implies that Herbert should probably go with his gut instinct and go out with Beth rather than Joan. This is true for both the short run and the long run.

4.   As a child, Pete played baseball because it was fun. Now that he has made it to the professional ranks, he receives $400,000 a year. Given his salary, Pete will probably experience

   c.   **an overjustification effect.** Pete used to play baseball for the fun of it (he was intrinsically motivated). Now he gets paid big money to play. Self-perception theory suggests that, when he interprets his own behavior, he will now begin to believe that he plays baseball at least partly for the money. This will undermine his intrinsic motivation – an effect known as overjustification. There is no reason to expect that he will choke under pressure or that he will engage in social comparison jealousy or self-handicapping. These processes are unaffected by the salary that he is earning.

5.   Research by McGuire and his colleagues shows that when asked "Who are you?" people spontaneously rely on

   c.   **distinguishing features.** The research by McGuire and his colleagues shows that, when spontaneously describing themselves, people tend to point out how they differ from others in their social environment. For example, a girl in a group of all boys is more likely to describe herself in terms of her sex than if she were in a group of all girls or in a group with a more equal mix of boys and girls. Answers to the question "Who are you?" reveal little evidence of the hindsight bias or of self-verification, and they do not appear to be affected by rewards for competence.

6.   Elena spends a lot of time in introspection. She is very much "in touch" with her attitudes, values, and opinions. Elena is someone who is high in

   c.   **private self-consciousness.** People high in private self-consciousness know their attitudes well and spend a lot of time introspecting about them. Elena seems to be such a person. She certainly is not someone high in public self-consciousness, concerned with her effects upon others, and there is no evidence that she is high in self-monitoring or self-handicapping.

7.   Jennifer is preparing for an important interview. In order to appear upbeat but also to feel upbeat, she sits alone before the interview and smiles for a while. Jennifer is making use of the

    d. facial feedback hypothesis. Research on the facial feedback hypothesis suggests that people's facial expressions can often influence their moods. Therefore, smiling might make Jennifer not only look more upbeat, but also feel more upbeat. The two-factor theory of emotion suggests that physiological arousal that is labeled cognitively gives rise to emotion. However, since there was no mention of physiological arousal or a cognitive label, the two-factor theory would be incorrect. The self-reference effect and the egocentric bias are unrelated to emotion.

8.   People from western cultures tend to be more _____ than people from eastern cultures.

    d. individualistic Research cited in the textbook suggests that people from western cultures are more individualistic than people from eastern cultures. People in eastern cultures tend to be more interdependent than westerners. There have been no differences noted in shyness or compassion between easterners or westerners.

9.   Monica thinks that she ought to spend more time with her family, but try as she may, she just can't seem to do it and also get her work done. Based on research by Higgins (1989) concerning the self-concept and self-guides one can predict that Monica is likely to feel

    a. disappointment. Monica is likely to feel a discrepancy between her ideal self (which wants to be with her family) and her actual self (which is not spending time with them). Higgins (1989) research on the self-concept and self-guides suggests that such ideal/actual self-discrepancies should lead to disappointment. The model does not predict other emotional reactions such as agitation, envy, and shame.

10.   The desire to have others perceive us as we perceive ourselves is called

    b. self-verification. Self-verification is the desire to have others perceive us as we truly perceive ourselves. Self-presentation encompasses the various strategies people use to shape what others think of them. Self-consciousness occurs when people focus on themselves. This self-consciousness can be public, where people focus on how others see them, or private, where people focus on how they see themselves. Self-monitoring is the tendency to change behavior in response to the self-presentation concerns of the situation.

11.   In their research on optimism and mental health Taylor and Brown (1988) argue that positive illusions about ourselves can

    d. be adaptive in that they promote mental health. Taylor and Brown (1988) argue that positive illusions are adaptive in that they promote happiness, caring for others, and productive work – in short, mental health. This view is at odds with what many psychologists previously claimed: That accurate perceptions of reality are crucial for mental health. More recently, some have noted the shortcomings to Taylor and Brown's argument. Colvin and colleagues (1995) have noted that positive illusions can lead to relationship problems, while Baumeister and colleagues (1996) have suggested that high self-esteem and its positive illusions may actually lead people to lash out after negative feedback.

12. People who drink alcohol often avoid the negative aspects of focusing on themselves and downplay the discrepancy between their real and ideal self-concepts. This process is called

   a. drunken self-inflation. Drunken self-inflation is the tendency to discount real and ideal self-discrepancies when drinking. Drinking is sometimes used as a self-handicapping strategy, but self-handicapping has little to do with focus of attention. Private self-awareness occurs when people focus on their self-concepts and is decreased when people drink alcohol, but may or may not be related to discrepancies between real and ideal self-concepts. As self-monitoring is the tendency to focus on the immediate social situation and adjust one's behavior accordingly, it has little to do with drinking alcohol.

13. James is a big fan of his college's football team. After the team wins the league championship, Jim wears his baseball cap with the college's logo for a week straight. Jim is probably

   d. basking in reflected glory. Cialdini's research on basking in reflected glory demonstrates that people like to identify with groups that they are a part of when those groups succeed. James is probably basking in reflected glory by identifying himself with the team as it wins. There is little reason to expect that Jim is high in self-esteem, and his self-esteem could not explain why he wore his cap more after the team won. Jim is not engaging in downward social comparisons either. These comparisons involve interactions with others who are doing worse than oneself. Finally, there is no evidence that James is a high self-monitor.

14. Jerry is a high school senior with slightly above-average grades. In order to feel good about his intellectual abilities, he selects a college with average-ability students. In doing so, Jerry makes it possible to engage in

   c. downward social comparisons. Attending a less selective school should give Jerry plenty of opportunity for contact with others who are not as smart as he is. It should also allow him to engage in downward social comparisons – comparisons with others that would put him in a positive light. Such comparisons can be self-enhancing. There is no evidence that Jerry is basking in reflected glory or engaging in overjustification or drunken self-inflation. These processes have little or nothing to do with comparisons that allow people to feel good about themselves.

15. During her job interview, Rachel goes out of her way to congratulate her prospective employers on their successful year and to agree with their strategies for the next fiscal year. Rachel's behavior is an example of

   c. ingratiation. Ingratiation is a tactic of strategic self-presentation. It includes such behaviors as flattery, agreement, and putting one's best foot forward. If successful, ingratiation results in liking by others. There is no evidence that Rachel's behavior exemplifies the cocktail party phenomenon, the hindsight bias, or basking in reflected glory. These processes have little to do with flattery and congratulation.

16. Preoccupied with their self-image, people who are high in self-monitoring go out of their way to learn about

   d. others with whom they'll interact. Since high self-monitors tailor their behavior to fit the situation they are in, they are very sensitive to the people with whom they interact. They recognize that other people are an important part of the situation. However, there is little reason to expect that self-monitors will try to learn about their autobiographical memories, self-discrepancies, or self-verifications. These concepts are probably unrelated to self-monitoring.

Answers to Essay Questions: Sample Essays

1. Describe how the self-concept develops from the perception of one's own behavior and from comparisons with other people.

    Self-perception theory describes how people often infer their beliefs and attitudes from their actions. This theory suggests that people make inferences about their own behavior in the same way that they make inferences about other people's behavior. They assume that if someone engages in a behavior, then he or she probably has attitudes and beliefs consistent with this behavior unless there is a good reason to believe otherwise. For example, if someone spends a lot of time playing basketball, then he or she would probably infer that basketball is an important part of his or her self-concept. Social comparison theory describes how people develop their attitudes and behaviors by comparing themselves with others. In particular, it suggests that people make comparisons with others who are similar, especially those who are doing just slightly better. By making these comparisons, we gain a sense of what our beliefs and abilities are.

2. Explain how the self improves and organizes our memories.

    Research on the self-reference effect demonstrates that when people encode information in ways that make it self-relevant (such as thinking about how it relates to themselves), they can remember that information better. Research on self-schemas shows that people's self-concepts (or more precisely their self-schemas) guide and organize their memories. Since these self-schemas are generally well developed, they make self-relevant information easier to encode when people try to learn it and easier to retrieve when people try to remember it. In this way the self provides the structures that organize memory and the mechanisms that improve memory.

3. Describe two ways in which people can enhance their self-image and cope with their faults and inadequacies. Explain how these self-enhancing biases can promote positive mental health.

    The main text discusses four ways in which people can enhance their self-image: basking in reflected glory, downward social comparison, self-handicapping, and self-evaluation maintenance. Basking in reflected glory occurs when people come to identify with a group that is succeeding. For example, when a student at a prestigious university points to the accomplishments of the professors and identifies with them, he or she is able to share in their success. Downward social comparison entails making contact with others who are doing worse than oneself. This type of comparison allows one to feel relatively better off. For example, the cancer patient who meets other patients in worse shape can derive some comfort in the thought that at least he or she is doing better than they are. Self-handicapping is a strategy that some people use in order to provide an excuse for poor performance on an upcoming threatening event. For example, the student who gets drunk the night before an exam will have a ready explanation for why he or she fails the exam the next day. Note that while this behavior may soften the negative impact of a poor performance, it may also cause the poor performance. Tesser's theory of self-evaluation maintenance draws on some of the above work but also suggests that people can have different reactions based on how important the domain is to their self-concept and how close they feel to people they are comparing themselves with. For example, if John is close to his brother he may take pride and bask in the reflected glory of his brother's basketball success if basketball is not important to John; however, if basketball is important to John and he plays on the same team but isn't doing well, he may feel jealousy and anger at his brother's success. Self-evaluation maintenance theory suggests that John will either distance himself from his brother or come to see basketball as less important in this situation. Taylor and Brown present evidence that such self-enhancing biases may be beneficial to our mental health. They suggest that we may need such biases to cope with the difficult problems we face in daily life. Their evidence suggests that people who do not show these biases tend to be depressed.

4

Perceiving Persons

LEARNING OBJECTIVES: GUIDELINES FOR STUDY

You should be able to do each of the following by the conclusion of Chapter 4.

1. Define social perception. Identify sources of "raw data" from which social perception arises (persons, situations, behavior). (*pp. 93-94*)

2. Describe the impact of appearance on people's perceptions of others. Distinguish "baby-faced" features from mature facial features, and contrast the traits that perceivers infer about others on the basis of these facial features. Summarize the three explanations that have been offered to account for the differences in social perceptions as a function of such features. (*pp. 94-95*)

3. Define scripts, and describe their functions in social perception. Explain how the manner in which perceivers divide the continuous stream of human behavior into discrete units can influence social perception. (*pp. 95-97*)

4. Explain how people use nonverbal cues to judge others. Identify the six "primary" emotions. Summarize the research concerning perception of angry faces. Discuss the roles of other nonverbal cues, including body language, eye contact, and touch. (*pp. 97-99*)

5. Describe people's ability to detect deception. Contrast the channels of communication that are most likely to reveal that someone is lying with the channels that perceivers typically try to use to detect deception. (*pp. 99-101*)

6. Define dispositions and attributions. Distinguish between personal and situational attributions. Identify the characteristics that make people more likely to make attributions for an event. Summarize Jones's correspondent inference theory and Kelley's covariation theory. (*pp. 101-104*)

7. Describe cognitive heuristics in general and the availability heuristic in particular. Explain how the availability heuristic can give rise to the false-consensus effect. Describe the base-rate fallacy. Define counterfactual thinking and identify when it is likely to occur. (*pp. 104-107*)

8. Define the fundamental attribution error. Summarize the explanations of this attribution bias, including the two-step process model and the role of culture. Describe the factors that make the fundamental attribution error less likely to occur. Compare the fundamental attribution error with the actor-observer effect. Discuss the two explanations of the actor-observer effect. (*pp. 107-112*)

9. Explain how attribution biases may stem from motivational factors, such as the desire to take more credit for success than for failure. Define what is meant by the "belief in a just world," and identify the factors that lead to defensive attributions. *(pp. 112-113)*

10. Explain the summation and averaging models of impression formation. Describe information integration theory. Explain the role of perceiver characteristics (including the effects of individual differences, priming, and mood) and of target characteristics (including the trait negativity bias) on impression formation. *(pp. 113-117)*

11. Define implicit personality theory. Explain how people's implicit personality theories affect their impressions of other people. Describe the effects of central traits and the primacy effect on these impressions. Identify two explanations for the primacy effect and explain the influence of the need for closure on this effect. *(pp. 117-119)*

12. Define the confirmation bias. Describe how belief perseverance, confirmatory hypothesis testing, and the self-fulfilling prophecy can each contribute to this bias and identify which factors can reduce the likelihood that these effects will occur. Compare belief perseverance to the primacy effect. *(pp. 119-125)*

13. Describe the problem of overconfidence in people's judgments. Distinguish between bias and error. Describe generally how people fare as social perceivers, and list a few reasons for being somewhat optimistic about people's competence as social perceivers. *(pp. 125-127)*

MAJOR CONCEPTS: THE BIG PICTURE

Below are four basic issues or principles that organize Chapter 4. You should know these issues and principles well.

1. To understand other people's emotions, motives, and personal dispositions, social perceivers rely on indirect clues. These indirect clues – the elements of social perception – include information about persons, situations, and behavior. People's perceptions of others are influenced by the others' physical appearance, by preconceptions about various types of situations, and by nonverbal communication.

2. People try to understand each other by attributing the causes of their behavior to personal factors or situational factors. Although these attributions often are consistent with the logic represented in theories of the attribution process, there are several ways in which people's attributions often depart from the logic of these theories, resulting in attribution biases.

3. Perceivers combine different pieces of information about a person to form a coherent overall impression. The integration of this information depends in part on characteristics of the perceiver, such as the perceiver's sensitivity to particular information, and in part on characteristics of the target, such as the presence or absence of particular types of traits.

4. Once an impression is formed, people become less likely to change their minds when confronted with nonsupportive evidence. Rather, they tend to interpret, seek, and even create information in ways that confirm their existing beliefs.

KEY TERM EXERCISE: THE CONCEPTS YOU SHOULD KNOW

Below are all of the key terms that appear in **boldface** in Chapter 4. To help you better understand these concepts, rather than just memorize them, write a definition for each term in your own words. After doing so, look at the next section where you'll find a list of definitions from the textbook for each of the key terms presented in random order. For each of your definitions, find the corresponding textbook definition. Note how your definitions compare with those from the textbook.

Key Terms

1. base-rate fallacy

2. central traits

3. situational attribution

4. belief in a just world

5. primacy effect

6. false-consensus effect

7. social perception

8. correspondent inference theory

9. information integration theory

10. availability heuristic

11. personal attribution

12. implicit personality theory

13. covariation principle

14. fundamental attribution error

15. confirmation bias

16. impression formation

17. actor-observer effect

18. nonverbal behavior

19. counterfactual thinking

20. priming

21. self-fulfilling prophecy

22.   attribution theory

23.   belief perseverance

24.   need for closure

Textbook Definitions

a.   A general term for the processes by which people come to understand one another.

b.   A tendency to estimate the likelihood that an event will occur by how easily instances of it come to mind.

c.   Behavior that reveals a person's feelings through facial expressions, body language, and vocal cues.

d.   A group of theories that describe how people explain the causes of behavior.

e.   Attribution to internal characteristics of an actor, such as ability, personality, mood, or effort.

f.   Attribution to factors external to an actor, such as the task, other people, luck.

g.   A theory holding that we make inferences about a person when his or her actions are freely chosen, are unexpected, and result in a small number of desirable effects.

h.   A principle of attribution theory holding that people attribute behavior to factors that are present when a behavior occurs and absent when it does not.

i.   The tendency to focus on the role of personal causes and underestimate the impact of situations on other people's behavior.

j.   The tendency to attribute our own behavior to situational causes and the behavior of others to personal factors.

k.   A tendency to imagine alternative events or outcomes that might have occurred but did not.

l.   The tendency for people to overestimate the extent to which others share their opinions, attributes, and behavior.

m.   The finding that people are relatively insensitive to consensus information presented in the form of numerical base rates.

n.   The belief that individuals get what they deserve in life, an orientation that leads people to disparage victims.

o.   The process of integrating information about a person to form a coherent impression.

p.   The theory that impressions are based on (1) perceiver dispositions and (2) a weighted average of a target person's traits.

q.   The tendency for recently used words or ideas to come to mind easily and influence the interpretation of new information.

r.   A network of assumptions people make about the relationships among traits and behaviors.

s.   Traits that exert a powerful influence on overall impressions.

t.   The tendency for information presented early in a sequence to have more impact on impressions than information presented later.

u.   A desire to reduce cognitive uncertainty, which heightens the importance of first impressions.

v.   The tendency to seek, interpret, and create information that verifies existing beliefs.

w.   The tendency to maintain beliefs even after they have been discredited.

x.   The process by which one's expectations about a person eventually lead that person to behave in ways that confirm those expectations.

ANSWERS FOR KEY TERM EXERCISE

Each of the key terms listed below is followed by the letter of the textbook definition that matches it.

1.	base-rate fallacy	m	13.	covariation principle	h
2.	central traits	s	14.	fundamental attribution error	i
3.	situational attribution	f	15.	confirmation bias	v
4.	belief in a just world	n	16.	impression formation	o
5.	primacy effect	t	17.	actor-observer effect	j
6.	false-consensus effect	l	18.	nonverbal behavior	c
7.	social perception	a	19.	counterfactual thinking	k
8.	correspondent inference theory	g	20.	priming	q
9.	information integration theory	p	21.	self-fulfilling prophecy	x
10.	availability heuristic	b	22.	attribution theory	d
11.	personal attribution	e	23.	belief perseverance	w
12.	implicit personality theory	r	24.	need for closure	u

PRACTICE QUIZ: TEST YOUR KNOWLEDGE OF THE CHAPTER

Multiple-Choice Questions

1. Charlene finishes second in a swim meet and wins the silver medal, but she is depressed because she can't stop thinking about the fact that she was so close to winning the gold medal. Liv finishes third and wins the bronze medal, and she feels great relief and satisfaction because she realizes how close she came to finishing fourth and therefore not winning a medal. Charlene's and Liv's reactions reflect

   a. belief in a just world.
   b. counterfactual thinking.
   c. the fundamental attribution error.
   d. the covariation principle.

2. Diane sees Carla make a strong speech *against* legalized gambling. She learns that Carla had free choice to make a speech on any issue she chose, and Diane knows that most of the students in Carla's class are in *favor* of legalized gambling. Diane infers that Carla truly is opposed to legalized gambling. This is most consistent with

   a. the self-fulfilling prophecy.
   b. the correspondent inference theory.
   c. the fundamental attribution error.
   d. the false-consensus effect.

3.   Yvonne has small eyes, low eyebrows, a small forehead, and an angular chin. Vickie has large round eyes, high eyebrows, round cheeks, a large forehead, smooth skin, and a rounded chin. According to research concerning social perception, Yvonne should have an advantage over Vickie if each of them

   a.   applied for a job as a day-care teacher.
   b.   auditioned for an acting job to play the part of someone who is seen as submissive.
   c.   was accused of negligence as an adult.
   d.   was accused of intentional wrongdoing as an adult.

4.   Joyce expected that her new roommate, Chrissie, would be somewhat cold and unfriendly. Because of this expectation, Joyce did not welcome Chrissie into her room very warmly. In turn, Chrissie did not act very warmly toward Joyce, and even began to be unfriendly toward Joyce and her friends. This best illustrates the

   a.   negative effects of counterfactual thinking.
   b.   self-fulfilling prophecy.
   c.   false-consensus effect.
   d.   correspondent inference theory.

5.   Facial expressions, body language, eye contact, and touch are all forms of

   a.   attribution theory.
   b.   the priming process.
   c.   nonverbal behavior.
   d.   situational attribution.

6.   Jose hires someone from an escort service to be his date for the evening at a company party and to act very warmly toward him. During the party, Jose comes to believe that his date's behavior suggests that she really is warm and friendly. Jose's inference is most likely an example of

   a.   a primacy effect.
   b.   the fundamental attribution error.
   c.   trait negativity bias.
   d.   a situational attribution.

7.   According to research conducted across different cultures concerning people's attributions, which of the following pairs of people should show the biggest discrepancy in terms of whether they attribute someone's negative behavior to the person or to the situation?

   a.   A child in India and a child in the United States.
   b.   An adult in India and an adult in the United States.
   c.   An adult in India and a child in the United States.
   d.   An adult in India and a very suspicious adult in the United States.

8.   Persons, situations, and behavior are the three major elements in

   a.   central traits.
   b.   cognitive heuristics.
   c.   self-fulfilling prophecies.
   d.   social perception.

9. Ed observes Mary Ann behave in a particular way and considers whether or not he has learned anything about her personal characteristics on the basis of this behavior. Based on the correspondent inference theory, Ed would be most likely to infer that her behavior does correspond to an enduring personal characteristic if

   a. Mary Ann was behaving in front of other people rather than alone.
   b. Mary Ann's behavior was likely to earn her both a lot of money and a great deal of respect.
   c. Mary Ann's behavior was consistent with a social norm.
   d. Mary Ann had a high degree of choice concerning whether or not to behave in that way.

10. While busy doing something else, and without fully realizing it, Sophia heard the lyrics to a song, which included words such as "punch," "fight," "threaten," and "hurt." Jennifer did not hear the song. Later, Sophia and Jennifer watched a video of a man pushing another man. Sophia interpreted the push as more hostile and threatening than did Jennifer. This outcome is an example of the effects of

   a. priming.
   b. the base-rate fallacy.
   c. the actor-observer difference.
   d. the trait negativity bias.

11. If we know that Juan's perception was influenced by a script, we can reasonably conclude that Juan

   a. was unable to detect deception accurately.
   b. was affected by his expectations.
   c. ignored cognitive heuristics.
   d. made attributions that were biased to make himself look good.

12. Research concerning the base-rate fallacy shows that, when asked to make predictions about the future actions of others, people tend to rely on

   a. graphic, dramatic events.
   b. numerical base rates.
   c. abstract laws of probability.
   d. hard statistical facts.

13. The day before Brenda's roommate Rhoda is supposed to turn in a term paper, Rhoda experiences a very painful headache and blurred vision and goes to the infirmary. Brenda has noticed that Rhoda gets these symptoms whenever she has to turn in a term paper. Brenda also has noticed that Rhoda gets similar symptoms whenever she is excited, stressed, or required to do a lot of work. None of the other students whom Brenda knows well experiences these symptoms. According to Kelley's covariation theory, Brenda should make a personal attribution for Rhoda's experiences because her experiences are

   a. low in consensus, low in consistency, and low in distinctiveness.
   b. high in consensus, high in consistency, and low in distinctiveness.
   c. low in consensus, high in consistency, and low in distinctiveness.
   d. high in consensus, high in consistency, and high in distinctiveness.

14. Of the following, the person most likely to make the fundamental attribution error when observing someone's behavior is

    a. Reed, who is distracted while observing the behavior.
    b. Pamela, who is focusing on the situation.
    c. Angie, who is not cognitively busy.
    d. Sirajul, who is an adult in India.

15. Lance suspects that Marcia has low self-esteem. Lance asks Marcia, "Do you sometimes feel that you can't do anything right?" When Marcia answers "yes," Lance concludes that he was right about Marcia having low self-esteem. This conclusion is an example of

    a. confirmatory hypothesis testing.
    b. the summation model of impression formation.
    c. the primacy effect.
    d. priming.

16. Michael often physically touches the people with whom he works, patting them on the back or elbowing them in the ribs. Research suggests that Michael's behavior may be a sign of

    a. dominance.
    b. priming.
    c. suspicion.
    d. personal attributions.

17. According to research concerning the belief in a just world, which of the following people should be *least* likely to be critical of or derogate the plight of a victim?

    a. Mick, who sees the victim as similar to himself in many respects
    b. Charlie, who is prompted to take the victim's perspective
    c. Ron, who is emotionally aroused by observing the victim
    d. Keith, who sees the consequences to the victim as being severe and negative

18. Stacey, a high school student, came home past her curfew. She claimed the fog was so bad that she couldn't drive. Her parents argued that she was just being thoughtless. This difference in views is consistent with the

    a. confirmation bias.
    b. false-consensus effect.
    c. self-fulfilling prophecy.
    d. actor-observer effect.

19. Researchers have found that when participants are asked whether there are more English words that start with the letter *r* or that have the letter *r* as the third letter, most participants guess that there are more words that start with the letter *r*. This phenomenon most clearly reflects the

    a. covariation theory.
    b. primacy effect.
    c. availability heuristic.
    d. confirmation bias.

20.   For the first time since he began college, Brad goes to his professor for help. His professor shows him some new study techniques. Brad thinks his instructor is a genuinely dedicated teacher. Brad's opinion is an example of a

    a.   situational attribution.
    b.   primacy effect.
    c.   personal attribution.
    d.   central trait.

Essay Questions

1.   While observing someone's behavior, why are people more likely to commit the fundamental attribution error when they are cognitively busy, or distracted?

2.   What is the primacy effect? Describe two major reasons for this effect.

3.   Imagine the following study. Participants read about a number of experiments, each of which supports the idea that introverted people make better psychiatrists than extroverted people. The participants are given time to think about this information. Later, they are informed that the experiments they had read were fictitious – they were fabricated by the experimenter for purposes of the experiment. Despite the fact that the information was discredited, however, the participants continue to believe that introverted people probably would make better psychiatrists than extroverted people. What social psychological concept best describes the results of this study? Why does this phenomenon occur?

ANSWERS TO THE PRACTICE QUIZ

Multiple-Choice Questions: Correct Answers and Explanations

1. Charlene finishes second in a swim meet and wins the silver medal, but she is depressed because she can't stop thinking about the fact that she was so close to winning the gold medal. Liv finishes third and wins the bronze medal, and she feels great relief and satisfaction because she realizes how close she came to finishing fourth and therefore not winning a medal. Charlene's and Liv's reactions reflect

    b. **counterfactual thinking.** Counterfactual thinking involves imagining alternative events or outcomes that might have occurred but did not, which is what the two swimmers were reacting to. Belief in a just world is the belief that individuals get what they deserve in life, but there is no evidence that the two swimmers are reacting to such a belief. The fundamental attribution error and the covariation principle both concern attribution theory, but the swimmers' reactions are not due to how they explained the causes of their performances in the meet, but rather are influenced by their thoughts of "what might have been."

2. Diane sees Carla make a strong speech *against* legalized gambling. She learns that Carla had free choice to make a speech on any issue she chose, and Diane knows that most of the students in Carla's class are in *favor* of legalized gambling. Diane infers that Carla truly is opposed to legalized gambling. This is most consistent with

    b. **the correspondent inference theory.** This theory proposes that when perceivers learn that an actor's behavior was performed under free choice, and that it departed from social norms, they are likely to infer that the behavior reflects the actor's true disposition. Because Carla had free choice, and because her speech against gambling departed from her class's norm of supporting gambling, Diane inferred that Carla's speech did indeed reflect her attitudes. Because Diane's attribution was consistent with this theory, there is no evidence of an attribution bias; options "c" and "d" therefore are incorrect as they each concern an attribution bias. The other option, the self-fulfilling prophecy, refers to the process by which one's expectations about a person eventually lead that person to behave in ways that confirm those expectations; there is nothing stated in the question about Diane's expectations or any effects on Carla's behavior.

3. Yvonne has small eyes, low eyebrows, a small forehead, and an angular chin. Vickie has large round eyes, high eyebrows, round cheeks, a large forehead, smooth skin, and a rounded chin. According to research concerning social perception, Yvonne should have an advantage over Vickie if each of them

    c. **was accused of negligence as an adult.** Yvonne's facial features are considered to be mature features, whereas Vickie's are considered baby-faced features. Research has shown that adults with baby-faced features are more likely to be perceived in ways consistent with negligence. Conversely, these same adults are more likely to be seen as appropriate for a day-care teacher, as submissive, and as less likely to engage in intentional wrongdoing.

4.   Joyce expected that her new roommate, Chrissie, would be somewhat cold and unfriendly. Because of this expectation, Joyce did not welcome Chrissie into her room very warmly. In turn, Chrissie did not act very warmly toward Joyce, and even began to be unfriendly toward Joyce and her friends. This best illustrates the

b.   **self-fulfilling prophecy.** The self-fulfilling prophecy occurs when one's expectations about a person eventually lead that person to behave in ways that confirm those expectations; this is what apparently happened here, as Joyce's expectations about Chrissie caused Chrissie to behave in ways that confirmed Joyce's expectations. Counterfactual thinking involves imagining alternative events or outcomes that might have occurred but did not; there is no evidence of that in this question. The false-consensus effect is the tendency for people to overestimate the extent to which others share their opinions, attributes, and behavior; again, there is no evidence of this indicated. The correspondent inference theory maintains that we make inferences about a person when his or her actions are freely chosen, are unexpected, and result in a small number of desirable effects; although this theory might be relevant to predicting how Joyce and Chrissie explain each other's behaviors, it is less clearly relevant to what happened between them than is the self-fulfilling prophecy.

5.   Facial expressions, body language, eye contact, and touch are all forms of

c.   **nonverbal behavior.** Nonverbal behavior communicates a person's feelings without words, such as through facial expressions, body language, eye contact, and touch. The other options are not comprised of these particular behaviors.

6.   Jose hires someone from an escort service to be his date for the evening at a company party and to act very warmly toward him. During the party, Jose comes to believe that his date's behavior suggests that she really is warm and friendly. Jose's inference is most likely an example of

b.   **the fundamental attribution error.** The fundamental attribution error is the tendency to underestimate the impact of situations on other people's behavior and to focus on the role of personal causes. José ignores the fact that his date was required to act friendly as part of the job (a situational cause) and instead attributes her behavior to her being a warm and friendly person (a personal cause). José does not, therefore, make a situational attribution. The primacy effect and trait negativity bias are concepts concerning the integration of a number of traits in the impression formation process, rather than attributions of a specific type of behavior.

7.   According to research conducted across different cultures concerning people's attributions, which of the following pairs of people should show the biggest discrepancy in terms of whether they attribute someone's negative behavior to the person or to the situation?

b.   **An adult in India and an adult in the United States.** According to cross-cultural research, adults in India tend to avoid the fundamental attribution error, whereas adults in the United States tend to make this error. All of the individuals in the other three choices for this question are relatively unlikely to commit the fundamental attribution error.

8. Persons, situations, and behavior are the three major elements in

   d. social perception. Social perception is the general term for the processes by which people come to understand each other, and the information used in these processes concerns persons, situations, and behaviors. This set of three elements is not of central importance in any of the three other choices, which are concerned with more specific concepts.

9. Ed observes Mary Ann behave in a particular way and considers whether or not he has learned anything about her personal characteristics on the basis of this behavior. Based on the correspondent inference theory, Ed would be most likely to infer that her behavior does correspond to an enduring personal characteristic if

   d. Mary Ann had a high degree of choice concerning whether or not to behave in that way. Correspondent inference theory proposes that when perceivers learn that an actor's behavior was performed under free choice, departs from social norms, and results in a small number of desirable effects, they are more likely to infer that the actor's behavior reflects their true disposition. Thus, Ed should make this inference if Mary Ann had a high degree of choice, but not if her behavior was likely to earn money and respect (which are multiple desirable effects) or if it was consistent with social norms. Whether she behaved in front of other people is information which, by itself, is not relevant to this theory.

10. While busy doing something else, and without fully realizing it, Sophia heard the lyrics to a song, which included words such as "punch," "fight," "threaten," and "hurt." Jennifer did not hear the song. Later, Sophia and Jennifer watched a video of a man pushing another man. Sophia interpreted the push as more hostile and threatening than did Jennifer. This outcome is an example of the effects of

    a. priming. Priming refers to the tendency for recently used words or ideas to influence the interpretation of new information. Sophia's recent exposure to aggressive words influenced her interpretation of the behavior depicted on the video. The base-rate fallacy and the actor-observer difference are not relevant to this question. Because Sophia and Jennifer were not presented with multiple traits about the man in the video, the trait negativity bias is not relevant either.

11. If we know that Juan's perception was influenced by a script, we can reasonably conclude that Juan

    b. was affected by his expectations. Scripts are preconceived notions about a sequence of events likely to occur in a particular situation. Perceivers' expectations about the likely occurrence of a sequence of events can influence their perceptions. Detection of deception, cognitive heuristics, and biased attributions are not as likely to depend on perceivers' preconceived notions about a sequence of events.

12. Research concerning the base-rate fallacy shows that, when asked to make predictions about the future actions of others, people tend to rely on

    a. graphic, dramatic events. The base-rate fallacy is the tendency to rely on graphic, dramatic events when making predictions, and to be relatively insensitive to numerical base rates, abstract laws of probability, and hard statistical facts.

13.   The day before Brenda's roommate Rhoda is supposed to turn in a term paper, Rhoda experiences a very painful headache and blurred vision and goes to the infirmary. Brenda has noticed that Rhoda gets these symptoms whenever she has to turn in a term paper. Brenda also has noticed that Rhoda gets similar symptoms whenever she is excited, stressed, or required to do a lot of work. None of the other students whom Brenda knows well experiences these symptoms. According to Kelley's covariation theory, Brenda should make a personal attribution for Rhoda's experiences because her experiences are

   c.   **low in consensus, high in consistency, and low in distinctiveness.** The fact that no other students get these symptoms indicates low consensus. The fact that Rhoda always gets these symptoms whenever she faces a deadline indicates high consistency. And the fact that Rhoda experiences similar symptoms in a number of different situations indicates low distinctiveness.

14.   Of the following, the person most likely to make the fundamental attribution error when observing someone's behavior is

   a.   **Reed, who is distracted while observing the behavior.** Distraction inhibits a perceiver's ability to adjust personal attributions to take into account situational causes, thus making the fundamental attribution error more likely to occur. The other three individuals are all more likely to take into account situational factors, and thus less likely to commit the fundamental attribution error.

15.   Lance suspects that Marcia has low self-esteem. Lance asks Marcia, "Do you sometimes feel that you can't do anything right?" When Marcia answers "yes," Lance concludes that he was right about Marcia having low self-esteem. This conclusion is an example of:

   a.   **confirmatory hypothesis testing.** Because Lance hypothesized that Marcia has low self-esteem, he asked Marcia a question that was likely to elicit confirmation of his hypothesis. The summation model and the primacy effect are not correct because this question does not concern Lance's integration of multiple traits about Marcia. Priming is not relevant because there is no mention of any recently used words or ideas influencing Lance's interpretation of new information.

16.   Michael often physically touches the people with whom he works, patting them on the back or elbowing them in the ribs. Research suggests that Michael's behavior may be a sign of

   a.   **dominance.** Research has shown that touch can be a sign of friendship, intimacy, and related feelings, or a sign of dominance and control. There is no evidence that touch is related to priming, which concerns the effects of recently used words on perceivers' perceptions, or to suspicion or personal attributions, both of which are concepts relevant to attribution theory.

17.   According to research concerning the belief in a just world, which of the following people should be *least* likely to be critical of or derogate the plight of a victim?

   b.   **Charlie, who is prompted to take the victim's perspective** Taking the victim's perspective is one way to reduce the tendency to be critical of a victim. The individuals described in the other choices for this question have an *increased* likelihood of derogating victims, due to people's tendency to want to believe in a just world – the belief that individuals get what they deserve in life, an orientation that leads people to disparage victims.

18. Stacey, a high school student, came home past her curfew. She claimed the fog was so bad that she couldn't drive. Her parents argued that she was just being thoughtless. This difference in views is consistent with the

    d. **actor-observer effect.** The actor-observer effect is the tendency to attribute one's own behavior to situational causes and others' behavior to personal causes. Stacey attributed her own behavior to a situational cause (the fog), whereas her parents attributed her behavior to a personal cause (her thoughtlessness). The confirmation bias concerns the impact of expectations, which is irrelevant to this question. The false-consensus effect concerns overestimating the consensus for one's opinions, attributes, and behaviors; there is no mention of estimates concerning consensus in this question. The self-fulfilling prophecy refers to the process by which one's expectations about a person eventually lead that person to behave in ways that confirm those expectations; there is no mention in this question about the effect of someone's expectations on another's behavior.

19. Researchers have found that when participants are asked whether there are more English words that start with the letter *r* or that have the letter *r* as the third letter, most participants guess that there are more words that start with the letter *r*. This phenomenon most clearly reflects the

    c. **the availability heuristic.** The availability heuristic is the tendency to estimate the likelihood of an event on the basis of how easily instances of it come to mind. Although the English language contains many more words with *r* as the third letter rather than the first, it is easier for most people to bring to mind words that start with *r*, and thus they judge these words to be more common. The covariation theory is an attribution model, so it cannot account for this phenomenon. The primacy effect and the confirmation bias are relevant to impression formation, not to these types of judgment.

20. For the first time since he began college, Brad goes to his professor for help. His professor shows him some new study techniques. Brad thinks his instructor is a genuinely dedicated teacher. Brad's opinion is an example of a

    c. **personal attribution.** A personal attribution focuses on the internal characteristics of an actor. Brad's explanation of the teacher's behavior indeed focuses on internal qualities of the teacher. This is in contrast to a situational attribution, which focuses on factors external to the actor. The primacy effect concerns the strong impact that information learned early in a sequence has on impressions; because there is no mention in this question of a sequence of events that began with his going to the teacher for help, there is no reason to believe the primacy effect is relevant. Central traits exert powerful influence on overall impressions, causing people to assume the presence of other traits as well. In this example, no specific traits (such as warm or cold) were specified and no other traits assumed.

Answers to Essay Questions: Sample Essays

1.   While observing someone's behavior, why are people more likely to commit the fundamental attribution error when they are cognitively busy, or distracted?

According to the two-step model of the attribution process, people first identify a behavior and make a quick personal attribution, and then correct or adjust this initial inference to account for situational influences. The first step then is simple and automatic and being cognitively busy should not interfere with the simple and automatic step of making a personal attribution. The second step, correcting the inference to take into account situational influences, however, requires attention, thought, and effort. Being cognitively busy reduces a perceiver's ability to give the second step the attention, thought, and effort needed to correct the initial inference to account for situational influences; therefore, the result is a personal attribution that does not take into sufficient account the situational influences that may have affected the behavior. In other words, the result is the fundamental attribution error. If, in contrast, perceivers are not cognitively busy (that is, if they are not distracted by other demands on their attention), then they will have a better chance of dedicating the attention, thought, and effort needed for the second step of the process. Thus, these perceivers would be more likely to take situational influences into account, thereby avoiding the fundamental attribution error.

2.   What is the primacy effect? Describe two major reasons for this effect.

The primacy effect refers to the tendency for information presented early in a sequence to have more impact on impressions than information presented later. One reason for this effect is that once perceivers think they have formed an accurate impression, they become less attentive to subsequent information. Thus, this later information has less impact on the overall impression. A second reason for the primacy effect is known as the change-of-meaning hypothesis. According to this hypothesis, once people form an initial impression, they interpret subsequent information in light of that impression. Thus, initial information influences the interpretation of later information, resulting in the initial information having a particularly strong influence on the overall judgment.

3.   Imagine the following study. Participants read about a number of experiments, each of which supports the idea that introverted people make better psychiatrists than extroverted people. The participants are given time to think about this information. Later, they are informed that the experiments they had read were fictitious – they were fabricated by the experimenter for purposes of the experiment. Despite the fact that the information was discredited, however, the participants continue to believe that introverted people probably would make better psychiatrists than extroverted people. What social psychological concept best describes the results of this study? Why does this phenomenon occur?

This study illustrates the concept of belief perseverance. Individuals exhibit belief perseverance when they stick to an initial belief even after it has been discredited. The reason this phenomenon occurs is that, once people come up with explanations to account for some theory or belief, those explanations take on a life of their own. The more they think about this belief, the more explanations or support they come up with to increase their confidence in the belief. Thus, even when the information on which the belief or theory was initially based is discredited, people may have generated enough alternative explanations or recalled enough other evidence consistent with the belief that they continue to believe it.

5

Perceiving Groups

LEARNING OBJECTIVES: GUIDELINES FOR STUDY

You should be able to do each of the following by the conclusion of Chapter 5.

1. Define discrimination, prejudice, and stereotypes. Explain the different mechanisms by which stereotypes form. Describe social categorization and the ingroup/outgroup distinction. Discuss advantages and disadvantages of social categorization. Delineate sociocultural and motivational factors that can influence social categorization. (*pp. 131-136*)

2. Describe how stereotypes distort perceptions of individuals. (*pp. 136-138*)

3. Describe how the mechanisms of illusory correlations, attributional processes, subtyping, and confirmation biases help perpetuate stereotypes. Identify target attributes that can encourage changes in stereotypic beliefs. (*pp. 138-141*)

4. Describe factors that can impact whether stereotypes are accessed in order to judge others, and whether they are automatic or intentional. Explain the conditions under which stereotype suppression may backfire. (*pp. 141-147*)

5. Explain how prejudice differs from a stereotype. Describe the Robbers Cave study and explain the significance of its results. (*pp. 147-148*)

6. Explain realistic conflict theory and relative deprivation. (*pp. 148-149*)

7. Explain social identity theory and how it accounts for ingroup favoritism. Identify factors that can influence social identity processes and explicate their influence. (*pp. 149-153*)

8. Identify when people first learn their gender identity and of the existence of gender stereotypes. Comment on the accuracy of gender stereotypes. (*pp. 153-155*)

9. Describe ways in which gender stereotypes are strengthened and maintained. Describe the impact of the media on gender stereotyping and explain social role theory. Explain ambivalent sexism. (*pp. 155-161*)

10. Explain modern racism and describe procedures that can be used to uncover it. (*pp. 161-165)*

11. Explain the contact hypothesis and the conditions that enable intergroup contact to reduce prejudice. (*pp. 165-168)*

12. Describe how discrimination is perceived by the target. Explain how people's self-esteem can be influenced by whether they believe a perceiver's evaluation of them is influenced by their race. Explain the concept of stereotype threat, including the reason it happens and its potential consequences. (*pp. 168-173*)

MAJOR CONCEPTS: THE BIG PICTURE

Below are five basic issues or principles that organize Chapter 5. You should know these issues and principles well.

1. Stereotypes are beliefs about others based on their group membership. People share the tendency to put individuals into social categories. This social categorization leads people to see outgroup members as all the same and to generalize from characterizations of individual members to characterizations of the group and vice versa. Stereotypes lead to the distortion of people's perception of others, and can be self-perpetuating. Further they are often activated without people's awareness and can affect people's perceptions without their awareness. With effort, people can sometimes overcome the use of stereotypes, but suppression of their use is difficult on a long-term basis.

2. Prejudice consists of negative feelings about others based on their group membership. Such feelings of prejudice can arise from conflicts with others, as demonstrated in the Robbers Cave experiment. They can also arise from an effort to maintain a positive sense of self-esteem and a positive group identity.

3. Sexism is discrimination based on a person's gender. Gender stereotypes are prevalent the world over and are often activated in our personal interactions. Although differences do exist between men and women on some traits, gender stereotypes typically exaggerate these differences. The media and social roles help perpetuate gender stereotypes. The impact of sexism is clearly seen in the context of occupational access: Both men and women are judged more favorably when they apply for jobs that are consistent with gender stereotypes.

4. Racism is discrimination based on a person's skin color or ethnic origin. Although most research has focused on Blacks and Whites the growing number of multiracial people in North America is bound to change this. While overt endorsement of racist statements on surveys has declined over the years subtle forms of prejudice are still pervasive and can take the form of ambivalence or even unconscious discrimination. Recently a number of researchers have made important advances in detecting such forms of modern racism by using computer tasks. Intergroup contact can lead to better intergroup relations, but only when the groups have equal status, and are characterized by personal interactions, the need to achieve common goals, and supportive social norms. The jigsaw classroom is one technique that has consistently improved race relations.

5. The targets of discrimination often cope with negative feedback by attributing it to prejudice. While this strategy appears to have positive consequences for self-esteem, targets may feel a lack of control over their lives. The targets of stereotyping are affected by the threat that the stereotype implies about their ability. Research on stereotype threat shows that when people believe others may view them stereotypically this can undermine their academic performance; however, when this stereotype threat is removed, the stereotyped perform just as well as the unstereotyped.

KEY TERM EXERCISE: THE CONCEPTS YOU SHOULD KNOW

Below are all of the key terms that appear in **boldface** in Chapter 5. To help you better understand these concepts, rather than just memorize them, write a definition for each term in your own words. After doing so, look at the next section where you'll find a list of definitions from the textbook for each of the key terms presented in random order. For each of your definitions, find the corresponding textbook definition. Note how your definitions compare with those from the textbook.

Key Terms

1. contact hypothesis

2. relative deprivation

3. modern racism

4. superordinate goals

5. contrast effect

6. illusory correlation

7. social identity theory

8. outgroup homogeneity effect

9. realistic conflict theory

10. stereotype

11. ingroup favoritism

12. prejudice

13. sexism

14. social role theory

15. social categorization

16. discrimination

17. jigsaw classroom

18. racism

19. group

20. subliminal presentation

21. ambivalent sexism

22.   ingroups

23.   outgroups

Textbook Definitions

a.   The tendency to discriminate in favor of ingroups over outgroups.
b.   A method of presenting stimuli so faintly or rapidly that people do not have any conscious awareness of having been exposed to them.
c.   Feelings of discontent aroused by the belief that one fares poorly compared to others.
d.   The classification of persons into groups on the basis of common attributes.
e.   Any behavior directed against persons because of their identification with a particular group.
f.   Prejudice and discrimination based on a person's racial background.
g.   The theory that hostility between groups is caused by direct competition for limited resources.
h.   Shared goals that can be achieved only through cooperation among individuals or groups.
i.   A form of prejudice that surfaces in subtle ways when it is safe, socially acceptable, and easy to rationalize.
j.   Two or more persons perceived as related because of their interaction with each other over time, membership in the same social category, or common fate.
k.   A belief that associates a group of people with certain traits.
l.   Negative feelings toward persons based solely on their membership in certain groups.
m.   A cooperative learning method used to reduce racial prejudice through interaction in group efforts.
n.   Discrimination based on a person's gender.
o.   The theory that small gender differences are magnified in perception by the contrasting social roles occupied by men and women.
p.   The theory that people favor ingroups over outgroups in order to enhance their self-esteem.
q.   The tendency to perceive stimuli that differ from expectations as being even more different than they really are.
r.   The tendency to assume that there is a greater similarity among members of outgroups than of ingroups.
s.   The theory that direct contact between hostile groups will reduce prejudice under certain conditions.
t.   An overestimate of the association between variables that are only slightly correlated or not correlated at all.
u.   Comprised of two elements: *hostile* sexism, which concerns negative, resentful feelings about women's abilities, value, and challenging of men's power, and *benevolent* sexism, which concerns affectionate, chivalrous, but potentially patronizing feelings of women needing and deserving protection.
v.   Groups to which we belong
w.   Different from groups to which we do not belong

ANSWERS FOR KEY TERM EXERCISE

Each of the key terms listed below is followed by the letter of the textbook definition that matches it.

1.	contact hypothesis	s	4.	superordinate goals	h
2.	relative deprivation	c	5.	contrast effect	q
3.	modern racism	i	6.	illusory correlation	t

7.	social identity theory	p		16.	discrimination	e
8.	outgroup homogeneity effect	r		17.	jigsaw classroom	m
9.	realistic conflict theory	g		18.	racism	f
10.	stereotype	k		19.	group	j
11.	ingroup favoritism	a		20.	subliminal presentation	b
12.	prejudice	l		21.	ambivalent sexism	u
13.	sexism	n		22.	ingroups	v
14.	social role theory	o		23.	outgroups	w
15.	social categorization	d				

PRACTICE QUIZ: TEST YOUR KNOWLEDGE OF THE CHAPTER

Multiple-Choice Questions

1. Social categorization and ingroup favoritism are two processes that lead to

    a. stereotypes.
    b. authoritarian personalities.
    c. contrast effects.
    d. contact hypotheses.

2. The blue gang and the red gang are having a dispute about who controls the turf around the vacant lot next to the high school. During this dispute, fighting between the two groups escalates. This result could be most easily predicted from

    a. social categorization theory.
    b. modern racism.
    c. confirmation biases.
    d. realistic conflict theory.

3. Lisa thinks that women are more critical than men. At parties, she is more likely to notice a sarcastic remark from a woman than from a man. Lisa's perceptions illustrate

    a. ingroup favoritism.
    b. the confirmation bias.
    c. contrast effects.
    d. androgyny.

4. Frank thinks that all his instructors are windbags, but he also thinks there are two kinds of instructors: those who are arrogant and those who are incompetent. Frank's classification of instructors is an example of

    a. a contrast effect.
    b. subtyping.
    c. ingroup bias.
    d. the confirmation bias.

5. Illusory correlations, attributions about men's and women's behavior, subtyping men and women who are not representative, and seeking information that supports one's views are four ways in which

    a. gender roles develop.
    b. gender stereotypes endure.
    c. all stereotypes are overcome.
    d. prejudice is minimized.

6. In the Robbers Cave experiment, young boys came to dislike each other intensely after a period of

    a. striving to attain superordinate goals.
    b. forming friendships with one another.
    c. competing with one another.
    d. fighting a common enemy.

7. Steve expects poor work from his Italian-American executives. One of these employees turns in a report of above-average quality. However, Steve thinks the report is fantastic. Steve's reaction may have resulted from

    a. realistic conflict.
    b. social roles.
    c. contrast effects.
    d. old-fashioned racism.

8. For Joel, being a part of the basketball team is very important. When asked to compare the basketball team to the football team, he states, "We're a lot better than they are." According to social identity theory, this ingroup favoritism should make Joel

    a. feel better about himself and the basketball team.
    b. pay less attention to football.
    c. guilty that he judged the football team so arbitrarily.
    d. concerned about the status of the football team.

9. Karen divides her class into small, racially mixed groups. Each student learns part of the assigned work and then teaches it to others in the group. This procedure is an example of

    a. a jigsaw classroom.
    b. a minimal group.
    c. ingroup favoritism.
    d. realistic conflict.

10. According to cross-cultural research, men are widely seen as more _____ than women.

    a. intelligent
    b. sensitive
    c. aggressive
    d. people-oriented

11. In the media, images of men are more likely than images of women to emphasize

    a. activity.
    b. strength.
    c. the face.
    d. the body.

12. The cognitive capacity to process information carefully and the motivation to be accurate are two factors that enable people to

    a. engage in modern racism.
    b. avoid using stereotypes.
    c. feel relative deprivation.
    d. form illusory correlations.

13. Stereotypes about men and women present

    a. a totally biased picture of men and women.
    b. a kernel of the truth that is oversimplified and exaggerated.
    c. an accurate description of the differences between men and women.
    d. unrealistic expectations for men and women.

14. According to _____ theory, gender stereotypes result from expectations created by a sex-based division of the labor market.

    a. realistic conflict
    b. social identity
    c. social role
    d. outgroup homogeneity

15. Recent research on the measurement of modern racism shows that it

    a. is easily measured with a questionnaire.
    b. is impossible to measure.
    c. can be measured with computer tasks without the respondent's awareness.
    d. is difficult to measure with a questionnaire, but possible if anonymity is assured.

16. According to theories of modern racism, discrimination against Blacks is most likely to occur when it is

    a. explicit and obvious.
    b. socially unacceptable.
    c. easy to rationalize.
    d. confrontational in form.

17. Tom is prejudiced against Blacks but doesn't admit it. He sees a Black store owner being robbed. Although he would ordinarily try to help in such emergencies, he does nothing. Tom's lack of action is an example of

    a. old-fashioned racism.
    b. reaction time.
    c. outgroup homogeneity.
    d. modern racism.

18. Gender schematics are more likely to see the world

    a. as divided into masculine and feminine categories.
    b. as biased against their gender.
    c. in distorted ways that favor their gender.
    d. as a place where their own gender dominates.

19. In one high school students from the country have always fought with students from the city. In order to reduce this intergroup hostility, the principal decides that the people in the two groups need to have personal contact on an equal-status basis. What else might he do to try to achieve more harmonious relations between the groups?

    a. Have them work together on a schoolwide project.
    b. Have them identify the strengths of their own group.
    c. Have them take classes designed to familiarize the groups with aspects of each other's lives.
    d. Have teachers identify students based on their group affiliation.

20. Research on stereotype threat by Steele and his colleagues shows that stereotypes can

    a. motivate people to try harder in order to improve their performance.
    b. undermine the academic performance of women and minorities.
    c. only affect members of groups who do not have power in society.
    d. lower the self-esteem of members of stereotyped groups.

Essay Questions

1. Describe how social categorization can lead people to see all members of an outgroup in the same way. Discuss the implications of this process for intergroup perceptions and interactions.

2. Explain how social identity theory accounts for favoritism of the ingroup over the outgroup.

3. Characterize modern racism. Describe when it is most, and least, likely to be evident.

ANSWERS TO THE PRACTICE QUIZ

Multiple-Choice Questions: Correct Answers and Explanations

1. Social categorization and ingroup favoritism are two processes that lead to

   a. **stereotypes.** Social categorization and ingroup favoritism are two mechanisms that produce stereotyping. Social categorization is the dividing of people into groups based on salient differences between the individuals. Research has demonstrated that once people are categorized into groups, their differences are exaggerated. Ingroup favoritism takes social categorization one step further. When people make social categorizations, they not only exaggerate group differences but they do so in a way that favors their own group. Social categorization and ingroup bias are less likely to produce contrast effects. These emerge when people face disconfirming information. They also are unrelated to authoritarian personalities, which are thought to arise from early childhood experience. Contact hypotheses suggest that intergroup contact can diminish stereotypes and prejudice.

2. The blue gang and the red gang are having a dispute about who controls the turf around the vacant lot next to the high school. During this dispute, fighting between the two groups escalates. This result could be most easily predicted from

   d. **realistic conflict theory.** The two gangs appear to be fighting over a scarce resource – the vacant lot. Realistic conflict theory tries to account for such situations, predicting that when such a conflict occurs animosity between the groups will increase. Social categorization could also predict animosity between the groups, but not the escalation of conflict during the dispute. Confirmation biases and modern racism would not make clear predictions about this situation, because there is insufficient information about the gangs' racial compositions or their expectations about one another.

3. Lisa thinks that women are more critical than men. At parties, she is more likely to notice a sarcastic remark from a woman than from a man. Lisa's perceptions illustrate

   b. **the confirmation bias.** The confirmation bias, or the tendency to pay particular attention to information that confirms one's beliefs, is evident in the fact that Lisa finds it easy to notice sarcastic remarks made by women at parties. This phenomenon is unlikely to result from ingroup favoritism, because Lisa is a woman herself, and there is no evidence that it is related to contrast effects or androgyny.

4. Frank thinks that all his instructors are windbags, but he also thinks there are two kinds of instructors: those who are arrogant and those who are incompetent. Frank's classification of instructors is an example of

b. **subtyping.** Frank seems to have a negative stereotype about instructors, but he has also differentiated them into two subcategories. Frank's classification of the instructors does not show evidence of contrast effects, ingroup bias, or confirmation bias. If his views depicted contrast effect, one would expect him to have an overly positive view of instructors if they gave a good lecture. If his views depicted ingroup bias, one would expect him to state how people in his group (i.e., students) are so much better than instructors. Finally, if his views depicted the confirmation bias, one would expect to find evidence that he quickly judges instructors to be windbags.

5. Illusory correlations, attributions about men's and women's behavior, subtyping men and women who are not representative, and seeking information that supports one's views are four ways in which

b. **gender stereotypes endure.** Illusory correlations work to exaggerate any gender differences that do exist. Research suggests that people make different attributions for men's and women's behaviors and these attributions bolster stereotypes. By subtyping people as "exceptions to the rule," people can maintain their stereotypes even when they are faced with people who do not fit the stereotypes. Finally, people tend to seek out information that supports their stereotypes about men and women. This confirmation bias causes stereotypes to endure. Gender roles may be reinforced by attributions and people's seeking of information, but it is unclear how illusory correlations or subtyping would lead to gender role development. These processes help stereotypes to endure, rather than allowing stereotypes to be overcome or allowing prejudice to be minimized.

6. In the Robbers Cave experiment, young boys came to dislike each other intensely after a period of

c. **competing with one another.** In this famous experiment, the researchers devised a situation whereby two groups of boys competed with one another. After this period of competition, the two groups began to show intense animosity and dislike for one another. In this early part of the experiment there was no evidence of striving to attain superordinate goals, forming friendships with one another, or fighting a common enemy.

7. Steve expects poor work from his Italian-American executives. One of these employees turns in a report of above-average quality. However, Steve thinks the report is fantastic. Steve's reaction may have resulted from

c. **contrast effects.** Steve's reaction is a good example of a contrast effect. He expected a poor outcome but was surprised by a decent outcome, and then he exaggerated the quality of this outcome. It is unclear how social roles or realistic conflict could have accounted for Steve's reaction, and old-fashioned racism might have led Steve to deny rather than enhance the quality of the report.

8. For Joel, being a part of the basketball team is very important. When asked to compare the basketball team to the football team, he states, "We're a lot better than they are." According to social identity theory, this ingroup favoritism should make Joel

a. **feel better about himself and the basketball team.** Social identity theory suggests that ingroup favoritism makes people feel better about their group which in turn makes them feel better about themselves. Social identity theory has little to say about where people focus their attention. It would suggest, however, that Joel would not feel guilty about his evaluation of the football team and that he would be unconcerned about their status.

9.   Karen divides her class into small, racially mixed groups. Each student learns part of the assigned work and then teaches it to others in the group. This procedure is an example of

    a.   **a jigsaw classroom.** In a jigsaw classroom the instructor arranges for students of different racial groups to interact together on joint tasks in an equal-status environment. Karen's class is an excellent example. None of her actions are related to minimal groups, ingroup favoritism, or realistic conflict. Instead, she seems to have developed an environment with real groups that undermines ingroup favoritism and realistic conflict.

10.   According to cross- cultural research men are widely seen as more _____ than women.

    c.   **aggressive.** Cross-cultural research suggests that, in almost all countries that have been studied, men are seen as more aggressive than women. In most of these countries, women are seen as more sensitive and people-oriented. There are no consistent differences in perceptions of the intelligence of men and women.

11.   In the media, images of men are more likely than images of women to emphasize

    c.   **the face.** Studies of the contents of advertisements show that men's faces and heads – but women's bodies – are more likely to be pictured in ads. There is no evidence that men are more often seen as active and strong.

12.   The cognitive capacity to process information carefully and the motivation to be accurate are two factors that enable people to

    b.   **avoid using stereotypes.** Some research suggests that, when people have the cognitive capacity to process information (they are not distracted) and try hard to be accurate, they can also avoid using stereotypes. By making this effort they are also less likely to display modern racism, to feel relative deprivation, and form illusory correlations.

13.   Stereotypes about men and women present

    b.   **a kernel of the truth that is oversimplified and exaggerated.** There are some differences between men and women (e.g., men tend to be more aggressive than women), but gender stereotypes exaggerate these differences and fail to take into account that there are more similarities between men and women than there are differences. Thus gender stereotypes are not totally biased, and they do not portray an accurate description of the differences between men and women. Gender roles sometimes present demanding and unrealistic expectations of men and women, but this feature is less characteristic of gender stereotypes.

14.   According to _____ theory, gender stereotypes result from expectations created by a sex-based division of the labor market.

    c.   **social role** Social role theory suggests that the sex-based division of labor provides a justification for gender stereotypes. From this perspective, gender roles, which contain a stereotypical component, create a sex-based division of labor. This division of labor is then used as a justification for the original stereotype. Realistic conflict theory, social identity theory, and outgroup homogeneity all have little to say about sex-based division of labor.

15. Recent research on the measurement of modern racism shows that it

    c. **can be measured with computer tasks without the respondent's awareness.** Recent research has shown that bias in the measurement of modern racism occurs when it is measured with a questionnaire, even if anonymity is assured. Several researchers, however, have developed computer tasks that measure modern racism without the respondent being aware that the measurement is occurring. These appear to have avoided the problems of questionnaire measures.

16. According to theories of modern racism, discrimination against Blacks is most likely to occur when it is

    c. **easy to rationalize.** Theories of modern racism suggest that many people are torn between egalitarian values and lingering beliefs in the inferiority of Blacks. For these people, overt endorsement of stereotypes is difficult because it conflicts with their egalitarian values, but when stereotyping and prejudice can be easily rationalized the lingering belief in the inferiority of Blacks is expressed. Modern racists are unlikely to discriminate against Blacks when the discrimination is explicit and obvious, socially unacceptable, or confrontational in form, because these kinds of discrimination may challenge their egalitarian values.

17. Tom is prejudiced against Blacks but doesn't admit it. He sees a Black store owner being robbed. Although he would ordinarily try to help in such emergencies, he does nothing. Tom's lack of action is an example of

    d. **modern racism.** Tom's actions illustrate modern racism because he failed to help the store owner in a situation that offered a good rationalization not to help. In this sort of situation, Tom would be unlikely to feel that he was not being egalitarian. Tom's behavior is less an example of old-fashioned racism because, if he were an old-fashioned racist, he would be more likely to admit his prejudice. Reaction time and outgroup homogeneity have no clear relationship to Tom's behavior.

18. Gender schematics are more likely to see the world

    a. **as divided into masculine and feminine categories.** Gender schematics categorize people and things as being masculine or feminine, and they use these categories more often than do people who are gender aschematic. There is no evidence that gender schematics see the world as biased against their gender, in distorted ways that favor their gender, or as a place where their own gender dominates.

19. In one high school students from the country have always fought with students from the city. In order to reduce this intergroup hostility, the principal decides that the people in the two groups need to have personal contact on an equal-status basis. What else might he do to try to achieve more harmonious relations between the groups?

    a. **Have them work together on a schoolwide project.** The principal has met most of the necessary conditions for establishing intergroup contacts that promote racial harmony, personal contacts, equal status, and norms that support positive relations. One condition he has not met is the establishment of superordinate goals. By having the students work together on a schoolwide project, he could meet this condition as well. Having students identify their group's strengths, having students become familiar with each other's lives, and having teachers identify students based on their group affiliation have not been shown to promote racial harmony. Currently, it is uncertain whether these proposals will help promote racial harmony or not.

20. Research on stereotype threat by Steele and his colleagues shows that stereotypes can

   b. **undermine the academic performance of women and minorities.** Research on stereotype threat shows that when members of a stereotype group are in a situation where others may stereotype them they perform below their potential; but, when this stereotype threat is lifted, their performance improves. Although most of the research on stereotype threat has been on groups that have less power in society (women and minorities), there is some evidence that stereotype threat can affect dominant groups as well. There is no evidence that stereotype threat lowers self-esteem, in fact the theory behind stereotype threat predicts that when people face stereotype threat they will protect their self-esteem rather than have their self-esteem lowered. Finally, although it is an interesting idea, there is no evidence that stereotype threat motivates people to try harder in order to improve their performance.

Answers to Essay Questions: Sample Essays

1. Describe how social categorization can lead people to see all members of an outgroup in the same way. Discuss the implications of this process for intergroup perceptions and interactions.

   Social categorization can lead people to see all members of an outgroup in the same way through the outgroup homogeneity effect. When people categorize others as belonging to social groups, they exaggerate the differences between these groups. They also tend to see their own group as being comprised of many different types of people, whereas they see the outgroup as being composed of people who are all basically the same. One reason for this outgroup homogeneity effect is that people usually have a lot more contact with people in their own group than they have with people in another group. Therefore, they get to know more types of people in their own group. A second reason for this effect is that even if people have contact with members of the outgroup, this contact might reflect a biased sample. They might only have contact with a certain type of member of the outgroup. The outgroup homogeneity effect has important implications. If people perceive all outgroup members as being the same, then they will evaluate the whole group based on the actions of one individual, and they will evaluate the individual based on their perceptions of the group.

2. Explain how social identity theory accounts for favoritism of the ingroup over the outgroup.

   Social identity theory suggests that people favor their own group over other groups because they want to maintain a positive social identity; they want to see their group as being a good group and as having status. This positive social identity, in turn, makes people feel better about themselves and raises their self-esteem. Thus people favor their own group over other groups in order to feel better not only about the group they belong to but also about themselves.

3.   Characterize modern racism. Describe when it is most, and least, likely to be evident.

Modern racism is a recent form of racism characterized by a tension between two values: an egalitarian value which maintains that all people are created equal and deserve equal treatment, and traditional racial prejudice which maintains that certain racial groups are inferior to other groups. The latter value, often expressed in old-fashioned racism, is not as often expressed in modern racism. Modern racists rarely endorse overt prejudice and discrimination because it contradicts their egalitarian values. Yet the influence of racist values can be seen in situations where prejudice and discrimination can be justified. Here modern racists will engage in discriminatory actions; but when the discrimination could challenge their egalitarian values, they will be less likely to discriminate.

6

Attitudes

LEARNING OBJECTIVES: GUIDELINES FOR STUDY

You should be able to do each of the following by the conclusion of Chapter 6.

1. Describe how attitudes are defined and how they are measured. Address both self-report and covert techniques. (*pp. 179-183*)

2. Discuss how attitudes are related to behaviors. Explain what types of attitudes are most likely to predict behavior, and under what circumstances. (*pp. 183-187*)

3. Define the peripheral and central routes to persuasion, and explain their differences. Describe how persuasion differs in the two routes. Explain how self-esteem and intelligence are related to persuasion. Identify factors that influence which route of processing is chosen. (*pp. 187-190*)

4. Explain how the source of a persuasive message affects whether people are likely to be persuaded by the message. Describe the circumstances under which the source of the message is less important than what it said, including the reasons behind the sleeper effect. (*pp190-196*)

5. Explain how the content of a message can affect whether people are persuaded by it. Compare primacy and recency effects. Describe how both the cognitive and emotional contents of a message affect its persuasiveness. (*pp. 196-201*)

6. Explain how characteristics of the audience can moderate the extent to which it is persuaded by a message. Describe how forewarning and inoculating the audience may affect levels of persuasion. (*pp. 201-205*)

7. Describe how role-playing can influence one's attitudes. (*pp. 205-206*)

8. Explain the elements of the classic version of cognitive dissonance theory. Discuss how this theory can account for insufficient justification, insufficient deterrence, effort justification, and the justification of difficult decisions. (*pp. 206-210*)

9. Explain the "new look" of cognitive dissonance and address how it expands upon Festinger's original theory. (*pp. 210-212*)

10. Describe three alternate routes to self-persuasion. Explain how each of these routes describes the ways in which people justify their behaviors. (*pp. 211-215*)

MAJOR CONCEPTS: THE BIG PICTURE

Below are three basic issues or principles that organize Chapter 6. You should know these issues and principles well.

1. The study of attitudes has been one of the foundations of social psychology. Researchers measure attitudes by asking people direct questions about their attitudes or by assessing people's behavior or physiological responses. In general, our attitudes are not as strong a predictor of our behaviors as one might think. However, attitudes do a better job of predicting behavior when the attitude is specific to a behavior or particularly important.

2. One of the earliest fields of study in social psychology focused on persuasion, the changing of people's attitudes through communication. Research in this field has found that there are two basic routes to persuasion: a central route that emphasizes the content of a message and systematic deliberate processing of information, and a peripheral route that emphasizes more rules of thumb or heuristic processing of information. The source of a message, its content, and the audience that hears the message all affect whether the message will be persuasive.

3. People are also persuaded by their own actions and the roles that they play. Cognitive dissonance theory maintains that when people engage in an action that conflicts with their attitudes they will feel tension, and that the easiest way to reduce this tension is to change their attitude. In this way the theory predicts that people will change their attitudes to match their behavior. Recent revisions to cognitive dissonance theory suggest that this attitude change occurs mostly when people take responsibility for their actions. Other approaches emphasize that people rationalize their behaviors by changing them to manage a positive impression with others, to maintain a positive view of themselves, or to be consistent with the way in which they perceive their own behavior.

KEY TERM EXERCISE: THE CONCEPTS YOU SHOULD KNOW

Below are all of the key terms that appear in **boldface** in Chapter 6. To help you better understand these concepts, rather than just memorize them, write a definition for each term in your own words. After doing so, look at the next section where you'll find a list of definitions from the textbook for each of the key terms presented in random order. For each of your definitions, find the corresponding textbook definition. Note how your definitions compare with those from the textbook.

Key Terms

1. theory of planned behavior

2. cognitive dissonance theory

3. persuasion

4. inoculation hypothesis

5. central route to persuasion

6. insufficient deterrence

7. peripheral route to persuasion

8.   attitude

9.   elaboration

10.   sleeper effect

11.   need for cognition (NC)

12.   insufficient justification

13.   psychological reactance

14.   attitude scale

15.   implicit attitudes

16.   facial electromyograph (EMG)

17.   bogus pipeline

Textbook Definitions

a.   A condition in which people freely perform an attitude-discrepant behavior without receiving a large reward.

b.   The process by which a person does not think carefully about a communication and is influenced instead by superficial cues.

c.   A personality variable that distinguishes people on the basis of how much they enjoy effortful cognitive activities.

d.   The theory that attitudes toward a specific behavior combine with subjective norms and perceived control to influence a person's actions.

e.   The process by which a person thinks carefully about a communication and is influenced by the strength of its arguments.

f.   An electronic instrument that records facial muscle activity associated with emotions and attitudes.

g.   A phony lie-detector device that is sometimes used to get respondents to give truthful answers to sensitive attitude questions.

h.   The process by which attitudes are changed.

i.   The theory that holding inconsistent cognitions arouses psychological tension that people become motivated to reduce.

j.   A delayed increase in the persuasive impact of a noncredible source.

k.   A multiple-item questionnaire designed to measure a person's attitude toward some object.

l.   Attitudes that we cannot report in questionnaires because we're not aware of having them

m.   A condition in which people refrain from engaging in a desirable activity, even when only mild punishment is threatened.

n.   The idea that exposure to weak versions of a persuasive argument increases later resistance to that argument.

o.   A positive or negative reaction to a person, object, or idea.

p.   The theory that people react against threats to their freedom by asserting themselves and perceiving the threatened freedom as more attractive.

q.   The process of thinking about and scrutinizing the arguments contained in a persuasive communication.

ANSWERS FOR KEY TERM EXERCISE

Each of the key terms listed below is followed by the letter of the textbook definition that matches it.

1.	theory of planned behavior	d	10.	sleeper effect	j
2.	cognitive dissonance theory	i	11.	need for cognition (NC)	c
3.	persuasion	h	12.	insufficient justification	a
4.	inoculation hypothesis	n	13.	psychological reactance	p
5.	central route to persuasion	e	14.	attitude scale	k
6.	insufficient deterrence	m	15.	implicit attitudes	l
7.	peripheral route to persuasion	b	16.	facial electromyograph (EMG)	f
8.	attitude	o	17.	bogus pipeline	g
9.	elaboration	q			

PRACTICE QUIZ: TEST YOUR KNOWLEDGE OF THE CHAPTER

Multiple-Choice Questions

1. Attitudes are often measured by means of self-reports, questionnaires on which respondents endorse their attitudes. Another technique often used is to collect covert measures. Covert measures are

    a. collected from the respondent's friends, who describe what his or her attitudes are.
    b. measures that are taken in addition to self-report measures.
    c. collected by use of a bogus pipeline.
    d. measures collected indirectly.

2. The theory of planned behavior suggests that one reason attitudes might not always predict behaviors is that

    a. people may not have strong enough attitudes.
    b. people's attitudes may be outside their awareness.
    c. people may have only false attitudes.
    d. people's intentions to act may be different from their attitudes.

3. In a television commercial for dental floss, the spokesperson (a well-known TV celebrity) says that eight out of ten dentists recommend the product. The reference to dentists is an attempt to establish

    a. communicator credibility.
    b. self-monitoring.
    c. insufficient deterrence.
    d. fear arousal.

4. Central and peripheral routes to persuasion are proposed by

    a. the dual-process theory.
    b. cognitive dissonance theory.
    c. self-perception theory.
    d. the theory of planned behavior.

5. In their campaigns, John Smith and Jane Doe both present arguments stressing the logic of their positions and detailing the many reasons for their views. These candidates are trying to persuade voters through

    a. attitude-discrepant behavior.
    b. heuristics.
    c. the peripheral route.
    d. the central route.

6. If we must make a choice between two equally desirable options, the positive attributes of the alternative we ultimately do *not* choose will cause

    a. a sleeper effect.
    b. a primacy effect.
    c. cognitive dissonance.
    d. attitude inoculation.

7. Harry is listening to a debate. Harry assumes that the person with the most arguments is the best-qualified candidate. Harry's reasoning is an example of

    a. cognitive dissonance.
    b. elaboration.
    c. a heuristic.
    d. impression management.

8. Jeanne has a negative attitude toward bikes but a positive attitude toward skateboards. If she has spent a lot of time biking and only a little time skateboarding, which attitude is likely to be the stronger one?

    a. Her attitude toward biking is likely to be stronger.
    b. Her attitude toward skateboarding is likely to be stronger.
    c. Both attitudes are likely to be strong.
    d. Both attitudes are likely to be weak.

9. Yvonne is buying a new car. The salesman sees a school sticker on her old car and says he went to the same university. The reference to a common alma mater is an attempt to create

    a. self-monitoring.
    b. communicator like ability.
    c. the need for cognition.
    d. fear arousal.

10. Mindy chose to write an essay for her English class that argued for a tuition hike even though she didn't want one. Her instructor sent the essay to the president of the university, who decided that if students could write so well then there should *not* be a tuition hike. Recent research on cognitive dissonance theory would suggest that Mindy will

    a. experience physiological arousal.
    b. feel responsible for her essay.
    c. experience no cognitive dissonance.
    d. change her attitude about tuition hikes.

11. Personal involvement and the sleeper effect are two limitations on the persuasive impact of

    a. fear-arousing communications.
    b. communicator credibility.
    c. attitude-discrepant behavior.
    d. self-perception processes.

12. The mayor and her challenger set up a debate three weeks before the election. They both agree that this will be the one and only debate. The challenger gets the opportunity to decide whether to go first or last in the debate. What advice would you give her?

    a. She should go first.
    b. She should go last.
    c. It doesn't matter whether she goes first or last.
    d. Whether she should go first or last depends on what she is going to say.

13. In theory, people who are high in the need for cognition should receive persuasive communications that rely on

    a. arguments.
    b. heuristics.
    c. attributions.
    d. mood.

14. Helen has always been upset by doctors who are late for appointments and believes that people should criticize them for this behavior. Yet she has taken a job as a sales representative for a drug company and must try to schmooze with the doctors on her route. In time, Helen is likely to

    a. learn to dislike doctors even more.
    b. dislike her job.
    c. be less concerned with doctors' tardiness.
    d. feel stress in most of her interactions.

15. Heuristics and body movements are two kinds of cues that determine persuasion in

    a. attitude-discrepant behavior.
    b. cognitive dissonance.
    c. the peripheral route.
    d. the central route.

16. Carly decides to write a paper for her English class that argues for capital punishment even though she is against it. Cognitive dissonance theory would predict that Carly is

    a. likely to favor capital punishment more.
    b. likely to favor capital punishment less.
    c. unlikely to change her views on capital punishment.
    d. likely to find the experience enjoyable.

17. People are most likely to be in a state of cognitive dissonance if they

    a. experience no physiological arousal.
    b. engage in attitude-inconsistent behavior.
    c. engage in attitude-consistent behavior.
    d. experience negative unforeseeable consequences.

18. Advertisers and others often use the "overheard communicator" technique to enhance a speaker's

    a. like ability.
    b. perceived competence.
    c. reactance.
    d. trustworthiness.

19. Gabriella decides to buy a portable tape player rather than a portable CD player. She wonders if she made the right decision. After discussing her purchase with a friend she is reminded that she is a good student and a good friend. Research on self-affirmation theory would predict that Gabriella will

    a. experience physiological arousal.
    b. feel bad about her decision.
    c. experience no cognitive dissonance.
    d. come to a stronger conviction that she made the right decision.

20. Self-perception theory suggests that people change their attitudes to match their behaviors because they

    a. feel a psychological tension.
    b. want to maintain a positive self-image.
    c. infer their attitudes from their behaviors.
    d. want to impress other people.

Essay Questions

1. Discuss whether attitudes lead to behaviors that are consistent with the attitudes. Describe aspects of attitudes that can strengthen their relationship to behavior.

2.   Compare and contrast the central and peripheral routes to persuasion.

3.   Explain how cognitive dissonance theory accounts for changes in people's attitudes based on changes in their behavior.

ANSWERS TO THE PRACTICE QUIZ

Multiple-Choice Questions: Correct Answers and Explanations

1.   Attitudes are often measured by means of self-reports, questionnaires on which respondents endorse their attitudes. Another technique often used is to collect covert measures. Covert measures are

   d.   measures collected indirectly. Covert measures, like facial movements, physiological recordings, and brain-wave patterns, are collected indirectly without the respondents being able to control their responses. The bogus pipeline is not a covert measure as respondents are aware their attitudes are being measured and can control their responses. This procedure attempts to get respondents to give accurate responses. Sometimes covert measures are collected by means of self-reports but usually they are not. Finally, asking a respondent's friends about the respondent's attitudes is usually viewed as assessing the friend's attitudes about the respondent's attitude via self-report.

2.   The theory of planned behavior suggests that one reason attitudes might not always predict behaviors is that

   d.   people's intentions to act may be different from their attitudes. The theory of planned behavior stresses that in order for an attitude to predict behavior, that attitude must lead to an intention to act in a specific situation. But such intentions to act do not always follow from people's attitudes, which prevents their attitudes from predicting their behavior. The theory of planned behavior does not encompass the strength of attitudes, the awareness of attitudes, or the falseness of attitudes.

3. In a television commercial for dental floss, the spokesperson (a well-known TV celebrity) says that eight out of ten dentists recommend the product. The reference to dentists is an attempt to establish

    a. **communicator credibility.** In referring to the expert's opinion, the spokesperson is drawing upon the credibility of the expert in an attempt to influence the audience. It does not appear that the spokesperson is arousing fear or attempting to deter (or use insufficient deterrence against) people's use of the product. Finally, the spokesperson does not seem to be using a self-monitoring strategy, attempting to present himself or herself in a way that is appropriate for the specific situation.

4. Central and peripheral routes to persuasion are proposed by

    a. **the dual-process theory.** The dual-process theory of persuasion suggests that people process information through one of two channels: a central channel in which the quality of the arguments affects people's response to a persuasive message, and a peripheral channel in which heuristics or simplistic rules affect people's response to a persuasive message. Cognitive dissonance theory, self-perception theory, and the theory of planned behavior do not propose central and peripheral routes to persuasion.

5. In their campaigns, John Smith and Jane Doe both present arguments stressing the logic of their positions and detailing the many reasons for their views. These candidates are trying to persuade voters through

    d. **the central route.** The central route to persuasion, as elaborated by the dual-process theory, leads to persuasion through the quality of the arguments that are presented for or against a position. John Smith and Jane Doe appear to be trying to use this route to persuasion. The peripheral route to persuasion, also elaborated by the dual-process theory, leads to persuasion through the use of heuristics or simplistic rules that people may use without even being aware of it. There is no evidence that John Smith and Jane Doe are trying to use heuristics or a peripheral route to persuasion. Finally, it does not appear that the campaigners are trying to use attitude-discrepant behavior to influence voters. This strategy would require the voters to engage in actions that would later lead to a change in their attitudes.

6. If we must make a choice between two equally desirable options, the positive attributes of the alternative we ultimately do not choose will cause

    c. **cognitive dissonance.** When people make a choice, the positive features of the option they did not choose are inconsistent with their choice. This inconsistency creates cognitive dissonance. For example, if I choose between a chocolate chip cookie and a molasses cookie, and pick the molasses cookie, the fact that I love chocolate would be inconsistent with my choice and would create cognitive dissonance. There is no evidence that the positive attributes of the alternative not chosen (chocolate chips in my example) create a sleeper effect, a primacy effect, or attitude inoculation.

7. Harry is listening to a debate. Harry assumes that the person with the most arguments is the best-qualified candidate. Harry's reasoning is an example of

    c. **a heuristic.** Here Harry is using a simplistic rule, or heuristic – whoever makes the most arguments is the best-qualified candidate. He is not elaborating on what the candidate is saying, and there is no evidence that Harry is experiencing cognitive dissonance or that he is concerned with impression management.

8. Jeanne has a negative attitude toward bikes but a positive attitude toward skateboards. If she has spent a lot of time biking and only a little time skateboarding, which attitude is likely to be the stronger one?

    a. Her attitude toward biking is likely to be stronger. Jeanne has spent more time biking and thus has more personal contact with biking. Research shows that attitudes about objects with which people have more personal contact tend to be stronger attitudes. Jeanne's attitude toward skateboarding is less likely to be strong because she has had little contact with skateboarding.

9. Yvonne is buying a new car. The salesman sees a school sticker on her old car and says he went to the same university. The reference to a common alma mater is an attempt to create

    b. communicator like ability. The salesman is establishing that in at least one respect, that he went to the same school, he is similar to Yvonne. This similarity may increase Yvonne's liking for the salesman, which in turn may increase his like ability. It does not appear that the salesman is arousing fear and need for cognition is a personality construct that distinguishes people on how much they enjoy effortful cognition, so neither of these answers is correct. The salesman may be engaging in self-monitoring or trying to present himself in a way that is appropriate to the situation, but the reference to his alma mater does not seem to be a self-monitoring strategy per se.

10. Mindy chose to write an essay for her English class that argued for a tuition hike even though she didn't want one. Her instructor sent the essay to the president of the university, who decided that if students could write so well then there should *not* be a tuition hike. Recent research on cognitive dissonance theory would suggest that Mindy will

    c. experience no cognitive dissonance. Even though Mindy chose to write a counterattitudinal essay, she is unlikely to experience cognitive dissonance because her actions had no negative consequences. In fact, her actions produced a result that was consistent with her attitude; her essay actually prevented the tuition hike she opposed. Because Mindy is unlikely to feel cognitive dissonance, she is also unlikely to experience physiological arousal, take responsibility for her essay, or change her attitude about tuition hikes.

11. Personal involvement and the sleeper effect are two limitations on the persuasive impact of

    b. communicator credibility. When people are personally involved with a topic, they are more likely to process information about that topic through the central route to persuasion. Processing information in this way should lead them to be less concerned with communicator credibility and more concerned with the content of the message. The sleeper effect is the tendency for people to lose track of which message was associated with which communicator such that over time, the effect of communicator credibility becomes increasingly less and people evaluate the message more on its own merit. Fear-arousing messages may have less affect for people who are personally involved with a topic, but there is no evidence that the sleeper effect influences fear-arousing communications. Finally, attitude-discrepant behavior and self-perception processes are more likely to occur when people are personally involved with a topic and thus probably not affected by the sleeper effect.

12. The mayor and her challenger set up a debate three weeks before the election. They both agree that this will be the one and only debate. The challenger gets the opportunity to decide whether to go first or last in the debate. What advice would you give her?

   a. **She should go first.** Because the election is just a few weeks away the challenger would probably be better off going first, so she could take advantage of the primacy effect. Research shows that when two messages are presented together and there is a time separation before people make a decision about the quality of the messages, as is the case in this example, people tend to prefer the first message – a primacy effect. Recency effects tend to occur when people make a decision about the quality of the messages immediately after the messages are presented. Primacy and recency effects are general effects and seem to be the result of the way people's memories work; as such, they do not seem to be affected by the content of messages.

13. In theory, people who are high in the need for cognition should be persuaded by communications that rely on

   a. **arguments.** The dual-process theory suggests that people who are high in the need for cognition are more likely to process information through the central route to persuasion and, therefore, are more likely to rely on the quality of arguments for or against a position. By the same token, they are less likely to rely on heuristics associated with the peripheral route to persuasion.

14. Helen has always been upset by doctors who are late for appointments and believes that people should criticize them for this behavior. Yet she has taken a job as a sales representative for a drug company and must try to schmooze with the doctors on her route. In time, Helen is likely to

   c. **be less concerned with doctors' tardiness.** On her route, Helen will probably meet a lot of doctors who are late for their appointments with her, but Helen will probably have to say things like, "That's OK. I don't mind that you are late for your appointment." This action that is discrepant with her attitude will likely set the wheels of justification in motion, and Helen will likely change her attitude to match her behavior. As she makes this transition, it is unlikely that she will dislike doctors more, dislike her job, or be stressed in most of her interactions.

15. Heuristics and body movements are two kinds of cues that determine persuasion in

   c. **the peripheral route.** When people are persuaded through the peripheral route they are persuaded without fully processing the incoming information. Instead of relying on the content of the information, they use simplistic rules, or heuristics, and rely on simple cues like body movements when processing information along this route. In contrast, persuasion in the central route is determined by the quality of the arguments not peripheral cues. Attitude-discrepant behavior and cognitive dissonance are likely to promote attitude change through self-justification.

16. Carly decides to write a paper for her English class that argues for capital punishment even though she is against it. Cognitive dissonance theory would predict that Carly is

   a. **likely to favor capital punishment more.** Early research testing cognitive dissonance theory found that when people write essays that are contrary to their attitudes, they often change their attitudes so that they are closer to their essays. Cognitive dissonance explained this finding by noting that the act of writing the essay is inconsistent with the writer's attitudes, which should produce cognitive dissonance. The easiest way to reduce this dissonance is for the people to change their attitudes; after all, they cannot take back their essays. Therefore, in this example, cognitive dissonance theory would predict that Carly will change her attitude about capital punishment and become more in favor of it; and because she has experienced cognitive dissonance, she probably has not found the experience enjoyable.

17.   People are most likely to be in a state of cognitive dissonance if they

   b.   **engage in attitude-inconsistent behavior.** An inconsistency between people's attitudes and their behavior is likely to produce cognitive dissonance. Cognitive dissonance is associated with physiological arousal, so if people experience no physiological arousal they probably have no cognitive dissonance. Attitude-consistent behavior does not produce cognitive dissonance because the attitudes and behavior in this case are consonant, not dissonant. Finally, research has shown that unforeseeable consequences often prevent cognitive dissonance in situations when it might otherwise be present.

18.   Advertisers and others often use the "overheard communicator" technique to enhance a speaker's

   d.   **trustworthiness.** People will often discount a persuasive communication if they know that the person is trying to persuade them. The "overheard communicator" technique tries to nullify this discounting by presenting the persuasive appeal as if it were not directed at the audience. This technique gives the impression that the communicator is quite sincere and trustworthy. The "overheard communicator" technique has not been shown to have an affect on like ability or the perceived competence of the communicator, nor has it been shown to create reactance.

19.   Gabriella decides to buy a portable tape player rather than a portable CD player. She wonders if she made the right decision. After discussing her purchase with a friend, she is reminded that she is a good student and a good friend. Research on self-affirmation theory would predict that Gabriella will

   c.   **experience no cognitive dissonance.** Self-affirmation theory proposes that people experience cognitive dissonance because their actions have threatened their self-image and that if their self-image is repaired after it has been threatened then they will no longer experience cognitive dissonance. In this case, making a difficult decision may have threatened Gabriella's confidence that she is a competent decision maker, thus perhaps initially creating cognitive dissonance; but when she was reminded she is a good student and a good friend, this information should have repaired her self-image and removed any cognitive dissonance she may have felt. Because Gabriella is unlikely to experience cognitive dissonance, she is unlikely to experience physiological arousal, feel bad about her decision, or come to a stronger conviction that she made the right decision.

20.   Self-perception theory suggests that people change their attitudes to match their behaviors because they

   c.   **infer their attitudes from their behaviors.** Self-perception theory proposes that people infer their own attitudes in the same way that they infer other people's attitudes: on the basis of behaviors. Therefore, self-perception theory suggests that people make inferences about their own attitudes from their behaviors. Self-perception theory does not propose that people change their attitudes because they feel a psychological tension, want to maintain a positive self-image, or want to manage the impressions of others.

Answers to Essay Questions: Sample Essays

1. Discuss whether attitudes lead to behaviors that are consistent with the attitudes. Describe aspects of attitudes that can strengthen their relationship to behavior.

   In general, attitudes show a weak relationship to behavior; they predict behaviors, but not very well. For one thing, people are not always thinking about their attitudes. Indeed, attitudes are better predictors of behavior when the attitudes are accessible – that is, when people are thinking about their attitudes. In addition, not all attitudes are well thought out and clear in the minds of the people who hold them. Some attitudes are closer to a weak impression than to a strong feeling that people have toward an object. Attitudes generally are better predictors if they are strong.

2. Compare and contrast the central and peripheral routes to persuasion.

   The dual-process model proposes that there are two basic routes by which persuasive communication leads to changes in attitudes: the central route and the peripheral route. The central route to persuasion leads to attitude change that occurs when the audience pays attention to the quality of the arguments and elaborates or thinks about the content of the message. When people are persuaded via the central route to persuasion, they systematically process the information with which they are presented. The peripheral route to persuasion leads to attitude change that occurs when the audience pays attention to heuristics that suggest what attitude change should take place. When people are persuaded via the peripheral route, they spend little time analyzing the information that is being presented and they may not even be aware that they are being persuaded.

3. Explain how cognitive dissonance theory accounts for changes in people's attitudes based on changes in their behavior.

   Cognitive dissonance theory proposes that when people have two thoughts that are psychologically inconsistent, they will experience physiological arousal and cognitive dissonance. In addition, the theory suggests that people will be motivated to reduce this cognitive dissonance by changing whatever thought is easiest to change. When people engage in a behavior that is inconsistent with their attitudes, they are likely to have conflicting thoughts such as "I just did that" and "I don't think people should do that." These two thoughts are psychologically inconsistent and, as such, lead to physiological arousal and cognitive dissonance. To reduce this dissonance, people are more likely to change their attitudes – that is, to think "Maybe it is OK if people do that." This thought is much easier to change than the thought that they had engaged in the action.

7

Conformity

LEARNING OBJECTIVES: GUIDELINES FOR STUDY

You should be able to do each of the following by the conclusion of Chapter 7.

1. Define social influence. Define, compare, and contrast conformity, compliance, and obedience. (*pp. 219-222*)

2. Compare normative with informational influence and public with private conformity. Explain each in the context of Sherif's and Asch's studies. (*pp. 222-226*)

3. Identify and explain each of the factors that have been shown to affect levels of conformity, including group size, awareness of norms, having an ally, age, gender, and cultural influences. Identify factors that distinguish collectivistic from individualistic cultures. (*pp. 226-231*)

4. Differentiate between majority and minority influence. Explain how to account for the effects of minority influence, and how majorities and minorities exert pressure to effect people's behavior. (*pp. 231-234*)

5. Describe the ways in which the discourse of making requests affects compliance, with reference to mindlessness. Explain how people may use the norm of reciprocity to encourage others to comply with their requests. (*pp. 234-236*)

6. Define and explain the sequential request strategies known as the foot-in-the-door technique, low-balling, the door-in-the-face technique, and the that's-not-all technique. Explain why each works. Refer to the principles of self-perception, commitment, perceptual contrast, and reciprocity. Address how to resist these strategies. (*pp. 236-240*)

7. Explain blind obedience. Describe the procedures used in Milgram's research on obedience to authority. Compare the predictions made about how participants would behave to what actually happened. Summarize how each of the following affected levels of obedience in the study: participants (e.g., their sex, personality), authority figure (e.g., his or her prestige, presence), proximity of victim, and experimental procedure (e.g., the roles of responsibility and gradual escalation). Explain why behavior in the Milgram study differed from that of the Gamson et al. study. (*pp. 240-249*)

8. Summarize social impact theory. Identify the factors that influence a source's strength, immediacy, and number, and the aspects of the target that facilitate resistance. Explain the relevance of this theory to conformity, compliance, and obedience. (*pp. 249-251*)

MAJOR CONCEPTS: THE BIG PICTURE

Below are four basic issues or principles that organize Chapter 7. You should know these issues and principles well.

1. Conformity is the tendency for people to change their behavior to be consistent with group norms. Sherif and Asch conducted two classic studies that illustrate different types of influence and conformity, including informational influence, normative influence, private conformity, and public conformity. A number of situational factors affect majority influence, and a number of other factors affect minority influence. Majorities and minorities may exert different kinds of pressure and elicit different types of conformity. Resistance to conformity is enhanced by having allies in dissent.

2. In conformity situations, people follow implicit group norms; but in compliance situations, people are influenced by direct *explicit* requests. The style of a request may affect the likelihood that someone will comply with the request even if its content is not very reasonable. People are more likely to comply when they feel indebted to a requester. A number of sequential request strategies can effectively trap people into compliance. Compliance techniques are more likely to work if they are subtle and if people are not vigilant.

3. In contrast to situations eliciting compliance, if the request is a command and the requester is (or seems to be) a figure of authority, the resulting social influence is obedience. Milgram's research on the forces of destructive obedience demonstrated dramatically how susceptible people are to obedience to authority, and how a number of situational factors can increase or decrease the chances that people will obey an authority's command to harm another human being. Just as processes of social influence breed obedience, they can also support acts of defiance against authority.

4. Social influence situations vary in their impact on people. Social Impact Theory maintains that three factors – strength, immediacy, and number – affect the impact of a social influence situation. Strength refers to the power that the influence source has over those being influenced. Immediacy refers to the proximity in time and space between the influence source and the target of influence; the closer the source, the greater its impact. And finally, number refers to the number of influence sources; the larger the number of sources, the greater their impact – at least up to a point.

KEY TERM EXERCISE: THE CONCEPTS YOU SHOULD KNOW

Below are all of the key terms that appear in **boldface** in Chapter 7. To help you better understand these concepts, rather than just memorize them, write a definition for each term in your own words. After doing so, look at the next section where you'll find a list of definitions from the textbook for each of the key terms presented in random order. For each of your definitions, find the corresponding textbook definition. Note how your definitions compare with those from the textbook.

Key Terms

1. individualism

2. that's-not-all technique

3. conformity

4. foot-in-the-door technique

5. idiosyncrasy credits

6. private conformity

7. collectivism

8. compliance

9. normative influence

10. low-balling

11. public conformity

12. social impact theory

13. door-in-the-face technique

14. obedience

15. informational influence

16. minority influence

Textbook Definitions

a. Tendency to change perceptions, opinions, or behavior in ways that are consistent with group norms.
b. Influence that produces conformity because a person believes others are correct in their judgments.
c. Influence that produces conformity because a person fears the negative social consequences of appearing deviant.
d. Change of mind that occurs when a person privately accepts the position taken by others.
e. A superficial change in observable behavior, without a corresponding change of opinion, produced by real or imagined group pressure.
f. A cultural orientation in which independence, autonomy, and self-reliance take priority over group allegiances.
g. A cultural orientation in which interdependence, cooperation, and social harmony take priority over purely personal goals.
h. Interpersonal "credits" a person earns by following group norms.
i. Changes in behavior that are elicited by direct requests.
j. A two-step compliance technique in which an influencer sets the stage for the real request by first getting a person to comply with a much smaller one.
k. A two-step compliance technique in which the influencer secures agreement with a request but then increases the size of that request by revealing hidden costs.
l. A two-step compliance technique in which an influencer prefaces the real request with one so large that it is sure to be rejected.
m. A two-step compliance technique in which the influencer begins with an inflated request, then immediately decreases its apparent size by offering a discount or bonus.
n. The process by which dissenters produce change within a group.

o.   Behavior change produced by the commands of authority.

p.   Theory that social influence depends on the strength, immediacy, and number of source persons relative to target persons.

ANSWERS FOR KEY TERM EXERCISE

Each of the key terms listed below is followed by the letter of the textbook definition that matches it.

1.	individualism	**f**	9.	normative influence	**c**
2.	that's-not-all technique	**m**	10.	low-balling	**k**
3.	conformity	**a**	11.	public conformity	**e**
4.	foot-in-the-door technique	**j**	12.	social impact theory	**p**
5.	idiosyncrasy credits	**h**	13.	door-in-the-face technique	**l**
6.	private conformity	**d**	14.	obedience	**o**
7.	collectivism	**g**	15.	informational influence	**b**
8.	compliance	**i**	16.	minority influence	**n**

PRACTICE QUIZ: TEST YOUR KNOWLEDGE OF THE CHAPTER

Multiple-Choice Questions

1.   Jane conducts a new experiment based on Milgram's study of destructive obedience. She manipulates the number of authorities and participants present in the room. She finds that when there are three people in authority present all giving similar commands to one participant, obedience rates are extremely high. However, when there are several participants and only one person in authority giving orders, obedience rates are quite low. These findings are most consistent with

a.   research findings on informational influence.
b.   social impact theory.
c.   the two-step compliance technique.
d.   reciprocation ideology.

2.   Which of the following people is *least* likely to conform to group pressure?

a.   An adolescent in eighth grade
b.   A person from an individualistic culture
c.   A person from a collectivistic culture
d.   A person whose attention has been drawn to the group norm

3.   Before registering for class, Susan asks her friends about a professor. They all say the professor is a great teacher. Not knowing the professor, Susan therefore comes to believe that he is a great teacher and looks forward to taking his class. This illustrates

a.   reciprocal concessions.
b.   perceptual contrast.
c.   informational influence.
d.   public conformity.

4. Although they are distinct techniques, the foot-in-the-door, door-in-the-face, low-balling, and that's-not-all techniques are similar in that they all involve

    a. starting with a small request and subsequently raising the costs.
    b. normative influence.
    c. two steps.
    d. the norm of reciprocity.

5. Joanie asked an acquaintance named Chachi if he would do a small favor for her. After he agreed and did the small favor, Joanie then asked him to do an even larger favor for her. This scenario describes

    a. the foot-in-the-door technique.
    b. reciprocal concessions.
    c. low-balling.
    d. minority influence.

6. Hector's friends all say a recent test was difficult. Hector thinks the test was easy. When asked what he thought, Hector agrees with his friends. This outcome illustrates

    a. normative influence.
    b. private conformity.
    c. reciprocity norms.
    d. obedience.

7. A dozen participants were gathered into a group. An authority figure approached the group and ordered the group to do something most of the participants thought was morally wrong. The group defied the authority, refusing to obey. According to social impact theory, a factor likely to have helped the group defy the authority is that the

    a. social impact of the authority was divided among the dozen targets.
    b. source of the social influence was not immediate.
    c. situation created normative influence rather than informational influence.
    d. situation was ambiguous.

8. Which of the following people should be *least* likely to conform to a unanimous majority in a situation similar to that faced by the participants in Asch's study concerning line judgments?

    a. Jeff, who is not confident about his eyesight
    b. Shari-Beth, who made her responses in public
    c. Jacob, who comes from a collectivistic culture
    d. Benjamin, who saw someone else dissent

9. When Milgram exposed participants to an authority who demanded that they harm another person by administering electric shocks of up to 450 volts to him, he initially found that the percentage of participants who obeyed the authority's orders to administer all of these shocks was

    a. 0.1 percent.
    b. 10 percent among the male participants and 50 percent among the female participants.
    c. 65 percent.
    d. more than 97 percent.

10. Karen needs to type a term paper. To persuade her roommate to let Karen use her typewriter, Karen first lends her some notes that the roommate needs and then asks if she can use her typewriter. Karen is using the

    a. social impact theory.
    b. that's-not-all technique.
    c. low-balling technique.
    d. norm of reciprocity.

11. Although neither group makes any explicit requests or demands of her, Joni expresses pro-conservative opinions when she is with her conservative friends and she expresses anti-conservative opinions when she is with her liberal friends. Joni's actions best illustrate

    a. compliance.
    b. individualism.
    c. conformity.
    d. obedience.

12. A majority is more likely to be persuaded to change its views if the dissenting minority

    a. has accumulated idiosyncrasy credits.
    b. seems very obstinate and unusual.
    c. keeps changing back and forth from conforming to dissenting.
    d. is perceived as an outgroup.

13. Which of the following is most accurate concerning gender differences in levels of conformity?

    a. Across situations, men are reliably more likely than women to conform to a group norm.
    b. Across situations, women are reliably more likely than men to conform to a group norm.
    c. When they think they are being observed, women conform more and men conform less than they do in more private situations.
    d. There is no evidence of gender differences in levels of conformity.

14. Sherif conducted a study in which participants in totally darkened rooms estimated how far a dot of light appeared to move. Asch conducted a study in which participants were asked to report which of three lines was identical in length to a standard line. Compared to the participants in Sherif's study, those in Asch's study exhibited more

    a. vulnerability to informational influence.
    b. private conformity.
    c. obedience.
    d. public conformity.

15. Though in the minority and new to the Senate, a group of senators argued consistently, persuasively, and successfully against a particular bill. Most of the other senators eventually agreed with them that the bill should not be approved. In this example, the first group of senators derived their power to influence from their

   a. idiosyncrasy credits.
   b. style of behavior.
   c. sheer number.
   d. reciprocation ideology.

16. Keana hopes that Naomi will pledge $5 and sign a petition in support of a community center. Keana first asks Naomi if she'd be willing to pledge $50 in support of a proposed community center. Naomi politely declines. Keana then asks Naomi if she'd be willing to pledge $5 and sign a petition in support of the community center. Naomi complies. Keana's ability to get Naomi to pledge $5 and sign the petition is likely to have been enhanced by Keana's use of the

   a. foot-in-the-door technique.
   b. low-balling technique.
   c. door-in-the-face technique.
   d. that's-not-all technique.

17. Oscar was walking in a relatively clean parking lot. Walking a few feet in front of him was a man named Felix. Oscar observed Felix stop to pick up and throw into a garbage can some litter that someone had thrown on the ground. Having seen Felix do this, Oscar, who was just about to throw his gum wrapper on the ground, stopped himself from doing this and instead threw the wrapper into the garbage can. Oscar was influenced by Felix's behavior because it

   a. made Oscar more aware of injunctive norms.
   b. elicited obedience in Oscar.
   c. made Oscar exhibit reciprocal concessions.
   d. was a sequential strategy.

18. Bickman and his colleagues had a stranger (actually a confederate) approach people on the street and order them to do something. People were most willing to comply with these orders when the

   a. stranger watched them closely.
   b. stranger was dressed in a uniform.
   c. the initial command was extreme and a subsequent one was smaller.
   d. participants were not authoritarian.

19. In which of the following situations is Matthew most likely to exhibit private conformity?

   a. Matthew is sure of the proper way to behave, but he is faced with a very large group that is behaving in a very different way.
   b. Matthew is not at all sure of the proper way to behave, and he is in the presence of three other people who are confident that their behavior is correct.
   c. Matthew is sure of the proper way to behave, but he is faced with a small but unanimous group that is behaving in a very different way.
   d. Matthew is commanded by an authority to behave in a particular way.

20. By their willingness to maintain independence from the majority, people in the minority force other group members to

    a. publicly, but not privately, conform.
    b. respond with informational influence.
    c. issue idiosyncrasy credits to them.
    d. think carefully about a problem.

Essay Questions

1. Sherif conducted a study in which participants in totally darkened rooms estimated how far a dot of light appeared to move. Asch conducted a study in which participants were asked to report which of three lines was identical in length to a standard line. Was the conformity found in Sherif's study private conformity, public conformity, or both? Was the conformity found in Asch's study private conformity, public conformity, or both? How can one tell the difference? Explain your answers.

2. Summarize the door-in-the-face technique. Give two reasons why this is such an effective strategy for eliciting compliance.

3. Summarize the ways in which Milgram varied the authority in different conditions of his research on destructive obedience. How did these variations affect the levels of obedience observed?

ANSWERS TO THE PRACTICE QUIZ

Multiple-Choice Questions: Correct Answers and Explanations

1.   Jane conducts a new experiment based on Milgram's study of destructive obedience. She manipulates the number of authorities and participants present in the room. She finds that when there are three people in authority present all giving similar commands to one participant, obedience rates are extremely high. However, when there are several participants and only one person in authority giving orders, obedience rates are quite low. These findings are most consistent with

      b.   social impact theory. Social impact theory holds that social influence depends on the strength, immediacy, and number of source persons relative to target persons. In Jane's study, the levels of obedience are affected by the number of source persons relative to target persons. Informational influence produces conformity because a person believes others are correct in their judgments. There is no evidence that the participants would have this belief; in addition, Jane's study is about obedience to commands rather than conformity to a group norm. There is no single (i.e., "the") two-step compliance technique but rather several, including the foot-in-the-door and the door-in-the-face techniques. These concern eliciting compliance to a request rather than obedience to an authority; moreover, there is nothing in this question about a technique involving two steps. A person's reciprocation ideology refers to his or her individual motives in using the norm of reciprocity; this is not relevant here.

2.   Which of the following people is *least* likely to conform to group pressure?

      b.   A person from an individualistic culture. An individualistic culture is one that values independence, autonomy, and self-reliance over group allegiances. People from such a culture are more likely to exert their independence and autonomy over group allegiances and hence to resist conformity than are people from a collectivistic culture, which is one that values interdependence, cooperation, and social harmony over purely personal goals. Adolescents are particularly vulnerable to peer pressure, so an adolescent in eighth grade is relatively likely to conform to group pressure. And making people aware of a group norm increases the likelihood that they will conform to the group norm.

3.   Before registering for class, Susan asks her friends about a professor. They all say the professor is a great teacher. Not knowing the professor, Susan therefore comes to believe that he is a great teacher and looks forward to taking his class. This illustrates

      c.   informational influence. Informational influence is influence that produces conformity because a person believes others are correct in their judgments. Faced with a clear consensus among her friends, and not having had any opportunity to form her own opinion about the professor, Susan reasonably assumes that her friends' judgments are valid; hence, she adopts their opinion. The notion of reciprocal concessions refers to the pressure to respond to changes in a bargaining position; there is no bargaining going on in this example. In the context of social influence, perceptual contrast refers to the tendency to perceive a request as smaller if it was preceded by a larger request than if it was not; this is not relevant in this example. Public conformity is a superficial change in observable behavior, without a corresponding change of opinion, produced by real or imagined group pressure; but there is no evidence that Susan was responding to real or imagined group pressure, and in any case Susan's opinion *did* change.

4.   Although they are distinct techniques, the foot-in-the-door, door-in-the-face, low-balling, and that's-not-all techniques are similar in that they all involve

    c.   two steps. All of these techniques involve a two-step, sequential trap. In the foot-in-the-door technique, the influencer first gets a person to comply with a relatively small request, and next makes a much larger request. The door-in-the-face technique involves the opposite sequence: first a large request (one so large that it is likely to be rejected), followed by a much smaller request. In low-balling, the influencer first secures an agreement, and next changes the agreement by revealing hidden costs. In the that's-not-all technique, the influencer first begins with an inflated request, then immediately decreases the apparent size of that request by offering a discount or bonus. Thus, each of these techniques involves two steps. As is particularly evident in the door-in-the-face technique, they do not all start with a small request and subsequently raise the costs. Normative influence, which is influence that produces conformity because a person fears the negative social consequences of appearing deviant, is not relevant here because these techniques do not involve groups (against which one could appear deviant) or conformity. And finally, the norm of reciprocity dictates that we should treat others as they treat us; but this is not relevant in the foot-in-the-door technique, in which the influencer does not do anything that would make the person feel the need to reciprocate.

5.   Joanie asked an acquaintance named Chachi if he would do a small favor for her. After he agreed and did the small favor, Joanie then asked him to do an even larger favor for her. This scenario describes

    a.   the foot-in-the-door technique. The foot-in-the-door technique is a two-step compliance technique in which an influencer prefaces the real request by first getting a person to comply with a much smaller one; this is what is described in this example. Reciprocal concessions refer to changes one makes in a bargaining position to reciprocate the opposing side's changes in their bargaining position; there is no bargaining going on in this example. Low-balling is a two-step compliance technique in which the influencer secures agreement with a request but then increases the size of that request by revealing hidden costs. In this example, Joanie did not change an already secured agreement by revealing extra costs; rather, she secured an agreement, and then made a *separate* request that did not change the original agreement. Finally, minority influence is the process by which dissenters produce change within a group. There is no issue between a group and some dissenter(s) in this question.

6.   Hector's friends all say a recent test was difficult. Hector thinks the test was easy. When asked what he thought, Hector agrees with his friends. This outcome illustrates

    a.   normative influence. Normative influence is influence that produces conformity because a person fears the negative social consequences of appearing deviant. Hector's behavior is consistent with this influence; rather than stand out from his friends, Hector decides to agree with them even though he had a different opinion. Because Hector's personal opinion was that the test was easy, there is no evidence of private conformity, which refers to a change of mind that occurs when a person privately accepts the position taken by others. The reciprocity norm dictates that we should treat others as they treat us; but there is no evidence that Hector was reciprocating for a previous favor or for previous conformity on the part of his friends. Finally, obedience is behavior change produced by the commands of authority; but Hector was not commanded by an authority.

7.   A dozen participants were gathered into a group. An authority figure approached the group and ordered the group to do something most of the participants thought was morally wrong. The group defied the authority, refusing to obey. According to social impact theory, a factor likely to have helped the group defy the authority is that the

a.   **social impact of the authority was divided among the dozen targets.** Social impact theory maintains that social influence depends on the strength, immediacy, and number of source persons relative to target persons. According to this theory, resistance to the social influence is more likely to occur to the extent that the social impact of the source (in this case, the authority figure) is divided among many targets (in this case, the dozen participants). In this example, the source of the social influence was immediate; the authority was described as having *approached* the group to give the order. Normative influence is influence that produces conformity because a person fears the negative social consequences of appearing deviant; but there is no evidence that this was a factor in this example. Indeed, the fear of appearing deviant might have prevented anyone from starting the resistance against the authority in the first place. The situation did not seem to have been ambiguous – most of the participants thought that the order they had received was morally wrong. Moreover, they probably would have been more likely to obey if the situation were ambiguous because they'd have had little reason to defy the command.

8.   Which of the following people should be *least* likely to conform to a unanimous majority in a situation similar to that faced by the participants in Asch's study concerning line judgments?

d.   **Benjamin, who saw someone else dissent.** The research of Asch and of others has shown that having an ally in dissent can break the spell cast by a unanimous majority and reduce the normative pressure to conform. Jeff, who is not confident in his eyesight, is vulnerable not only to normative influence in this study but also to informational influence because he would not be sure what the correct answers are. Thus, Jeff would be especially likely to conform. Because the conformity typically elicited in the situation faced by Asch's participants is public conformity, Shari-Beth would be likely to publicly conform. Finally, since collectivistic cultures value interdependence, cooperation, and social harmony over purely personal goals, Jacob, who is from such a culture, would be more likely to conform in order to cooperate and preserve social harmony with the group.

9.   When Milgram exposed participants to an authority who demanded that they harm another person by administering electric shocks of up to 450 volts to him, he initially found that the percentage of participants who obeyed the authority's orders to administer all of these shocks was

c.   **65 percent.** Although psychiatrists who were told about Milgram's experimental procedure *predicted* that only about 0.1 percent of participants would obey through the maximum level of shock, 65 percent of the participants did so all the way to 450 volts. This was true of both male and female participants.

10.   Karen needs to type a term paper. To persuade her roommate to let Karen use her typewriter, Karen first lends her some notes that the roommate needs and then asks if she can use her typewriter. Karen is using the

d.   **norm of reciprocity.** The norm of reciprocity dictates that we should treat others as they treat us. Karen apparently assumes that if she does her roommate a favor, then her roommate will feel obligated to return the favor later. Social impact theory maintains that social influence depends on the strength, immediacy, and number of source persons relative to target persons; but Karen has not manipulated any of these factors, so this theory is not relevant here. The that's-not-all technique is a two-step compliance technique in which the influencer begins with an inflated request, then immediately decreases the apparent size of that request by offering a discount or bonus; but Karen has not offered a discount or bonus. The low-balling technique is a two-step compliance technique in which the influencer secures agreement with a request but then increases the size of that request by revealing hidden costs; but Karen has not increased the size of her request in any way.

11. Although neither group makes any explicit requests or demands of her, Joni expresses pro-conservative opinions when she is with her conservative friends and she expresses anti-conservative opinions when she is with her liberal friends. Joni's actions best illustrate

  c. **conformity.** Conformity is the tendency to change perceptions, opinions, or behavior in ways that are consistent with group norms. In this example, the norm (pro- versus anti-conservative) varies among Joni's friends, and she changes her opinions to be consistent with the norm of each friendship group. Compliance refers to changes in behavior that are elicited by direct requests; but in this example, Joni was not requested to act in a particular way. Individualism is a cultural orientation in which independence, autonomy, and self-reliance take priority over group allegiances; but this is not relevant in this example. And obedience is behavior change produced by the commands of authority; but Joni was not commanded by an authority to change her opinions.

12. A majority is more likely to be persuaded to change its views if the dissenting minority

  a. **has accumulated idiosyncrasy credits.** Idiosyncrasy credits are interpersonal "credits" a person earns by following group norms. Research has shown that by first conforming and then dissenting, minorities may be effective in influencing the majority. Minorities are *less* effective if they seem very obstinate or unusual, do not appear to be sure of themselves because they keep changing back and forth from conforming to dissenting, or are perceived as an outgroup.

13. Which of the following is most accurate concerning gender differences in levels of conformity?

  c. **When they think they are being observed, women conform more and men conform less than they do in more private situations.** This is one of the few reliable sex differences reported in the literature.

14. Sherif conducted a study in which participants in totally darkened rooms estimated how far a dot of light appeared to move. Asch conducted a study in which participants were asked to report which of three lines was identical in length to a standard line. Compared to the participants in Sherif's study, those in Asch's study exhibited more

  d. **public conformity.** Public conformity is a superficial change in observable behavior, without a corresponding change of opinion, produced by real or imagined group pressure. Because the correct answers in Asch's study were so obvious, the participants' conformity reflected the desire to *seem* to agree with the majority; privately, they knew the correct answers. Because the correct answers were obvious to them, the participants in Asch's study were protected from informational influence, which is influence that produces conformity because a person believes others are correct in their judgments. In contrast, Sherif's participants were not at all sure what the correct answers were, so they looked to the other participants to provide them with information about these answers. Thus vulnerable to informational influence, the participants in Sherif's study exhibited private conformity, which is a change of mind that occurs when a person privately accepts the position taken by others; but Asch's participants did not *privately* accept the position taken by the others. Obedience is a behavior change produced by the commands of authority; but there were no commands given by an authority in either of these two studies.

15. Though in the minority and new to the Senate, a group of senators argued consistently, persuasively, and successfully against a particular bill. Most of the other senators eventually agreed with them that the bill should not be approved. In this example, the first group of senators derived their power to influence from their

   b. **style of behavior.** According to Moscovici, people in the *majority* derive social influence power by virtue of their sheer number and inherent power, but people in the *minority* derive social influence power from the style of their behavior. These senators, who were in the minority, argued in a consistent and persuasive style. Idiosyncrasy credits are interpersonal "credits" a person earns by following group norms, but there is no evidence that these senators had any such credits or that they had followed group norms; indeed, because they were new to the Senate, they probably hadn't had time to earn any idiosyncrasy credits, and they certainly were not earning any by arguing consistently against the majority in this example. A person's reciprocation ideology refers to his or her individual motives in the use of the norm of reciprocity; but this is not relevant here because no mention is made either of the senators' motives or attitudes about this norm or of any behaviors that the senators might want to reciprocate.

16. Keana hopes that Naomi will pledge $5 and sign a petition in support of a community center. Keana first asks Naomi if she'd be willing to pledge $50 in support of a proposed community center. Naomi politely declines. Keana then asks Naomi if she'd be willing to pledge $5 and sign a petition in support of the community center. Naomi complies. Keana's ability to get Naomi to pledge $5 and sign the petition is likely to have been enhanced by Keana's use of the

   c. **door-in-the-face technique.** All of the possible answers to this question are two-step compliance techniques. It is important to recognize the differences among them. In the door-in-the-face technique, an influencer prefaces the real request with one so large that it is sure to be rejected. This is the technique described here – by prefacing the request to pledge $5 and sign a petition with a request for a much larger pledge, Keana increased the chances that Naomi would comply with the smaller, second request. In contrast, in the foot-in-the-door technique an influencer prefaces the real request by first getting a person to comply with a much smaller one; this is the *opposite* of what transpired in this example. In the technique of low-balling, the influencer secures agreement with a request but then increases the size of that request by revealing hidden costs; Keana did not secure an agreement first and then reveal hidden costs. And finally in the that's-not-all technique, the influencer begins with an inflated request, then immediately decreases the apparent size of that request by offering a discount or bonus. Keana did not immediately decrease the apparent size of her request by offering a discount or bonus; rather, she first made one request, which was rejected, and then made a different, smaller request.

17. Oscar was walking in a relatively clean parking lot. Walking a few feet in front of him was a man named Felix. Oscar observed Felix stop to pick up and throw into a garbage can some litter that someone had thrown on the ground. Having seen Felix do this, Oscar, who was just about to throw his gum wrapper on the ground, stopped himself from doing this and instead threw the wrapper into the garbage can. Oscar was influenced by Felix's behavior because it

   a. made Oscar more aware of injunctive norms. Injunctive norms specify how people in general *should* behave, for example, they should clean up litter. Research by Cialdini and others has shown that making people aware of group or situational norms increases the likelihood that they will be influenced by these norms. Because no authority commanded anyone in this example, there was no evidence of obedience, which is a behavior change produced by the commands of authority. The notion of reciprocal concessions refers to the pressure to respond to changes in a bargaining position; but there was no bargaining going on in this example. And finally, although several compliance techniques involve a sequential strategy, in which two or more related requests are made in a sequence, no such requests were made in this example.

18. Bickman and his colleagues had a stranger (actually a confederate) approach people on the street and order them to do something. People were most willing to comply with these orders when the

   b. stranger was dressed in a uniform. The presence of a uniform suggests authority. Even when those authorities are not very powerful, they can elicit obedience. Bickman found that obedience levels were high even when the stranger gave the order and then turned the corner, not waiting to see if the orders had been followed. In this study, the stranger did not make an initial extreme command followed by a subsequent, smaller command. Nor did this study measure how authoritarian (a personality dimension characterized by attitudes and behaviors concerning authority, rigidity, dissent, ethnocentrism, etc.) the participants were.

19. In which of the following situations is Matthew most likely to exhibit private conformity?

   b. Matthew is not at all sure of the proper way to behave, and he is in the presence of three other people who are confident that their behavior is correct. Private conformity is most likely to occur when there is no obviously correct or incorrect opinion. Because it is not clear to Matthew what the correct or incorrect opinion is, he is vulnerable to private conformity, particularly because the confidence of the other people should make their opinion a source of informational influence for him. If Matthew were sure of the proper way to behave, he would have been less likely to exhibit private conformity. The presence of a large group, or of a small but unanimous group, that was behaving in a very different way would increase the chances of *public* conformity, but Matthew's confidence would leave him less vulnerable to private conformity. If Matthew were commanded by an authority, he might exhibit obedience, which is a behavior change produced by the commands of authority; but he would not exhibit private conformity.

20. By their willingness to maintain independence from the majority, people in the minority force other group members to

   d. think carefully about a problem. When faced with a persistent minority, majorities often think about a problem more carefully than they would otherwise. As a result, the overall quality or creativity of group decisions is enhanced. Minority influence is more likely to lead to private, rather than public, conformity. Minorities are not particularly likely to cause other group members to respond with informational influence, which is influence that produces conformity because a person believes others are correct in their judgments; instead, the group members are likely to apply their sheer number and power and use normative influence. Idiosyncrasy credits are interpersonal "credits" a person earns by following group norms, but minorities are not in a position of power to "issue" credits to the rest of the group. Indeed, by going against the majority, the minorities are acting in a way that should *cost* them idiosyncrasy credits.

Answers to Essay Questions: Sample Essays

1.   Sherif conducted a study in which participants in totally darkened rooms estimated how far a dot of light appeared to move. Asch conducted a study in which participants were asked to report which of three lines was identical in length to a standard line. Was the conformity found in Sherif's study private conformity, public conformity, or both? Was the conformity found in Asch's study private conformity, public conformity, or both? How can one tell the difference? Explain your answers.

Private conformity is a change of mind that occurs when a person privately accepts the position taken by others. Public conformity is a superficial change in observable behavior, without a corresponding change of opinion, produced by real or imagined group pressure. The conformity found in Sherif's study was primarily private conformity, whereas that found in Asch's study was primarily public conformity. The situation was very ambiguous for the participants in Sherif's study; they could not be sure how far the dot of light really moved. Hence, these participants looked to the other participants to provide them with information about what the correct answers were. Thus vulnerable to the informational influence that the participants provided for each other, the participants in Sherif's study exhibited private conformity to the group norm. One can tell that this was private and not merely public conformity because, when participants in Sherif's study were later asked to make the same judgments alone (in a situation where there would be little pressure against deviating from a group norm), they continued to make judgments consistent with the group norm. By contrast, the situation in Asch's study was not ambiguous; the correct answers were obvious to the participants. When these participants conformed to the judgments given by the majority, they were publicly, but not privately, conforming. That is, they continued to believe their original judgments, but they responded by giving a different judgment so as not to deviate from the rest of the group. One can tell that the conformity was more public than private here because, when participants were asked to write down their answers privately (in a situation where there was much less pressure against deviating from a group norm), levels of conformity dropped sharply.

2.   Summarize the door-in-the-face technique. Give two reasons why this is such an effective strategy for eliciting compliance.

The door-in-the-face technique is a two-step compliance technique in which an influencer prefaces the real request with one so large that it is sure to be rejected. One reason this technique works may have to do with the principle of perceptual contrast. The contrast effect is the tendency to perceive stimuli that differ from expectations or other stimuli as even more different than they really are. In this case, after exposure to the very large request, the second request may seem even smaller than it would otherwise. Cialdini and his colleagues concluded that perceptual contrast is only partly responsible for the effectiveness of the door-in-the-face technique. A second, and possibly more compelling, reason for the effectiveness of this technique concerns reciprocal concessions – namely, the pressure to respond to changes in a bargaining position. When the influencer backs down from the original large request and makes a subsequent smaller request, the person who rejected the original request may perceive the influencer's second request as a concession or gesture of compromise and thus feel pressure to respond in kind by complying with this second request.

3. Summarize the ways in which Milgram varied the authority in different conditions of his research on destructive obedience. How did these variations affect the levels of obedience observed?

Milgram varied the apparent status of the experimenter (the authority) by moving his lab from the prestigious Yale University to a rundown urban office building with no university affiliation. The rate of total obedience dropped from 65 percent at Yale to 48 percent at the office building – still a surprisingly high level of obedience. When the authority of the experimenter was diminished even more by replacing him with what appeared to be another participant, there was a dramatic drop in total obedience to 20 percent. In another condition, the experimenter issued his commands to the participants by telephone. This condition also showed a dramatic drop in obedience from the original condition – 21 percent of the participants obeyed all the way.

8

Group Processes

You should be able to do each of the following by the conclusion of Chapter 8.

1. Distinguish between a group and a collective. Explain how the presence of others affects people's performance on easy and hard tasks, and how Zajonc accounts for these effects. Describe three alternative accounts for this phenomenon. (*pp. 255-258*)

2. Describe how working with others on a task affects people's productivity. Identify factors that can reduce the likelihood that people will engage in social loafing. Explain how the presence of others can lead to increased arousal and social facilitation or decreased arousal and social loafing, depending on whether each member of the group is evaluated separately or the group is evaluated as a whole. (*pp. 258-264*)

3. Define deindividuation. Explain how being in a crowd can lead people to engage in destructive behaviors. Describe how environmental cues and a sense of identity can affect this process. (*pp. 264-267*)

4. Describe the reasons that people join a group, and discuss the process of adjustment to a new group. Explain the processes of group development. (*pp. 267-269*)

5. Describe roles, norms, and cohesiveness, and explain their influence on group behavior. Summarize research on the relationship between cohesiveness and group performance. (*pp. 269-271*)

6. Describe group polarization and delineate the processes that can create it. (*pp. 271-273*)

7. Define groupthink. Describe its antecedents, behavioral symptoms, and consequences. Explicate recent work on groupthink addressing the role of cohesiveness and personality of group members. Address how groupthink can be prevented. (*pp. 273-278*)

8. Describe the different types of tasks that groups perform, and the relationship between group performance and the type of task in which a group is engaged. Discuss goal setting in groups, and the advantages and disadvantages of brainstorming. (*pp. 278-281*)

9. Describe the roles of biased sampling, communication networks, information-processing biases, and diversity in group communication and performance. (*pp. 281-285*)

10. Define a social dilemma. Describe the prisoner's dilemma and resource dilemmas. Discuss mixed motives in the context of these dilemmas, and delineate psychological and structural factors that influence behavior in social dilemmas. (*pp. 285-290*)

11.   Discuss how threat capacity and perceptions of others can lead to the escalation of group conflict. (*pp. 290-292*)

12.   Explain how GRIT, negotiating, and finding common ground can lead to the reduction of group conflict. Distinguish between an arbitrator and a mediator. (*pp. 292-296*)

MAJOR CONCEPTS: THE BIG PICTURE

Below are three basic issues or principles that organize Chapter 8. You should know these issues and principles well.

1.   The presence of others can have a major impact on people's behavior. It improves our performance on simple tasks, but impairs our performance on difficult tasks. If people work with others on a joint project, they tend to slack off and do less work than if they worked individually. And, when people form together in an unorganized crowd, they often lose their sense of identity and can be spurred to violent and destructive acts.

2.   People tend to interact most with others in their group. This group interaction is facilitated by the existence of roles for various members, shared norms for group activity, and group cohesiveness. Interacting with others with shared convictions can strengthen these convictions and lead people to lose perspective on problems and engage in an excessive tendency to seek concurrence, called groupthink. Research on the performance of groups shows that they often do not perform as well as most people think; however, diversity in an integrated group can enhance the group's performance.

3.   People bring different motives to their group interactions. These motives can lead to cooperation, competition, or conflict. Research on social dilemmas suggests that people often respond in kind to others, and that they can be cooperative but will also take unfair rewards if they can get away with it. Conflict between groups can escalate, even if one or both groups have the capacity to harm the other and have little to gain from the conflict. This escalation is often fueled by distorted views of the other group. Fortunately, conflict can also be reduced. Strategies such as negotiating, finding common ground, and using graduated and reciprocated initiatives in tension-reduction (GRIT) are effective in resolving conflict.

KEY TERM EXERCISE: THE CONCEPTS YOU SHOULD KNOW

Below are all of the key terms that appear in **boldface** in Chapter 8. To help you better understand these concepts, rather than just memorize them, write a definition for each term in your own words. After doing so, look at the next section where you'll find a list of definitions from the textbook for each of the key terms presented in random order. For each of your definitions, find the corresponding textbook definition. Note how your definitions compare with those from the textbook.

Key Terms

1.   social dilemma

2.   evaluation apprehension theory

3.   mere presence theory

4.   social loafing

5.   graduated and reciprocated initiatives in tension-reduction (GRIT)

6.   deindividuation

7.   collective

8.   resource dilemma

9.   group polarization

10.   groupthink

11.   social facilitation

12.   brainstorming

13.   distraction-conflict theory

14.   entrapment

15.   integrative agreement

16.   collective effort model

17.   prisoner's dilemma

18.   process loss

Textbook Definitions

a.   A group-produced reduction in individual output on easy tasks where contributions are pooled.

b.   The condition in which commitments to a failing course of action are increased to justify investments already made.

c.   Which concern how two or more people share a limited resource.

d.   A technique that attempts to increase the production of creative ideas by encouraging group members to speak freely without criticizing their own or others' contributions.

e.   A situation in which a self-interested choice by everyone creates the worst outcome for everyone.

f.   A process whereby the presence of others enhances performance on easy tasks but impairs performance on difficult tasks.

g.   People engaged in common activities but with minimal direct interaction.

h.   The theory that individuals will exert effort on a collective task to the degree that they think their individual efforts will be important, relevant, and meaningful for achieving outcomes that they value.

i.   A theory holding that the presence of others will produce social facilitation effects only when those others are seen as potential evaluators.

j.   A group decision-making style characterized by an excessive tendency among group members to seek concurrence.

k.   A negotiated resolution to a conflict in which all parties obtain outcomes that are superior to what they would have obtained from an equal division of the contested resources.

l.   A theory holding that the mere presence of others is sufficient to produce social facilitation effects.

m.   The loss of a person's sense of individuality and the reduction of normal constraints against deviant behavior.

n.   A strategy for unilateral, persistent efforts to establish trust and cooperation between opposing parties.

o.   The exaggeration through group discussion of initial tendencies in the thinking of group members.

p.   A theory holding that the presence of others will produce social facilitation effects only when those others distract from the task and create attentional conflict.

q.   In the prisoner's dilemma, participants are given a series of choices in which they have the option of cooperating or competing.

r.   A group may perform worse than it would if every individual performed up to his or her potential.

ANSWERS FOR KEY TERM EXERCISE

Each of the key terms listed below is followed by the letter of the textbook definition that matches it.

1.	social dilemma	e	10. groupthink	j
2.	evaluation apprehension theory	i	11. social facilitation	f
3.	mere presence theory	l	12. brainstorming	d
4.	social loafing	a	13. distraction-conflict theory	p
5.	graduated and reciprocated initiatives in tension-reduction(GRIT)	n	14. entrapment	b
6.	deindividuation	m	15. integrative agreement	k
7.	collective	g	16. collective effort model	h
8.	resource dilemma	c	17. prisoner's dilemma	q
9.	group polarization	o	18. process loss	r

PRACTICE QUIZ: TEST YOUR KNOWLEDGE OF THE CHAPTER

Multiple-Choice Questions

1.   Dave is a novice tennis player. He is more anxious when being watched by a group of instructors than by a group of novice players. This difference in anxiety illustrates the process of

   a.   social comparison.
   b.   evaluation apprehension.
   c.   social loafing.
   d.   mere presence.

2.   Groups vary in specific characteristics, but all groups can be defined by three essential components:

   a.   attitudes, values, and norms.
   b.   roles, values, and ideologies.
   c.   roles, norms, and cohesiveness.
   d.   values, goals, and cohesiveness.

3.   Ben manages an automobile assembly plant. Since he started requiring workers to inscribe their names on the cars they assemble, quality control has found fewer defective cars. Ben reduced social loafing by making

    a.   integrative agreements.
    b.   superordinate goals.
    c.   contributions identifiable.
    d.   cohesive work teams.

4.   When people work with others on a task, they

    a.   work harder than when they work alone.
    b.   work just as hard as when they work alone.
    c.   don't work as hard as when they work alone.
    d.   work on different tasks than when they work alone.

5.   The marketing staff reports to the marketing director, who in turn reports to the president. This system is an example of

    a.   a communication network.
    b.   production blocking.
    c.   performance matching.
    d.   an integrative agreement.

6.   One consequence of deindividuation is that people experience a decrease in

    a.   social comparison.
    b.   anonymity.
    c.   self-awareness.
    d.   goal striving.

7.   Kathy hopes to join a sorority at her college. One reason she wants to join this group is that she

    a.   is following an implicit norm.
    b.   is looking to develop superordinate goals.
    c.   likes the other members and desires an opportunity to interact with them.
    d.   is vulnerable to groupthink.

8.   The kind of reciprocity that usually reduces cooperation and escalates conflict between parties involves the use of

    a.   perceived competence.
    b.   threat capacity.
    c.   public goods.
    d.   persuasive arguments.

9. The mere presence account of social facilitation suggests that people do better on easy tasks and worse on hard tasks when performing in front of others than when performing alone because

   a. they are concerned about the impression they are making.
   b. they are distracted by the other people.
   c. the presence of other people produces arousal, which in turn affects performance.
   d. they don't work as hard in the presence of others.

10. When people discuss a topic with others in their own social group who agree with them, they are likely to

    a. shift their position away from the initial leanings of the group.
    b. reverse their position altogether.
    c. exhibit no change in their position.
    d. enhance or exaggerate the initial leanings of the group.

11. Linda thinks that capital punishment is wrong and should not be allowed. When she talks to her friends who agree with her views, she most likely will

    a. develop arguments in favor of capital punishment.
    b. believe more strongly that capital punishment is wrong.
    c. be unaffected by her friends' views.
    d. challenge her friends' views.

12. Highly cohesive groups, group structure, and stressful situations are the three major contributing factors in the development of

    a. group roles.
    b. free riders.
    c. groupthink.
    d. superordinate goals.

13. Jane's company is developing a new product. There are indications that the product may be defective and could result in substantial liability for the company. Jane argues that the company's strong record of developing and marketing products suggests that they will pull through this time as well. The board members quickly decide to go ahead with the product despite its dangers. Their reasoning is an example of

    a. group roles.
    b. mutual cooperation.
    c. social loafing.
    d. groupthink.

14. The people in Everytown are celebrating the victory of their town's soccer team in a championship tournament. A large crowd of people join together in the town center to celebrate the victory and begin to feel anonymous. Because people are in this crowd they are more likely to

    a. engage in destructive behaviors.
    b. be reserved because they are concerned about how others will think of them.
    c. celebrate the victory through group cooperation.
    d. be concerned with the evaluations of others.

15. Priscilla and Carol are preparing for a big exam. Priscilla checks out a library book that Carol wants so that Carol can't get it. Carol steals Priscilla's notes so that Priscilla can't use them. Priscilla and Carol are

    a. engaged in a conflict spiral.
    b. both exhibiting an individualist orientation.
    c. engaged in a public goods dilemma.
    d. restrained by threat capacity.

16. When two people are faced with a situation in which mutual cooperation by both is beneficial to both, competition by both is harmful to both, but competition by only one is beneficial to the competitor and harmful to the cooperator, the situation can be described as

    a. the prisoner's dilemma.
    b. the tragedy of the commons.
    c. a public goods dilemma.
    d. a free-rider problem.

17. The red gang and the blue gang have been fighting for some time. On Friday, when the blue gang decides to share its hangout with the red gang, the red gang is likely to attribute this behavior to

    a. the kindness of the blue gang.
    b. an attempt to reduce conflict between the two gangs.
    c. ulterior motivation on the part of the blue gang.
    d. a change of leadership in the blue gang.

18. Specific behaviors, either formal or informal, that are expected for different positions within a group are called

    a. norms.
    b. social roles.
    c. disjunctive tasks.
    d. superordinate goals.

19. Stating one's intentions to reduce tension and taking unilateral cooperative actions to reduce tension are steps in

    a. GRIT.
    b. groupthink.
    c. integrative agreements.
    d. social dilemmas.

20. Stephanie and Keith both want to use their jointly owned wagon at the same time. Their mother tells them that dessert depends on their taking turns with the wagon. Her use of dessert to foster turn-taking illustrates the application of

   a. integrative agreements.
   b. superordinate goals.
   c. group polarization.
   d. social dilemmas.

Essay Questions

1. Describe three ways in which the presence of others can have an impact on people's behavior.

2. Explain how interacting with others who have shared convictions can lead to the strengthening of those convictions.

3. Discuss two techniques that can lead to the reduction of conflict between groups.

ANSWERS TO THE PRACTICE QUIZ

Multiple-Choice Questions: Correct Answers and Explanations

1. Dave is a novice tennis player. He is more anxious when being watched by a group of instructors than by a group of novice players. This difference in anxiety illustrates the process of

   b. **evaluation apprehension.** Because Dave is more nervous in front of experts, he is probably concerned about others evaluating him. After all, the experts can be harsher and more detailed critics than the novices. There is no evidence to show that he is comparing himself with others or engaging in social comparison. Social loafing is unlikely to occur in this situation because Dave is not working on a joint task where individual productivity is unobservable. Finally, the mere presence explanation of the social facilitation phenomenon does not distinguish between types of people, so Dave's differential reaction to experts and novices is inconsistent with mere presence.

2.   Groups vary is specific characteristics, but all groups can be defined by three essential components:

   c.   **roles, norms, and cohesiveness.** The main text argues that all groups can be characterized by the three components: roles, norms, and cohesiveness. Values, ideologies, and goals are all likely to be important to groups but they are not one of the three essential components.

3.   Ben manages an automobile assembly plant. Since he started requiring workers to inscribe their names on the cars they assemble, quality control has found fewer defective cars. Ben reduced social loafing by making

   c.   **contributions identifiable.** Social loafing is the tendency for people to work less productively when they work with others on a joint product. Research shows that social loafing is reduced when people's contributions are identifiable. When Ben required workers to put their names on the cars they assemble, he made their contributions identifiable and thereby reduced social loafing. There is no evidence that Ben used integrative agreements, superordinate goals, or cohesive work teams.

4.   When people work with others on a task, they

   c.   **don't work as hard as when they work alone.** When people work with others on a joint task, they tend to work less productively than when they work alone. This phenomenon is called social loafing. There is no evidence that people shift the tasks they are working on when they work with others.

5.   The marketing staff reports to the marketing director, who in turn reports to the president. This system is an example of

   a.   **a communication network.** A communication network is the chain of transmission of messages within an organization. This example clearly shows who communicates with whom, but it contains no evidence of production blocking, performance matching, or an integrative agreement.

6.   One consequence of deindividuation is that people experience a decrease in

   c.   **self-awareness.** When people experience deindividuation they become less self-aware. This decrease in self-awareness is probably responsible for many of the effects of deindividuation: increased aggression, increased helpfulness, etc. There is no evidence that deindividuation leads to a decrease in social comparison or goal striving and it increases anonymity.

7.   Kathy hopes to join a sorority at her college. One reason she wants to join this group is that she

   c.   **likes the other members and desires an opportunity to interact with them.** The main text suggests several reasons for which people may want to join a group. Two closely linked reasons mentioned here are: because they want to engage in the activities of the group, and because they like the members of the group and want to spend time with them. Kathy may want to join the sorority for both of these reasons. There is no documented evidence, however, that people join groups to follow implicit norms, to develop superordinate goals, or because they are vulnerable to groupthink.

8. The kind of reciprocity that usually reduces cooperation and escalates conflict between parties involves the use of

    b. threat capacity. When two groups emphasize threat capacity (i.e., how much they could hurt each other), they are likely to escalate conflict between themselves. This form of reciprocity often leads to a cycle of deepening tension between the groups. An arms race is a clear example of the way threat capacity can lead to increased tension and conflict. Perceived competence and persuasive arguments have little to do with reciprocity or reducing cooperation. And, public goods, what people fail to share in the public goods dilemma, have some connection to reciprocity, but have little to do with the escalation of conflict between parties.

9. The mere presence account of social facilitation suggests that people do better on easy tasks and worse on hard tasks when performing in front of others than when performing alone because

    c. the presence of other people produces arousal, which in turn affects performance. This explanation of social facilitation suggests that the mere presence of other people causes one to become aroused and that this arousal improves performance on easy tasks and impairs performance on difficult tasks. It does not, however, propose that people's performance is affected by the impression they are making, by the distraction they face, or by how hard they are working.

10. When people discuss a topic with others in their own social group who agree with them, they are likely to

    d. enhance or exaggerate the initial leanings of the group. Group polarization is exaggeration through group discussion of initial tendencies in the thinking of group members. Because of group polarization, it is very unlikely that people would shift or reverse their position, or even have no change in their position, when discussing their views with like-minded others.

11. Linda thinks that capital punishment is wrong and should not be allowed. When she talks to her friends who agree with her views, she most likely will

    b. believe more strongly that capital punishment is wrong. Linda is likely to believe more strongly that capital punishment is wrong after discussing this topic with her friends who agree with her because such discussion is likely to lead to group polarization, the tendency for people to gain conviction in their views when discussing them with like-minded others. It is unlikely that Linda would come to favor capital punishment, that her views would be unaffected, or that her friends would challenge her views.

12. Highly cohesive groups, group structure, and stressful situations are the three major contributing factors in the development of

    c. groupthink. Groupthink develops when pressures are exerted to maintain and justify positive feelings about the group, which can sometimes lead to the adoption of ineffective problem-solving strategies. Highly cohesive groups, group structure, and stressful situations are all factors that contribute to such pressures. Group roles are likely to be affected by group structure and stressful situations, but are probably not affected by cohesiveness. And there is no particular reason to believe that highly cohesive groups, group structure, and stressful situations have any effect on the development of free riders or superordinate goals.

13. Jane's company is developing a new product. There are indications that the product may be defective and could result in substantial liability for the company. Jane argues that the company's strong record of developing and marketing products suggests that they will pull through this time as well. The board members quickly decide to go ahead with the product despite its dangers. Their reasoning is an example of

   d. groupthink. The board members appear to be overestimating the ability of the group to carry off the project. They also seem to be using a closed-minded approach that rationalizes the correctness of their decision. Finally, because the group makes the decision so quickly there appears to be some pressure toward uniformity in the group. These are all behavioral symptoms of groupthink. Although people in this situation might be enacting slightly different roles, their reasoning has little to do with their respective roles. In addition, the actions of the group seem to have little to do with either social loafing or mutual cooperation.

14. The people in Everytown are celebrating the victory of their town's soccer team in a championship tournament. A large crowd of people join together in the town center to celebrate the victory and begin to feel anonymous. Because people are in this crowd they are more likely to

   a. engage in destructive behaviors. When people gather together into a crowd, their behavior often becomes violent and destructive. This phenomenon, known as deindividuation, may be responsible for the wanton and disturbing acts committed during riots. When people experience deindividuation, they seem to lose awareness of their own inner standards; this loss of awareness may be responsible for the increase in destructive behaviors. Deindividuation does not, however, cause people to become reserved, to engage in group cooperation, or to be concerned with evaluations by others.

15. Priscilla and Carol are preparing for a big exam. Priscilla checks out a library book that Carol wants so that Carol can't get it. Carol steals Priscilla's notes so that Priscilla can't use them. Priscilla and Carol are

   a. engaged in a conflict spiral. Priscilla and Carol appear to be in conflict and this conflict appears to be escalating. They are in a conflict spiral. They are *not* both exhibiting an individualist orientation. Although they are clearly looking out for themselves in this situation (as a person with an individualist orientation would), they are also trying to undermine the other person. Their behavior is consistent with a competitive orientation; however, we do not know their general pattern of behavior from this one instance, and therefore we do not have enough evidence to determine what their orientation is. Nor are they engaged in a public goods dilemma. In a public goods dilemma there is a pool of resources and people must contribute to the pool or the resources will be used up. There is no pool of resources in this example. Finally, Priscilla and Carol are not restrained by threat capacity. Even though they clearly have the ability to harm one another, it appears that neither one is aware that the other person might harm them in retaliation (a crucial feature of threat capacity), and in any event they do not appear to be restrained by the other person's ability to do harm.

16. When two people are faced with a situation in which mutual cooperation by both is beneficial to both, competition by both is harmful to both, but competition by only one is beneficial to the competitor and harmful to the cooperator, the situation can be described as

   a. the prisoner's dilemma. The prisoner's dilemma is a classic paradigm in which two people have the option of cooperating or competing. If one player cooperates and the other player competes, the player who competes gets a big payoff. If both players cooperate, then they both receive a moderate payoff. But if they both compete, they both lose a substantial amount. People usually respond to others in kind in this paradigm. The tragedy of the commons, the public goods dilemma, and the free-rider problem are all dilemmas faced by large social groups, so they are easily represented by two people.

17. The red gang and the blue gang have been fighting for some time. On Friday, when the blue gang decides to share its hangout with the red gang, the red gang is likely to attribute this behavior to

   c. ulterior motivation on the part of the blue gang. When two groups are in conflict with one another, they tend to make conflict-maintaining attributions and to see the worst in each other's actions. In this case, the red gang is likely to be suspicious of the blue gang and think that the blue gang has ulterior motives for this gesture of friendship. Because these groups have a history of conflict, it is unlikely that the red gang will think the blue gang is being kind, attempting to reduce conflict, or changing its leadership. These attributions are all positive, or at least neutral, and the red gang would be likely to search for a less flattering attribution for the blue gang's behavior.

18. Specific behaviors, either formal or informal, that are expected for different positions within a group are called

   b. social roles. Social roles are the specific behaviors carried out by individuals in a group that are expected by most of the group members. Norms are shared expectations for the group that help define the social roles, but they are not the behaviors themselves. Superordinate goals are also shared by the group, but they are not associated with positions within the group. Finally, disjunctive tasks are not related to expectations in a group.

19. Stating one's intentions to reduce tension and taking unilateral cooperative actions to reduce tension are steps in

   a. GRIT. GRIT is the acronym for the strategy known as graduated and reciprocated initiatives in tension-reduction. This strategy allows one party without the cooperation of the other party, to attempt to reduce conflict. It involves clear statements of one's desire to reduce tension, followed by unilateral cooperative actions. If any of these actions elicits cooperation from the other party, then a higher-level cooperative action is initiated in response. GRIT has been shown to be effective in reducing tension between parties. Groupthink and social dilemmas have little to do with reducing tension, and integrative agreements may be enacted to reduce tension but are not a unilateral solution.

20. Stephanie and Keith both want to use their jointly owned wagon at the same time. Their mother tells them that dessert depends on their taking turns with the wagon. Her use of dessert to foster turn-taking illustrates the application of

   b. superordinate goals. Superordinate goals are common goals that people share and must work together to obtain. It seems likely that Stephanie and Keith both want dessert, and their turn-taking is definitely an activity on which they will have to work together. There is little evidence of group polarization or social dilemmas in this example; and although the mother's solution may be innovative, it does not constitute an integrative agreement because no bargaining is involved.

Answers to Essay Questions: Sample Essays

1. Describe three ways in which the presence of others can have an impact on people's behavior.

    The presence of others can affect people's performance, productivity, and inclination to engage in destructive acts. When people are in the presence of others they tend to do better on easy tasks and worse on hard tasks than when they do these tasks alone. This phenomenon, known as social facilitation, may be the result of arousal, distraction, or evaluation apprehension that develop in the presence of others. When people work together on a joint task with others and individual contributions are not identifiable, people tend to be less productive. This phenomenon, known as social loafing, may be the result of a decreased sense of personal responsibility for the outcome of the group's work. Finally, when people are grouped together with others they do not know as in a crowd, they tend to engage in destructive actions. This phenomenon, known as deindividuation, seems to result from the distraction from internal standards of conduct that results from the presence of others.

2. Explain how interacting with others who have shared convictions can lead to the strengthening of those convictions.

    Group polarization is the exaggeration through group discussion of initial tendencies in the thinking of group members. This exaggeration or enhancement of convictions appears to result from three processes. First, people hear more persuasive arguments that are consistent with their views when they discuss these views with people who share them. Second, their views may be strengthened when people draw on the support of others as evidence that the views are valid and should be held. Third, an ingroup (consisting of people who share their views) and an outgroup (consisting of people who do not share their views) may be formed. As this social categorization process occurs, the differences between the two groups may be accentuated, and thus strengthening the convictions of the individual members.

3. Discuss two techniques that can lead to the reduction of conflict between groups.

    Two techniques that can lead to the reduction of conflict between groups are graduated and reciprocated initiatives in tension-reduction (GRIT) and negotiation. GRIT is a peacemaking strategy that can be used even if the other side is hostile toward the party using it. GRIT involves four basic components. First, a general statement is issued about the group's intention to reduce conflict. Second, the group carries out an announced tension-reducing initiative even if there is no immediate reciprocation. Third, if the other group initiates cooperation, the group using GRIT responds with at least as much cooperation. But fourth, the group using GRIT must retain enough retaliatory capability to prevent the other group from exploiting the cooperative overtures. Alternatively, negotiation attempts to reduce conflict without actually engaging in destructive activity. Negotiation works best when the negotiators use flexible behavior at the negotiation table to arrive at integrative agreements, resolutions in which all parties obtain outcomes that are superior to what they would have obtained from an equal distribution of the contested resources.

9

Attraction and Close Relationships

LEARNING OBJECTIVES: GUIDELINES FOR STUDY

You should be able to do each of the following by the conclusion of Chapter 9.

1. Explain the need to belong. Describe social anxiety and the need for affiliation. Address the relationship between affiliation and stress. (*pp. 301-304*)

2. Summarize the social difficulties of shyness and loneliness. Discuss factors that impact loneliness (e.g., age, transitions) and coping strategies that are employed. (*pp. 304-305*)

3. Explain the role of rewards in interpersonal attraction. Describe the role of familiarity in attraction, making reference to the proximity and mere exposure effects. (*pp. 305-307*)

4. Distinguish between objective and subjective factors that influence perceptions of beauty. Discuss reasons for people's bias toward beauty. Describe the what-is-beautiful-is-good stereotype and why it endures. Explain the benefits and costs of beauty. (*pp. 307-313*)

5. Explain the influence of similarity and dissimilarity on attractiveness. Describe the matching and complementarity hypotheses. Discuss the role of reciprocity in relationships and the hard-to-get effect. (*pp. 313-318*)

6. Explain mate preferences from an evolutionary perspective as well as the criticisms of this account. (*pp. 318-321*)

7. Define intimate relationships, and explain how they develop. (*pp. 321-322*)

8. Explain social exchange theory. Describe the influence of comparison level, comparison level alternatives, and investment on perceptions of and commitment to relationships. Explain equity theory. (*pp. 322-325*)

9. Distinguish between exchange and communal relationships. Explain the different types of attachment styles. (*pp. 325-327*)

10. Summarize different approaches to classifying love. Describe Lee's love styles, Sternberg's triangular theory of love, and Hatfield's distinction between passionate and companionate love. (*pp. 327-329*)

11. Describe passionate love. Explain the relationship between arousal and attraction. Distinguish between "being in love" versus "love," and discuss the influence of love on choosing to marry. Describe companionate love. Define self-disclosure, and describe typical patterns of disclosure in relationships. (*pp. 329-334*)

12. Discuss differences between the sexes regarding sexuality. Define jealousy, and address the influences of gender on jealousy and reactions to jealousy. (*pp. 334-337*)

13. Discuss communication patterns that can lead to conflict in relationships. Explain negative affect reciprocity and the demand/withdraw interaction pattern. Summarize the types of attributions made in happy and unhappy couples. Describe patterns of marital satisfaction and their relation to break-ups. Summarize work on how people cope with the end of an intimate relationship. (*pp. 337-339*)

MAJOR CONCEPTS: THE BIG PICTURE

Below are three basic issues or principles that organize Chapter 9. You should know these issues and principles well.

1. Being with others appears to be a fundamental human motive. We are drawn to affiliate with others and are quite good at regulating the level of interactions with others that we desire. We are especially likely to seek affiliation when we experience stress and can affiliate with people who share our fate. But not everyone is able to gain the intimacy that they desire. Loneliness is a persistent problem for some.

2. There are many factors that lead us to be attracted to others. We are attracted to people who we live near and encounter frequently. We are also attracted to people we find physically attractive. Certain features tend to be seen as more attractive by most people – even babies appear to find these features more attractive. However, there also appear to be significant variations due to culture, time, and circumstances in what people find attractive. When getting acquainted with others, we tend to like those who are similar rather than those who are different or opposite. We also like people who like us; and this is especially true if they are somewhat selective in whom they like. Finally, evolutionary perspectives suggest that men and women have important differences in what they find attractive. Men focus more on physical attractiveness as a sign of fertility and become jealous when they believe their partner has become unfaithful. Women focus on a man's ability to care for children and on his financial resources and become jealous when their partner forms an intimate relationship with someone else.

3. Social psychologists have devised several models to explain the development of intimate relationships. One model, social exchange theory, tries to explain relationship formation in terms of a marketplace. People develop intimate relationships if they provide more rewards and fewer costs than not being in the relationship or being in another relationship. Other researchers argue that in some relationships we are only initially concerned with exchange, while in other relationships we take a more communal approach and are concerned with meeting the needs of our partner. Still others note that our relationship styles may mirror the attachments that we had with our caregivers in early childhood. There are many different ways to classify love in relationships, but a common classification recognizes passionate love, an emotionally intense state of absorption in the other person – characteristic of early relationships, and companionate love, a secure, trusting, and stable partnership – characteristic of later on relationships.

KEY TERM EXERCISE: THE CONCEPTS YOU SHOULD KNOW

Below are all of the key terms that appear in **boldface** in Chapter 9. To help you better understand these concepts, rather than just memorize them, write a definition for each term in your own words. After doing so, look at the next section where you'll find a list of definitions from the textbook for each of the key terms presented in random order. For each of your definitions, find the corresponding textbook definition. Note how your definitions compare with those from the textbook.

Key Terms

1.   intimate relationship

2.   hard-to-get effect

3.   passionate love

4.   loneliness

5.   matching hypothesis

6.   mere exposure effect

7.   equity theory

8.   self-disclosure

9.   need for affiliation

10.   reciprocity

11.   communal relationship

12.   companionate love

13.   social exchange theory

14.   attachment style

15.   excitation transfer

16.   jealousy

17.   triangular theory of love

18.   exchange relationship

19.   what-is-beautiful-is-good stereotype

Textbook Definitions

a. A relationship in which the participants expect and desire strict reciprocity in their interactions.

b. The theory that people are most satisfied with a relationship when the ratio between benefits and contributions is similar for both partners.

c. The belief that physically attractive individuals also possess desirable personality characteristics.

d. A quid-pro-quo mutual exchange – for example, liking those who like us.

e. The tendency to prefer people who are highly selective in their social choices over those who are more readily available.

f. The process whereby arousal caused by one stimulus is added to arousal from a second stimulus and the combined arousal is attributed to the second stimulus.

g. The reaction to a perceived threat to a relationship.

h. The proposition that people are attracted to and form relationships with those who are similar to them in particular characteristics, such as physical attractiveness.

i. A secure, trusting, stable partnership.

j. The desire to establish and maintain many rewarding interpersonal relationships.

k. A feeling of deprivation about existing social relations.

l. A theory proposing that love has three basic components – intimacy, passion, and commitment – which can be combined to produce eight subtypes.

m. Revelations about the self that a person makes to other people.

n. A perspective that views people as motivated to maximize benefits and minimize costs in their relationships with others.

o. The way a person typically interacts with significant others.

p. The phenomenon whereby the more often people are exposed to a stimulus, the more positively they evaluate that stimulus.

q. Romantic love characterized by high arousal, intense attraction, and fear of rejection.

r. A close relationship between two adults involving at least one of the following: emotional attachment, fulfillment of psychological needs, and interdependence.

s. A relationship in which the participants expect and desire mutual responsiveness to each other's needs.

ANSWERS FOR KEY TERM EXERCISE

Each of the key terms listed below is followed by the letter of the textbook definition that matches it.

1.	intimate relationship	r	11.	communal relationship	s
2.	hard-to-get effect	e	12.	companionate love	i
3.	passionate love	q	13.	social exchange theory	n
4.	loneliness	k	14.	attachment style	o
5.	matching hypothesis	h	15.	excitation transfer	f
6.	mere exposure effect	p	16.	jealousy	g
7.	equity theory	b	17.	triangular theory of love	l
8.	self-disclosure	m	18.	exchange relationship	a
9.	need for affiliation	j	19.	what-is-beautiful-is-good stereotype	c
10.	reciprocity	d			

PRACTICE QUIZ: TEST YOUR KNOWLEDGE OF THE CHAPTER

Multiple-Choice Questions

1. Muhammad does not like Joe. Howard does not like Joe. Muhammad and Howard like each other. Joe does not like either Muhammad or Howard. This pattern is consistent with

   a. balance theory.
   b. internal attributions.
   c. contrast effects.
   d. psychological reactance.

2. The kind of attachment in which people report that they desire attachment but are afraid of being hurt is called

   a. secure.
   b. avoidant.
   c. anxious/ambivalent.
   d. fearful.

3. When people like her, Jenny likes them. When people dislike her, Jenny dislikes them. Jenny's likes and dislikes exemplify

   a. assimilation.
   b. reciprocity.
   c. resource exchange.
   d. complementarity.

4. Jealousy is most likely to develop in a relationship when

   a. there is a perceived threat to the relationship.
   b. one partner is insecure.
   c. the couple is involved in a long-distance relationship.
   d. one partner has too much social power.

5. All but one of the following have been suggested as explanations for the bias for beauty. Which is the exception?

   a. The aesthetic appeal of an individual affects others' responses to him or her.
   b. Men are interested in physical appearance, whereas women are interested in interpersonal warmth.
   c. People believe in the what-is-beautiful-is-good stereotype.
   d. Interactions with physically attractive people are likely to be more rewarding because physically attractive people tend to have higher levels of social skills than do physically unattractive people.

6.   Exchange relationships are characterized by

a.   deep affection and commitment.
b.   a high degree of self-disclosure.
c.   strict payment and repayment of benefits by one partner to the other.
d.   insecurity due to the nature of the interaction.

7.   When Gene meets an attractive member of the other sex, his only thoughts concern how he can have a good time without making a commitment. Gene's approach illustrates

a.   companionate love.
b.   social exchange theory.
c.   self-disclosure reciprocity.
d.   jealousy.

8.   Jamal and Veronica have been married for ten years. While their marriage was exciting and wild in its early days, they have since settled into a routine of care, nurturance, and friendship with one another. The changes in Jamal and Veronica's relationship illustrate the difference between

a.   passionate and companionate love.
b.   secure and insecure attachments.
c.   self-disclosure and social penetration.
d.   exchange and communal relationships.

9.   Luis and Shelia consoled each other when their parents passed away, supported each other's careers, and provided comfort for each other in times of loneliness. Research on _____ shows that these rewarding interactions are strongly associated with the couple's satisfaction and commitment.

a.   self-disclosure reciprocity
b.   the triangular theory of love
c.   the social exchange framework
d.   the two-factor theory of emotion

10.   Ruth thinks that people find her physically unattractive. Tina thinks that people find her physically attractive. Both Ruth and Tina received very favorable evaluations of their work on some task. Compared to Ruth, Tina should have felt better about the quality of her work if

a.   the evaluator was of the opposite sex.
b.   the task was social rather than cognitive.
c.   they both think that the evaluator was physically attractive.
d.   they both think that the evaluator was unaware of their physical appearance.

11. Bobby and Joan have been going out for some time. They began dating very casually, but then Bobby revealed that he was having trouble with his roommates and Joan revealed that she was still broken up by her father's death two years ago. As they shared these experiences Bobby and Joan became closer. Their actions illustrate

    a. self-disclosure reciprocity.
    b. the triangular theory of love.
    c. social rewards in their relationship.
    d. the two-factor theory of emotion.

12. Graciella tends to play "hard to get" and appears not to like most people. Social psychological research suggests that

    a. people will be attracted to Graciella to the extent that she shows no interest in them.
    b. Graciella will be seen as more attractive by people who think that she is committed to someone else.
    c. Graciella will be viewed as more attractive if she seems moderately selective rather than extremely selective in her social choices.
    d. people such as Graciella, who play hard to get, are extremely attractive to others.

13. David is a heterosexual forty-five-year-old man. Research suggests that he is most likely to be attracted to

    a. a woman whose needs are opposite his; for example, if David needs to control others, he should be most attracted to someone who likes to be controlled.
    b. a woman whose personality is opposite his.
    c. a financially successful forty-five-year-old woman.
    d. a woman whom he thinks has the same attitudes as he does.

14. Brenda and Chris have been having difficulty in their relationship. Brenda thinks that Chris puts less than his share of time into the relationship and doesn't try to please her. Chris gets quiet and sulks when Brenda makes these accusations. Brenda and Chris's relationship seems to display

    a. negative reciprocity.
    b. the demand/withdraw interaction pattern.
    c. lack of social support.
    d. anxious/ambivalent attachment.

15. In order to manage conflict in a relationship, each partner should try to

    a. self-disclose about the other partner's problems.
    b. ignore the other partner's problems.
    c. understand the other partner's point of view.
    d. make his or her demands for the relationship known to the other partner.

16.   Intimacy, passion, and commitment are three components of

    a.   passionate love.
    b.   companionate love.
    c.   the triangular theory of love.
    d.   communal relationships.

17.   Jim often forgets to finish the chores he has agreed to do around the house and sometimes is insensitive toward Molly. Molly usually brushes off such instances, saying that it isn't Jim's fault he's often too stressed out. Such attributions for Jim's behavior are

    a.   indications of trouble in Jim and Molly's relationship.
    b.   characteristic of happy couples.
    c.   likely to create communication difficulties.
    d.   are likely to cause trouble for Molly but not for Jim.

18.   People who have an interdependent self-concept – who include others in their definition of themselves – are likely to

    a.   make self-serving attributions.
    b.   have enduring relationships.
    c.   have low self-esteem.
    d.   have high self-esteem.

19.   Stanley will have an especially great desire to affiliate with other people if he

    a.   is not under any stress.
    b.   is somewhat worried about learning his test results and has the opportunity to be with similar others who are in the same situation.
    c.   expects that he is going to be put in a situation that will be very embarrassing to him.
    d.   is experiencing a great deal of fear about an upcoming situation and has the opportunity to be with others who are very dissimilar to him and who are not facing a similar situation.

20.   José and Lucinda have a happy marriage. They spend a lot of time together and see themselves as being interdependent. If José were to pass away, Lucinda is likely to

    a.   be able to handle it well.
    b.   be more broken up than the typical spouse.
    c.   never recover.
    d.   form other relationships quickly.

Essay Questions

1.   Compare and contrast companionate and passionate love.

2. Describe two communication patterns that may lead to conflict in relationships.

3. Discuss the positive and negative consequences of having an interdependent relationship.

ANSWERS TO THE PRACTICE QUIZ

Multiple-Choice Questions: Correct Answers and Explanations

1. Muhammad does not like Joe. Howard does not like Joe. Muhammad and Howard like each other. Joe does not like either Muhammad or Howard. This pattern is consistent with

   a. **balance theory.** Balance theory proposes that people desire consistency in their thoughts, feelings, and social relationships. A balanced pattern of attraction requires that we like someone whose relationships with others parallel our own. Usually, we like those who are friends of our friends and enemies of our enemies. Consistent with this, Muhammad and Howard see each other as enemies of their enemy, Joe, and therefore like each other. Joe's dislike of the other two men reciprocates their dislike of him, and so this pattern, too, is balanced. Internal attributions locate the cause of a condition or event in the person rather than in external circumstances; but attributions are not described in this question. Contrast effects concern the tendency to perceive stimuli that differ from expectations or other stimuli as even more different than they really are; but, again, there is no evidence of this phenomenon in this question. Psychological reactance refers to the theory that people react against threats to specific behavioral freedoms by perceiving a threatened freedom as more attractive and trying to re-establish it; in this question, however, no freedom was threatened.

2. The kind of attachment in which people report that they desire attachment but are afraid of being hurt is called

   c. **anxious/ambivalent.** Anxious/ambivalent attachments are characterized by a strong desire for a relationship, together with a fear that the relationship will not work out properly. Secure attachments are characterized by warmth and affection, together with a sense of independence and self-worth. And avoidant attachments are characterized by a reluctance to develop relationships. Although people may be fearful in a relationship, this trait is not usually called an attachment style.

3.   When people like her, Jenny likes them. When people dislike her, Jenny dislikes them.
     Jenny's likes and dislikes exemplify

     b.   reciprocity. Reciprocity is a quid-pro-quo mutual exchange between what we give and
           what we receive – for example, liking those who like us. Consistent with this idea, Jenny
           likes those who like her and dislikes those who dislike her. Assimilation in the context of
           attraction often refers to the phenomenon in which people of average physical attractive-
           ness are judged as more attractive when they are observed together with very attractive-
           looking people and as less attractive when they are observed together with unattractive-
           looking people; but this phenomenon is not relevant to this question. Resource exchange
           involves the resources that people possess; but this question does not give any informa-
           tion about the resources Jenny possesses or is seeking. Complementarity refers to a fit
           between opposites; it is consistent with the idea that "opposites attract." However, this
           question gives no indication that Jenny is attracted to people who have needs or person-
           ality traits opposite, or complementary, to hers.

4.   Jealousy is most likely to develop in a relationship when

     a.   there is a perceived threat to the relationship. Jealousy usually results from a per-
           ceived threat to a relationship. When the relationship is in jeopardy, one or both partners
           may feel fearful of being supplanted or apprehensive about the potential loss of affec-
           tion. An insecure partner may contribute to perceived threats, but insecurity in and of it-
           self is not enough to cause jealousy. There is no clear evidence that long-distance rela-
           tionships or social power promote jealousy.

5.   All but one of the following have been suggested as explanations for the bias for beauty.
     Which is the exception?

     **b.   Men are interested in physical appearance, whereas women are interested in inter-
           personal warmth.** Both men and women are attracted to and react more favorably to-
           ward people who are physically attractive. Therefore, the difference between men and
           women alleged in this question could not explain the general bias for beauty. The other
           three alternatives have been offered as explanations for this bias. (A fourth explanation
           is that people desire to increase their own perceived attractiveness through association
           with attractive others.)

6.   Exchange relationships are characterized by

     c.   strict payment and repayment of benefits by one partner to the other. Exchange re-
           lationships are defined by the strict equity in exchanges between partners. They are usu-
           ally casual or business-type relationships and, as such, they are not characterized by
           deep affection and commitment or a high degree of self-disclosure. These relationships
           can be quite stable and are not typically characterized by insecurity.

7.   When Gene meets an attractive member of the other sex, his only thoughts concern how he
     can have a good time without making a commitment. Gene's approach illustrates

     b.   social exchange theory. Social exchange theory suggests that people try to maximize
           their rewards and minimize their costs in a relationship. Therefore, when Gene tries to
           maximize his fun while minimizing his commitment, his approach illustrates social ex-
           change theory. Companionate love emphasizes a concern for the other person that has
           developed into a deep friendship, so this characteristic does not fit Gene. Likewise, self-

disclosure reciprocity and jealousy do not emphasize maximizing rewards and minimizing costs in a relationship.

8. Jamal and Veronica have been married for ten years. While their marriage was exciting and wild in its early days, they have since settled into a routine of care, nurturance, and friendship with one another. The changes in Jamal and Veronica's relationship illustrate the difference between

   a. passionate and companionate love. Passionate love often characterizes the early days of a relationship and contains a strong emotional component, much like the exciting and wild days of Jamal and Veronica. Companionate love is usually seen later in a relationship and is characterized by a deep loving friendship, much like the routine of care, nurturance, and friendship in Jamal and Veronica's relationship. There is no evidence that Jamal and Veronica have insecure attachments; and while their strong relationship might indicate a secure attachment, there is no illustration of the difference between these kinds of attachments. Likewise, Jamal and Veronica's description can tell us little about self-disclosure and social penetration or about exchange and communal relationships.

9. Luis and Shelia consoled each other when their parents passed away, supported each other's careers, and provided comfort for each other in times of loneliness. Research on _____ shows that these rewarding interactions are strongly associated with the couple's satisfaction and commitment.

   c. the social exchange framework. Luis and Shelia have given each other comfort, support, and companionship – clear rewards that they receive from their relationship. Rewards, along with costs and comparison level, are one of the building blocks of social exchange. It seems likely that Luis and Shelia have self-disclosed to each other, but this is not stated in the question. Similarly, there is no evidence of the triangular theory of love or the two-factor theory of emotion.

10. Ruth thinks that people find her physically unattractive. Tina thinks that people find her physically attractive. Both Ruth and Tina received very favorable evaluations of their work on some task. Compared to Ruth, Tina should have felt better about the quality of her work if

    d. they both think that the evaluator was unaware of their physical appearance. People who think that they are judged as physically attractive often discount the praise they receive for their work because they suspect that the evaluation they received was influenced by their physical appearance. If these people think that the evaluator was unaware of their physical appearance, however, then they have no reason to suspect that the favorable evaluation was due to their looks, and so they feel better about their work. People who think of themselves as physically unattractive, in contrast, often feel better about the quality of their work after getting a favorable evaluation from someone who they think was aware, rather than unaware, of their physical appearance. Neither the sex of the evaluator nor the evaluator's physical attractiveness is as important as Ruth's and Tina's thoughts about whether the evaluator was aware of their physical appearance. Tina would probably feel worse than Ruth about a favorable evaluation if the task was social rather than cognitive.

11. Bobby and Joan have been going out for some time. They began dating very casually, but then Bobby revealed that he was having trouble with his roommates and Joan revealed that

she was still broken up by her father's death two years ago. As they shared these experiences Bobby and Joan became closer. Their actions illustrate

a.   **self-disclosure reciprocity.** When Bobby revealed something important about himself, that he was having fights with his roommates, Joan responded by revealing something even more personal about herself – her feelings about the loss of her father. This back-and-forth exchange of personal, meaningful information, which gradually gets more personal and more meaningful, is self-disclosure reciprocity. The triangular theory of love and the two-factor theory of emotion do not entail information exchange in a relationship. One of the social rewards in a relationship is having someone who listens, but this concept also does not explain the exchange of information between Bobby and Joan.

12.   Graciella tends to play "hard to get" and appears not to like most people. Social psychological research suggests that

c.   **Graciella will be viewed as more attractive if she seems moderately selective rather than extremely selective in her social choices.** As the main text indicates, the hard-to-get effect – the tendency to prefer people who are highly selective in their social choices over those who are more readily available – has been very hard to get in social psychological research. People are especially unlikely to be attracted to someone who plays hard to get if the person has shown no interest in them or if the person is fully committed to someone else. In contrast, someone who appears to be moderately selective tends to be viewed as more attractive than someone who appears to be extremely selective.

13.   David is a heterosexual forty-five-year-old man. Research suggests that he is most likely to be attracted to

d.   **a woman whom he thinks has the same attitudes as he does.** Perceived (though not necessarily actual) similarity in attitudes is associated with attraction. Because complementarity, which is a fit between opposites, does not tend to affect attraction, there is no reason to assume that David will like someone whose needs or personality are opposite his. Cross-cultural research has found that men prefer mates who are younger than they are, and that they rate the financial status or potential of a mate as less important than women do. Thus, there is little reason to assume that David will be especially attracted to a woman who is forty-five years old and is financially successful.

14.   Brenda and Chris have been having difficulty in their relationship. Brenda thinks that Chris puts less than his share of time into the relationship and doesn't try to please her. Chris gets quiet and sulks when Brenda makes these accusations. Brenda and Chris's relationship seems to display

b.   **the demand/withdraw interaction pattern.** Brenda seems to be making demands in this relationship that Chris feels he cannot meet. In turn, Chris seems to be withdrawing. This demand/withdraw pattern of interaction has been associated with conflict in relationships. There is no evidence of negative reciprocity, or the escalation of the perception of negative affect in the partner, in Brenda and Chris's relationship. Likewise, we might guess that Chris and Brenda offer each other little social support or have an anxious/ambivalent attachment, but there is no clear evidence for either of these conclusions in the question.

15. In order to manage conflict in a relationship, each partner should try to

c. **understand the other partner's point of view.** When partners make an effort to understand each other's point of view, conflict in a relationship can be diminished. It is unclear whether self-disclosing about a partner's problems, ignoring the partner's problems, or making demands known to the partner will diminish conflict. Making demands known to the partner could be particularly troublesome if it leads to the demand/withdraw pattern of behavior.

16. Intimacy, passion, and commitment are three components of

c. **the triangular theory of love.** The three components of love according to the triangular theory of love are intimacy, passion, and commitment. This theory does not discuss passionate love, companionate love, or communal relationships.

17. Jim often forgets to finish the chores he has agreed to do around the house and sometimes is insensitive toward Molly. Molly usually brushes off such instances, saying that it isn't Jim's fault he's often too stressed out. Such attributions for Jim's behavior are

b. **characteristic of happy couples.** Happy couples usually make relationship-enhancing attributions for each other's actions. In other words, they tend to minimize the negative actions and weaknesses of their partners and maximize the positive actions and strengths of their partners.

18. People who have an interdependent self-concept – who include others in their definition of themselves – are likely to

b. **have enduring relationships.** People who are interdependent and include others in their definition of themselves have particularly strong attachments to others. These attachments make it more likely that these people will have enduring relationships. There is no evidence that people who include others in their definition of themselves have higher or lower self-esteem, or are more likely to engage in self-serving biases.

19. Stanley will have an especially great desire to affiliate with other people if he

b. **is somewhat worried about learning his test results and has the opportunity to be with similar others who are in the same situation.** Stress increases a person's desire to affiliate with others if he or she believes that being with others is likely to reduce the stress. This is particularly true when the stress is manageable and not related to embarrassment or other social anxieties, and if the individual believes that the other people are similar to him or her and can help him or her assess the situation.

20. José and Lucinda have a happy marriage. They spend a lot of time together and see themselves as being interdependent. If José were to pass away Lucinda is likely to

b. **be more broken up than the typical spouse.** Interdependent relationships are more likely to endure, but when such relationships end, either in death or in a breakup, the partners are more likely to have difficulty coping with the loss. These people do seem to recover eventually, even though they are unlikely to form other relationships quickly.

Answers to Essay Questions: Sample Essays

1.   Compare and contrast companionate and passionate love.

Passionate love is more typical of the early stages of a relationship. It is characterized by high states of arousal and strong emotions. Being passionately loved is joyous; being rejected is heartbreaking. Companionate love, on the other hand, is more typical of the later stages of a relationship. It is comfortable and warm, characterized by stability, security, trust, and deep friendship. Most people admire both kinds of love. They enjoy the intense emotion of passionate love and the stable trust of companionate love.

2.   Describe two communication patterns that may lead to conflict in relationships.

One communication pattern that may lead to conflict is negative affect reciprocity. In this pattern, one partner notices a small negative reaction in the other partner and follows it with a negative reaction of his or her own. This back-and-forth exchange continues. One version of this pattern, where there is more reciprocity of the man's negative affect by the woman and less reciprocity of the woman's negative affect by the man, seems to be particularly damaging. A second communication pattern that can lead to conflict is the demand/withdraw interaction pattern. In this interaction pattern, one partner initiates and demands discussion, while the other partner seeks to avoid discussion. The demanding partner nags and criticizes; the withdrawing partner remains silent and defensive. This pattern can lead to a regular pattern of conflict with little or no resolution.

3.   Discuss the positive and negative consequences of having an interdependent relationship.

When two people are involved in an interdependent relationship, such that they include their partner in their definition of themselves, their commitment is likely to be stronger and more enduring. They are more likely to spend time together, to engage in shared activities, and to influence each other. However, when such a relationship ends, either in a breakup or at death, they tend to have more difficulty coping with the loss of the relationship. Perhaps it is because these individuals have lost a more significant part of themselves – relative to others not involved in an interdependent relationship – that they have greater difficulty dealing with this outcome.

10

Helping Others

LEARNING OBJECTIVES: GUIDELINES FOR STUDY

You should be able to do each of the following by the conclusion of Chapter 10.

1. Explain how evolutionary theory accounts for helping behaviors. (*pp. 347-350*)

2. Discuss how helping others is related to helping the self. Explain the role of the cost-benefit ratio in helping behavior. Describe the effect of overhelping on perceptions of the receiver. (*pp. 350-353*)

3. Compare and contrast egoistic and altruistic motives for helping. Explain the empathy-altruism hypothesis. Identify the factor that helps reveal whether egoistic or altruistic motives are present. Delineate why a distinction between types of motives is important. Discuss how external rewards can influence helping. (*pp. 353-359*)

4. Explain how being in a group of people affects the likelihood that helping behavior will occur. Also explain how being in a group affects the ability of people to notice whether help is needed, to interpret an ambiguous helping situation, and to take responsibility for helping. Identify additional factors that influence the helping behavior of individuals in a group. (*pp. 359-365*)

5. Describe how place, time pressure, and mood can influence helping. (*pp. 365-370*)

6. Explain the ways in which models and social norms influence people's decisions to help others. (*pp. 370-373*)

7. Explain how personality, moral reasoning, and family background may affect a person's likelihood of helping others. (*pp. 373-376*)

8. Describe how characteristics of people who need help, such as their attractiveness and their responsibility for their plight, influence the likelihood that others will help them. (*pp. 376-378*)

9. Explain how the interaction between the person in need and the helper affects helping. Identify how similarity, closeness, and gender affect helping. (*pp. 378-381*)

10. Explain why help is sometimes seen as threatening and sometimes seen as supportive by those receiving it. (*pp. 381-382*)

11. Explain how feeling connected to others affects the likelihood that helping behavior will occur. (*pp. 382-384*)

MAJOR CONCEPTS: THE BIG PICTURE

Below are five basic issues or principles that organize Chapter 10. You should know these issues and principles well.

1.   There are several motivational factors that affect why people help. Evolutionary factors may lead us to help those who are close relatives, those with whom we have reciprocal relationships, and those who are part of our group. Egoistic factors might also lead to helping because helping makes most people feel good. Helping may even reflect a desire to steal some of the limelight from a very competent other, as overhelping will reflect negatively on them. On the other hand, it seems that at times we help for altruistic motives. This is especially true when we have empathy for those we help. The debate between whether we help for altruistic or egoistic motives continues and is not resolved at the present time. Distinguishing among the motivations to help is important because different motives are likely to affect behavioral and emotional responses to helping, attribution for helping, and the role of rewards in helping.

2.   The situation can also influence helping. For instance, research shows that the presence of others actually inhibits helping by making it harder to recognize the need for help, causing situations to be more ambiguous, and diffusing individual responsibility for helping. Other situations that inhibit helping include time pressure and living in a city. Situations can also influence helping by affecting our emotions. Positive moods, guilt, and, in some situations, other negative moods can all lead to helping. Finally, role models and social norms can be powerful situational factors that lead to individuals to help others.

3.   Despite the strong situational influences on helping, some people are simply more likely to help than others. Indeed, there is some evidence that helping may have a genetic component. In addition, other personality characteristics, such as empathy and moral reasoning, appear to work together in promoting helping.

4.   Some people are more likely to receive help than others. Attractive individuals, as well as those seen as innocent victims, are more likely to receive help. People are also more likely to help those who are similar to themselves. Men are more likely to help in situations that are somewhat dangerous, whereas women tend to help friends and relatives more often.

5.   People exhibit varied reactions to receiving help. Sometimes they see help as supportive; at other times they see it as threatening. For instance, help received from a similar other on an important task is often seen as threatening rather than supportive. People also vary in the extent to which they seek help. People who have received supportive help often seek help in the future, whereas people who have received threatening help will seek help again only if they are pessimistic about their own abilities to control the future.

KEY TERM EXERCISE: THE CONCEPTS YOU SHOULD KNOW

Following are all of the key terms that appear in **boldface** in Chapter 10. To help you better understand these concepts, rather than just memorize them, write a definition for each term in your own words. After doing so, look at the next section where you'll find a list of definitions from the textbook for each of the key terms presented in random order. For each of your definitions, find the corresponding textbook definition. Note how your definitions compare with those from the textbook.

Key Terms

1. guilt

2. audience inhibition

3. norm of social responsibility

4. threat-to-self-esteem model

5. altruistic

6. empathy-altruism hypothesis

7. social norm

8. good mood effect

9. bystander effect

10. negative state relief model

11. pluralistic ignorance

12. diffusion of responsibility

13. kinship selection

14. arousal: cost-reward model

15. egoistic

Textbook Definitions

a. The proposition that people react to emergency situations by acting in the most cost-effective way to reduce the arousal of shock and alarm.

b. The proposition that people help others in order to counteract their own feelings of sadness.

c. The theory that reactions to receiving assistance depend on whether help is perceived as supportive or threatening.

d. The effect whereby the presence of others inhibits helping.

e. Feelings of discomfort or distress produced by people's belief that they have violated their own personal standards or their fear that others will perceive such violations.

f. The belief that others will or should take the responsibility for providing assistance to a person in need.

g. Motivated by the desire to increase another's welfare.

h. A moral standard emphasizing that people should help those who need assistance.

i. The proposition that empathic concern for a person in need produces an altruistic motive for helping.

j. Reluctance to help for fear of making a bad impression on observers.

k. A general rule of conduct reflecting standards of social approval and disapproval.

l. Motivated by the desire to increase one's own welfare.

m.   The effect whereby a good mood increases helping behavior.

n.   The state in which people mistakenly believe that their own thoughts and feelings are different from those of others, even though everyone's behavior is the same.

o.   Preferential helping of genetic relatives, so that genes held in common survive.

ANSWERS FOR KEY TERM EXERCISE

Each of the key terms listed below is followed by the letter of the textbook definition that matches it.

1.	guilt	e	9.	bystander effect	d
2.	audience inhibition	j	10.	negative state relief model	b
3.	norm of social responsibility	h	11.	pluralistic ignorance	n
4.	threat-to-self-esteem model	c	12.	diffusion of responsibility	f
5.	altruistic	g	13.	kinship selection	o
6.	empathy-altruism hypothesis	i	14.	arousal: cost-reward model	a
7.	social norm	k	15.	egoistic	l
8.	good mood effect	m			

PRACTICE QUIZ: TEST YOUR KNOWLEDGE OF THE CHAPTER

Multiple-Choice Questions

1.   Reciprocal helping and kinship selection are two main kinds of helping, according to the

a.   arousal: cost-reward model.
b.   empathy-altruism hypothesis.
c.   negative state relief model.
d.   evolutionary perspective.

2.   Beth wants to borrow notes for the class she skipped on Friday. If she tells a classmate that she needs the notes because she skipped class rather than offering a good excuse (e.g., she was home sick) the classmate will probably be

a.   less likely to help because Beth doesn't deserve help.
b.   more likely to help because Beth was honest.
c.   more likely to help because Beth is so cool.
d.   no more or less likely to help.

3.   Norm is in a bad mood because he broke his roommate's stereo. He sees an elderly woman who needs help crossing the street. Because Norm is in a bad mood, he is

a.   less likely to help.
b.   more likely to help.
c.   no more or less likely to help.
d.   more likely to help but less likely to notice that the elderly woman needs help.

4. Bob has to drive his beat-up old Dodge Dart across the country. He knows that the car is likely to break down and that he may need help. According to research on bystander intervention, Bob would be best advised to

   a. take the rural route and avoid cities.
   b. make sure others know it was his decision to drive the car.
   c. drive through as many cities as possible.
   d. "dress down" so that if he does need help, others won't find him intimidating.

5. Michelle feels sorry for homeless people. To ease their suffering, she organizes a campaign to find clothing, food, and shelter for them. Michelle's actions illustrate

   a. reciprocity norms.
   b. good mood effects.
   c. empathic concern.
   d. kinship selection.

6. When people are in a good mood, they are

   a. less likely to help.
   b. more likely to help.
   c. no more or less likely to help.
   d. more likely to help but less likely to notice that others need help.

7. David and Lisa are both good friends of Ron, who has been in an accident. According to research concerning gender differences in helping, which of the two is more likely to stop by and help Ron with his daily chores when he comes home from the hospital?

   a. David is more likely to do so.
   b. Lisa is more likely to do so.
   c. David and Lisa are equally likely to stop by.
   d. It depends on the severity of Ron's accident.

8. Bobby helps his classmates with their homework because he wants them to like him. Bobby's behavior is

   a. cost-free.
   b. heroic.
   c. altruistic.
   d. egoistic.

9. According to research by Gilbert and Silvera (1996), people sometimes provide more help than another person truly needs. They argue that this help is motivated by

   a. altruism.
   b. the desire to maintain a positive mood.
   c. intentions to undermine the other person.
   d. the desire to look helpful.

10. Fred, a helpful person, is hurrying home to give his daughter a lecture on how she should be a helpful person. He is twenty minutes late, however. Research by Darley and Batson (1973), in which seminary students who were lecturing about the parable of the Good Samaritan encountered a person in apparent distress, would suggest that if Fred sees someone who needs help he is likely to

   a. help, because he is a helpful person.
   b. help, because he is thinking about lecturing his daughter on helpfulness.
   c. not help, because he doesn't want to look foolish.
   d. not help, because he is late.

11. Although tennis is not important to Randy, he would still like to play better. His brother spends three weekends coaching Randy. Randy is likely to interpret his brother's actions as a form of

   a. empathic concern.
   b. self-threatening help.
   c. supportive help.
   d. negative state relief.

12. Personal distress and perspective taking are two components of

   a. docility.
   b. empathy.
   c. pluralistic ignorance.
   d. audience inhibition.

13. Noticing incidents, interpreting situations, and taking responsibility for action are three steps specified by the

   a. just-world belief.
   b. self-evaluation maintenance model.
   c. empathy-altruism hypothesis.
   d. bystander intervention model.

14. A crowd of people has gathered at a bar. Suddenly smoke fills the whole room. The people are most likely to interpret the situation as an emergency if

   a. the crowd is very large.
   b. they are enjoying themselves.
   c. they know each other.
   d. they are mingling rather than staying in one place.

15. When a large group of people fails to help an innocent victim of a crime, the most likely cause is

   a. callousness of the people in the group.
   b. the tendency to blame the victim of the crime.
   c. diffusion of responsibility for helping.
   d. lack of empathy for the victim.

16. Isaac and Tina are making supper and run out of flour. Who is most likely to ask the neighbor for help?

    a. Isaac is most likely to do so.
    b. Tina is most likely to do so.
    c. Isaac and Tina are equally likely to ask for help.
    d. Whether Isaac or Tina asks for help depends on the gender of their neighbor.

17. Tasha has received threatening help in the past. How does this experience affect her desire to seek help?

    a. She is more likely to seek help later.
    b. She is less likely to seek help later.
    c. She is no more or less likely to seek help later.
    d. Whether she seeks help depends on her perceived control of the situation.

18. Molly thinks she's a first-rate parent. A friend points out that Molly should teach her children self-control by setting standards for them. Molly is likely to see this advice as

    a. empathic concern.
    b. self-threatening help.
    c. supportive help.
    d. negative state relief.

19. The social norm that motivates us out of a sense of duty and obligation to help those who are dependent on us is the norm of

    a. reciprocity.
    b. equity.
    c. social responsibility.
    d. justice.

20. Feeling a sense of connection to other people should

    a. increase helping.
    b. decrease helping.
    c. neither increase nor decrease helping.
    d. sometimes increase helping and sometimes decrease helping.

Essay Questions

1. Describe how a person's mood can affect the likelihood that he or she will help others. Analyze the effect of both positive and negative moods.

2. Discuss three ways in which the presence of others can affect the likelihood that people will help someone in need.

3. Explain why help from others may sometimes be perceived as threatening.

ANSWERS TO THE PRACTICE QUIZ

Multiple-Choice Questions: Correct Answers and Explanations

1. Reciprocal helping and kinship selection are two main kinds of helping, according to the

    d. evolutionary perspective. According to the evolutionary perspective, people help others because doing so enhances the possibility that they will be able to pass on their genes. Kinship selection is the helping of relatives and, since relatives share genes, helping a relative increases the chance that one's genes will be passed on. Reciprocal helping is helping someone who will help you in the future and thus can also increase the chances of passing on one's genes. The arousal: cost-reward model, the empathy-altruism hypothesis, and the negative state relief model do not try to explain kinship selection or reciprocal helping.

2. Beth wants to borrow notes for the class she skipped on Friday. If she tells a classmate that she needs the notes because she skipped class rather than offering a good excuse (e.g., she was home sick) the classmate will probably be

    a. less likely to help because Beth doesn't deserve help. Research shows that when people are blamed or judged to be responsible for their bad outcomes others are less likely to help them. If the classmate assumes Beth is to blame for skipping class, which seems likely, then the classmate will probably be less likely to help her.

3. Norm is in a bad mood because he broke his roommate's stereo. He sees an elderly woman who needs help crossing the street. Because Norm is in a bad mood, he is

    b. more likely to help. Research shows that when adults are in a bad mood they are more likely to help others, perhaps as a way to improve their mood. There is no documentation regarding the effect of mood on noticing that others need help.

4. Bob has to drive his beat-up old Dodge Dart across the country. He knows that the car is likely to break down and that he may need help. According to research on bystander intervention, Bob would be best advised to

   a. **take the rural route and avoid cities.** Research shows that people are more likely to help in rural areas than in cities, so Bob should take the rural routes because he is more likely to receive help there. If people knew it was his decision to drive this particular car, they might be less likely to help because they might infer that the breakdown was his responsibility. Finally, there is no clear evidence that "dressing down" will increase Bob's chances of being helped.

5. Michelle feels sorry for homeless people. To ease their suffering, she organizes a campaign to find clothing, food, and shelter for them. Michelle's actions illustrate

   c. **empathic concern.** Empathic concern involves other-oriented feelings, which Michelle demonstrates. Research shows that such feelings often lead to helping. It is unlikely that Michelle's actions result from a reciprocity norm, as it seems unlikely that she was previously helped by these homeless people. It is also unlikely that her actions are the result of good mood effects, because her empathic concern for the homeless is really more likely to put her in a bad mood. Finally, it is unlikely that her actions result from kinship selection, as the homeless people she is trying to help do not appear to be her relatives.

6. When people are in a good mood, they are

   b. **more likely to help.** Research shows that when people are in a good mood they are more likely to help others, perhaps as a way to maintain their good mood. There is no documentation regarding the effect of mood on noticing that others need help.

7. David and Lisa are both good friends of Ron, who has been in an accident. According to research concerning gender differences in helping, which of the two is more likely to stop by and help Ron with his daily chores when he comes home from the hospital?

   b. **Lisa is more likely to do so.** Research shows that women are more likely than men to provide supportive and caring help, especially to friends and family members. The seriousness of the accident is unlikely to affect the gender difference in helping, although when helping could be dangerous or embarrassing, men are more likely to help than women.

8. Bobby helps his classmates with their homework because he wants them to like him. Bobby's behavior is

   d. **egoistic.** Bobby seems to be helping because of what he can get out of doing so. This kind of helping is called egoistic helping. There is no indication that the helping is cost-free; he does have to expend some time and energy helping his classmates. And his helping surely isn't altruistic or heroic if he is helping solely for his own sake.

9. According to research by Gilbert and Silvera (1996), people sometimes provide more help than another person truly needs. They argue that this help is motivated by

   c. **intentions to undermine the other person.** Research by Gilbert and Silvera (1996) shows that people sometimes overhelp other people out of a desire to hurt the other person. Help given to a competent person can take away the credit that they would have received if they had completed a task on their own. This type of helping is definitely not altruistic, and there is no evidence that mood or the desire to look helpful play any role in this behavior.

10.   Fred, a helpful person, is hurrying home to give his daughter a lecture on how she should be a helpful person. He is twenty minutes late, however. Research by Darley and Batson (1973), in which seminary students who were lecturing about the parable of the Good Samaritan encountered a person in apparent distress, would suggest that if Fred sees someone who needs help he is likely to

d.   **not help, because he is late.** Darley and Batson's (1973) classic study showed that even seminary students who were late for an appointment to give a speech on the Good Samaritan parable (which teaches the importance of helping others) were unlikely to help a person coughing and groaning in a doorway. This study suggests then that Fred will be unlikely to help, regardless of whether he is a helpful person or is planning to lecture his daughter on the need to be helpful. There is no reason to believe that fear of looking foolish would undermine Fred's helpfulness in this situation.

11.   Although tennis is not important to Randy, he would still like to play better. His brother spends three weekends coaching Randy. Randy is likely to interpret his brother's actions as a form of

c.   **supportive help.** Because tennis is not important to Randy, it is unlikely that his brother's help will be perceived as self-threatening. Self-threatening help occurs when the help challenges an important area of one's self-concept. Empathic concern and negative state relief help have not been documented as ways in which people perceive help that they are receiving; therefore, it is difficult to say whether Randy would interpret his brother's help as empathic concern or negative state relief help.

12.   Personal distress and perspective taking are two components of

b.   **empathy.** When people feel empathy they take the other person's perspective and experience personal distress. Docility is a sense of withdrawal and thus has little to do with perspective taking or personal distress. Pluralistic ignorance is the mistaken belief that one's thoughts and feelings are different from others', and audience inhibition is the reluctance to help stemming from fear of making a bad impression. Both of these concepts are unrelated to perspective taking.

13.   Noticing incidents, interpreting situations, and taking responsibility for action are three steps specified by the

d.   **bystander intervention model.** The bystander intervention model proposes that people help when they notice an incident, interpret the situation as one in which help is needed, and take responsibility for helping. Just-world beliefs do not involve noticing incidents or interpreting situations, and the self-evaluation maintenance model and empathy-altruism hypothesis do not involve noticing incidents.

14.   A crowd of people has gathered at a bar. Suddenly smoke fills the whole room. The people are most likely to interpret the situation as an emergency if

    c.   they know each other. The people are most likely to interpret the situation as an emergency if they know each other because they will have an easier time reading each other's reactions; these reactions will be less ambiguous. A large crowd would tend to be more distracting, making it harder for people to recognize the situation as an emergency. And there is no clear evidence that people who are mingling or enjoying themselves would have an easier or harder time recognizing an emergency.

15.   When a large group of people fails to help an innocent victim of a crime, the most likely cause is

    c.   diffusion of responsibility for helping. The bystander intervention model was developed to help explain why large groups of people do not help in such instances. One of the important factors in this model is diffusion of responsibility, which describes the tendency for groups of people to be less likely to help than individuals would be. In a group, people tend to believe that other people will help and thus everyone is less likely to help. There is no clear evidence that groups who do not help are especially callous, are especially likely to blame the victim of a crime, or lack empathy for the victim.

16.   Isaac and Tina are making supper and run out of flour. Who is most likely to ask the neighbor for help?

    b.   Tina is most likely to do so. Research has shown that women are more likely than men to ask for help especially in case of simple requests. There is no clear evidence that the gender of the helper effects this basic finding.

17.   Tasha has received threatening help in the past. How does this experience affect her desire to seek help?

    d.   Whether she seeks help depends on her perceived control of the situation. Research shows that people who receive threatening help will seek help only if they think they have little control of the situation. Therefore, they are likely to seek help in some situations but not in others.

18.   Molly thinks she's a first-rate parent. A friend points out that Molly should teach her children self-control by setting standards for them. Molly is likely to see this advice as

    b.   self-threatening help. Self-threatening help is help that challenges an important aspect of one's self-concept. For Molly, being a good parent seems to be an important part of her self-concept, and her friend's advice seems to be challenging her belief that she is a first-rate parent; so the help her friend is giving is likely to be perceived as self-threatening. For the same reason, it is unlikely that Molly will see the help as supportive. In addition, there is no evidence that the help is based on empathic concern or negative state relief.

19. The social norm that motivates us out of a sense of duty and obligation to help those who are dependent on us is the norm of

   c. social responsibility. The norm of social responsibility is a moral standard emphasizing that we should help those in need, thus motivating us to help out of a sense of duty or obligation. The norm of reciprocity is the sense that we should help others who have helped us, and the norm of equity prescribes that those who have the most should help those who have the least. These two norms have less to do with helping people out of a sense of duty because they are dependent. Finally all of these norms describe different notions of justice, but there is no specific norm of justice.

20. Feeling a sense of connection to other people should

   a. increase helping. Feelings of interdependence and connection with other people usually lead to greater helping of those people. At present, there is no indication that feelings of connection to other people lead to decreased helping.

Answers to Essay Questions: Sample Essays

1. Describe how a person's mood can affect the likelihood that he or she will help others. Analyze the effect of both positive and negative moods.

   Both a good mood and a bad mood can increase the likelihood that people will help others. When people are in a good mood, positive thoughts are primed, thus leading to helping behavior. Alternatively, people may help others when they are in a good mood because they want to stay in a good mood. Adults in a bad mood are also more likely to help others, partly in order to dispel their bad mood. Children are less likely to help when they are in a bad mood; only at a later developmental stage will helping others lead to a more positive mood. However, negative moods don't always lead to more helping among adults. Negative moods are less likely to promote helping if one blames an individual for his or her bad mood. Also, negative moods are less likely to increase helping if they cause one to become very self-focused.

2. Discuss three ways in which the presence of others can affect the likelihood that people will help someone in need.

   When a group of people that do not know each other are faced with an emergency, each individual in the group is less likely to help than if they faced the emergency alone. The presence of others can lead to a decrease in helping in three ways. First, when other people are around, everyone is likely to be distracted and thus less likely to notice the emergency. Second, when other people are around, the ambiguous actions of others are often taken as cues that the situation may not be an emergency. Each person may believe that he or she is the only one who thinks it is an emergency, even though everyone thinks it is an emergency – a state called pluralistic ignorance. This state can make it difficult for people to interpret the situation as an emergency. Third, when people are around, individuals are less likely to take responsibility for helping in an emergency – a phenomenon called diffusion of responsibility. In this situation, everyone seems to say, "Someone else will do it."

3.   Explain why help from others may sometimes be perceived as threatening.

Although help is usually thought of as a positive thing to receive from others, at times it can be seen as threatening. For example, when people receive help in domains in which they feel competent, or in domains important to them, then the help may be perceived as self-threatening. This sort of help can seem to be an insult or a challenge to the competence of the person receiving help. Self-threatening help has been shown to lower self-esteem, especially if it is given by a similar other. Also, when the help seems to be assumptive help – help that the recipient neither asked for nor provided any evidence of needing – the recipient might feel threatened, especially if the recipient has reason to believe that the person offering help has prejudged him or her as inferior or needy based on a stereotype.

11

Aggression

LEARNING OBJECTIVES: GUIDELINES FOR STUDY

You should be able to do each of the following by the conclusion of Chapter 11.

1. Define aggression, anger, hostility, and violence. Distinguish between instrumental aggression and emotional aggression. (*pp. 391-393*)

2. Identify differences in aggression that exist across cultures and across societies within those cultures. Explain the accounts that are given for these differences. (*pp. 393-396*)

3. Explain the differences in aggression between men and women. In doing so, make reference to the different types of aggression (overt and relational) in which men and women engage. (*pp. 396-398*)

4. Explain instinct theories of aggression and the evolutionary account. Describe the role of genetics in aggression, as well as that of hormones and neurotransmitters. (*pp. 398-402*)

5. Define positive reinforcement and negative reinforcement. Describe the conditions under which punishment should be most effective. Explain whether corporal punishment is effective. (*pp. 402-403*)

6. Summarize the social learning theory of aggression. Discuss the influence of socialization on gender differences and on cultural variation in aggression. Define the "culture of honor." Comment on the current state of the "nature versus nurture" debate as it relates to aggression. (*pp. 403-407*)

7. Explain the frustration-aggression hypothesis in terms of the concepts of displacement and catharsis. Identify problems with this hypothesis. Summarize Berkowitz's reformulation of the hypothesis. (*pp. 407-409*)

8. Explain the effects of negative and positive affect on aggression. Describe the effects of temperature on aggression. Describe the negative affect escape model. Explain the process of excitation transfer, and discuss its implications for aggression. Summarize the arousal-affect model, and discuss how it integrates findings linking affect to aggression and the predictions it makes about what combinations of arousal and affect facilitate aggression. (*pp. 409-412*)

9. Describe Berkowitz's cognitive-neoassociation analysis, and discuss the weapons effect and other aggression-enhancing situational cues. Explain how higher-order cognitive processes can facilitate or inhibit aggression. Consider the roles of mitigating information and of alcohol in these processes. Define multisystematic therapy. (*pp. 413-415*)

10. Summarize the immediate as well as long-term effects on aggression of exposure to nonsexual violence in the media. Explain the concepts of habituation and cultivation, and the effects of prosocial television. (*pp. 416-421*)

11. Define pornography, and distinguish between violent and nonviolent pornography. Explain the conditions under which brief exposure to nonviolent pornography should increase or decrease aggression. Describe the effects of reducing constraints against male-to-female aggression after exposure to nonviolent pornography, and discuss the impact of dehumanizing pornography. (*pp. 421-422*)

12. Summarize the findings concerning the effects of exposure to violent pornography on male-to-male and male-to-female aggression. Explain why exposure to violent pornography can have such strong effects on aggression. Describe the effects of such exposure on men's attitudes toward women, and discuss the implications of these attitudes for sexual aggression. Also, describe the kinds of information or education that might reduce these effects. (*pp. 422-424*)

13. Discuss the prevalence and consequences of violence among intimates, such as sexual aggression among college students, physical aggression between partners, and child abuse. Discuss how gender, alcohol, rape myth attitudes, and orientations toward sexual relations are associated with sexual aggression among college students. Discuss effective ways of reducing violence in the family, thereby breaking cycles of violence. (*pp. 424-429*)

MAJOR CONCEPTS: THE BIG PICTURE

Below are six basic issues or principles that organize Chapter 11. You should know these issues and principles well.

1. Pinning down what is meant exactly by "aggression" can be rather difficult. This chapter emphasizes the role of one's intention to harm another person in its definition of aggression. Other concepts defined and discussed include violence, anger, and hostility. Two types of aggression are distinguished – aggression that is a means to some other end, and aggression that is impulsive and not intended to achieve some other end.

2. There are a number of ways in which patterns of aggression are similar and different across cultures and gender. Rates of violent crimes vary widely across countries, and across different regions within a particular culture – as in subcultures within a society that emphasize the use of violence to protect or establish one's honor. There are also significant variations in rates of aggression as a function of age, economic class, and race. In virtually every culture ever studied, men are much more likely than women to commit, and to be victims of, violent crime. Males tend to be more physically aggressive than females, but this difference is weakened under a variety of conditions. For more indirect, relational forms of aggression, females are often more aggressive than males.

3. Various theories and research findings concerning the origins of aggression differ in their perspectives. These perspectives vary in terms of the degree to which they emphasize the "nature" or "nurture" origins of aggression. Perspectives emphasizing the former include those that regard aggression as an innate instinct, as a characteristic favored by natural selection and other processes of evolution, as produced by genetic heritability, and as influenced by biological factors such as hormones and neurotransmitters. Perspectives emphasizing the latter include social learning theory, which focuses on the influence of models of aggression. These perspectives are not necessarily mutually exclusive, and they can be seen together as illustrating the interaction between nature and nurture, or biological and social factors.

4. There are numerous situational influences on aggression. Among these influences are frustration, negative and positive affect, and arousal. Thought – both automatic and deliberate – can also play an important role in influencing aggression.

5. The media have many important effects on aggression. Depictions of nonsexual violence can increase aggressive behavior among adults and children, and it can lead to changes in people's sensitivity to and attitudes about violence. Exposure to pornographic materials can also influence aggressive behavior and attitudes. The nature of the relationship between exposure to such materials and aggressive behavior depends in part on the arousal elicited by the materials, whether the pornography is nonviolent or violent, and whether the people depicted in the pornography are portrayed as enjoying or suffering through their experience.

6. Violence is not limited to strangers or competing groups. A great deal of violence occurs within familiar contexts and intimate relationships, as is evident in research concerning sexual aggression among college students, physical aggression between spouses or partners, and child abuse.

KEY TERM EXERCISE: THE CONCEPTS YOU SHOULD KNOW

Below are all of the key terms that appear in **boldface** in Chapter 11. To help you better understand these concepts, rather than just memorize them, write a definition for each term in your own words. After doing so, look at the next section where you'll find a list of definitions from the textbook for each of the key terms presented in random order. For each of your definitions, find the corresponding textbook definition. Note how your definitions compare with those from the textbook.

Key Terms

1. displacement

2. instrumental aggression

3. pornography

4. cognitive neoassociation analysis

5. mitigating information

6. emotional aggression

7.   cultivation

8.   cycle of family violence

9.   aggression

10. catharsis

11. arousal-affect model

12. social learning theory

13. weapons effect

14. habituation

15. frustration-aggression hypothesis

16. hostile attribution bias

Textbook Definitions

a.   Behavior intended to injure another person who does not want to be injured.

b.   Inflicting harm in order to obtain something of value.

c.   Inflicting harm for its own sake.

d.   The proposition that behavior is learned through the observation of others as well as through the direct experience of rewards and punishments.

e.   The idea that (1) frustration always elicits the motive to aggress and (2) all aggression is caused by frustration.

f.   Aggressing against a substitute target because aggressive acts against the source of the frustration are inhibited by fear or lack of access.

g.   A reduction of the motive to aggress that is said to result from any imagined, observed, or actual act of aggression.

h.   The proposal that aggression is influenced by both the intensity of arousal and the type of emotion produced by a stimulus.

i.   The view that unpleasant experiences create negative affect, which in turn stimulates associations connected with anger and fear. Emotional and behavioral outcomes then depend, at least in part, on higher-order cognitive processing.

j.   The tendency of weapons to increase the likelihood of aggression by their mere presence.

k.   Information about a person's situation indicating that he or she should not be held personally responsible for aggressive actions.

l.   Adaptation to something familiar, so that both physiological and psychological responses are reduced.

m.   The process by which the mass media (particularly television) construct a version of social reality for the public.

n.   Explicit sexual material.

o.   The transmission of aggressive behavior across generations.

p.   Individuals who tend to perceive hostile intent in others.

ANSWERS FOR KEY TERM EXERCISE

Each of the key terms listed below is followed by the letter of the textbook definition that matches it.

1.	displacement	f	9.	aggression	a
2.	instrumental aggression	b	10.	catharsis	g
3.	pornography	n	11.	arousal-affect model	h
4.	cognitive neoassociation analysis	i	12.	social learning theory	d
5.	mitigating information	k	13.	weapons effect	j
6.	emotional aggression	c	14.	habituation	l
7.	cultivation	m	15.	frustration-aggression hypothesis	e
8.	cycle of family violence	o	16.	hostile attribution bias	p

PRACTICE QUIZ: TEST YOUR KNOWLEDGE OF THE CHAPTER

Multiple-Choice Questions

1. The region of the United States that typically has the highest rates of violence is the

    a. Northeast.
    b. South.
    c. Midwest.
    d. West.

2. The idea that arousal produced by one stimulus can increase a person's emotional reaction to another stimulus is called

    a. excitation transfer.
    b. incompatible responses.
    c. emotional aggression.
    d. displacement.

3. Research consistent with the cognitive neoassociation analysis has shown that even among people in a neutral mood, aggression can be provoked by

    a. mitigating information.
    b. music that reduces their arousal.
    c. catharsis.
    d. the presence of weapons.

4. Research on the effects of pornography on aggression has found that

    a. the effects of violent pornography tend to be strong only among men who fit the rapist's profile.
    b. catharsis is much stronger in response to violent pornography than in response to non-violent pornography.
    c. nonviolent pornography tends to increase aggression primarily when arousal is low.
    d. violent pornography tends to have greater immediate effects on male-to-female aggression than on male-to-male aggression.

5. In some samples of preschool children studied, children living with a stepparent or foster parent were much more likely to be fatally abused than were children living with both biological parents. This finding is most consistent with

   a. negative affect theory.
   b. a cycle of family violence.
   c. the concept of catharsis.
   d. evolutionary psychology.

6. Brad is more likely than his peers to interpret other people's motives as hostile and to think aggressive thoughts whenever he finds himself in a conflict. He also is more likely to lash out with emotional aggression in such situations. Brad's aggressive behavior is most clearly explained by

   a. Konrad Lorenz's theory of aggression.
   b. social learning theory.
   c. the cognitive neoassociation analysis.
   d. cultivation.

7. According to social learning theory, an effective way to strengthen existing restraints against aggression is to

   a. discourage displaced aggression.
   b. encourage catharsis through socially acceptable means of displacing aggression.
   c. punish acts of aggression quickly, consistently, and with obvious hostility.
   d. demonstrate nonaggressive responses to a provoking situation.

8. The idea that repeated exposure to violent crimes on the local and national television news leads individuals to become overly fearful, distrustful, and more likely to feel threatened is most consistent with the concept of

   a. cultivation.
   b. habituation.
   c. social learning.
   d. displacement.

9. John read a magazine containing several pictures of very attractive nude models. John found this to be a very pleasant but not particularly arousing experience. Immediately afterward, John was put in a situation in which he had the opportunity to aggress against another man who had acted toward John in a way that might be considered insulting. Compared to someone who had *not* just seen the pictures, the degree of John's retaliatory aggression against this individual would likely have been

   a. increased.
   b. reduced.
   c. increased, unless the material that John read elicited feelings of empathy.
   d. reduced if John had already had a great deal of experience with pornography, but increased if he had not.

10. When Carl thinks of any of the *Lethal Weapon* movies, he imagines violence and mayhem. His thoughts are so strong that he's ready to start a fight at the drop of a hat. For Carl, these movies are most clearly

    a. a source of frustration.
    b. an aggression-enhancing situational cue.
    c. a trigger for death instincts.
    d. an outlet for catharsis.

11. Jerry angered Tom, and now Tom has an opportunity to retaliate by aggressing against Jerry. Assume that Jerry could do each of the following just before Tom has the chance to aggress against him. Of these actions, which, according to the research, should be most successful in reducing the degree of aggression that Tom would use against Jerry in retaliation?

    a. Jerry tricks Tom into drinking a great deal of alcohol, and then tells Tom that he hadn't meant to anger Tom.
    b. Jerry shows Tom a series of violent cartoons in which both characters depicted in the cartoon are killed.
    c. Jerry shows Tom a picture of a kitten who has lost its mother, causing Tom to feel sympathy and empathy for the kitten.
    d. Jerry gives Tom a punching bag and has Tom punch it for a few minutes.

12. When a witness went to the police and told them that she saw Jim leaving the scene of the crime, Jim did not get very upset but instead hired someone to kill her before she could testify in court. Jim's actions illustrate

    a. emotional aggression.
    b. instrumental aggression.
    c. a cycle of family violence.
    d. excitation transfer.

13. According to research by Malamuth, men who fit the rapist's profile report more sexually coercive behavior in the past and more sexually aggressive intentions for the future than do men who do not fit this profile. Men who fit the rapist's profile are also more likely than other men to

    a. express attitudes toward women that are very positive, whereas their behaviors are more negative.
    b. be habituated to violent pornography, such that they are no longer aroused by exposure to it.
    c. be vulnerable to the weapons effect.
    d. have high levels of arousal in response to violent pornography.

14. Whenever people stop Lynda from getting what she wants, she verbally attacks them. But she attacks people only when they have stood in her way. Lynda's behavior is an example of the

    a. frustration-aggression hypothesis.
    b. arousal-affect model.
    c. cycle of family violence.
    d. negative affect theory.

15. On the hottest day of the summer, Spike, who is usually not very aggressive, is walking down the street. There is a lot of noise on the street, and the pollution is bad. When Tony sees Spike and comes over to ask him a question, Spike is verbally aggressive to Tony. Spike's aggression is most likely a reaction to

    a. death instincts.
    b. habituation.
    c. noxious stimuli.
    d. mitigating information.

16. After the home team loses the championship game, many fans of the home team run into the streets and vandalize the neighborhood while yelling, drinking, and fighting. This behavior is *least* likely to reflect

    a. emotional aggression.
    b. excitation transfer.
    c. instrumental aggression.
    d. the relationship between frustration and aggression.

17. Freud believed that aggression was the result of

    a. the life instinct deflecting the death instinct outward rather than inward.
    b. people's instinctual enjoyment of inflicting pain on others.
    c. the processes of sexual selection.
    d. imitating the behaviors of one's opposite-sex parent.

18. In a bar, Mick aggressed successfully against a man named Walt. A few minutes later, Mick encountered some other men in the bar whom he found to be annoying. According to social learning theory, Mick's motivation to aggress against these other men may have been relatively high because his previous act of aggressing against Walt was likely to

    a. reduce Mick's levels of arousal and negative affect.
    b. reinforce aggressive actions for Mick.
    c. strengthen Mick's positive affect.
    d. produce catharsis for Mick.

19. When Kentaro asked Florence if he could borrow her class notes for a day, Florence told Kentaro not to bother her and called him annoying. Kentaro was about to make an insulting retort, but did not when he remembered that Florence recently had heard bad news about a loved one back home. Kentaro's decision not to retaliate against Florence's insults best illustrates the

    a. negative affect theory.
    b. impact of appropriate rewards and punishments in social learning.
    c. effects of mitigating information.
    d. role of gender norms.

20. Which of the following would the social psychological research on aggression suggest is most likely to reduce aggression in society?

    a. Reducing the prevalence of displays of weapons
    b. Exposing people to movies in which the use of violence by "the bad guys" is met with even stronger, successful violence by "the good guys"
    c. Encouraging parents to respond to their children's aggression by punishing them quickly with spanking and other kinds of non-abusive but very strong physical punishments
    d. Teaching people to be true to themselves by responding directly to their emotional states

Essay Questions

1. How are men and women similar or different in terms of aggression?

2. Explain what is meant by the weapons effect. Describe an experiment, discussed in the main text, that illustrates the weapons effect.

3. A group on campus has asked you to provide a list of the factors that make brief exposure to nonviolent pornography more or less likely to lead to aggressive behavior. How would you summarize the research findings relevant to this question?

ANSWERS TO THE PRACTICE QUIZ

Multiple-Choice Questions: Correct Answers and Explanations

1. The region of the United States that typically has the highest rates of violence is the

   b. South. Over the years, the highest rates of recorded violence in the United States have been reported in the South, followed by the West. This is consistent with the idea that there exists a strong "culture of violence" among White men in the South, as well as in the West.

2. The idea that arousal produced by one stimulus can increase a person's emotional reaction to another stimulus is called

   a. excitation transfer. Excitation transfer occurs when arousal experienced in one setting carries over to another setting. This residual arousal can enhance aggressive responding. Incompatible responses are mutually exclusive (experiencing one precludes the other). The different responses described in this question are related, not incompatible. As emotional aggression and displacement concern behaviors, they are not relevant here.

3. Research consistent with the cognitive neoassociation analysis has shown that even among people in a neutral mood, aggression can be provoked by

   d. the presence of weapons. Seeing weapons can lead to automatic associations with aggression and violence, thus making aggressive responses more likely. Mitigating information, factors that reduce arousal, and catharsis all should reduce aggression, not provoke it.

4. Research on the effects of pornography on aggression has found that

   d. violent pornography tends to have greater immediate effects on male-to-female aggression than on male-to-male aggression. Male-to-male aggression is no greater after exposure to violent pornography than after exposure to highly arousing but nonviolent pornography; male-to-female aggression, however, is markedly increased. The effects of violent pornography are not limited to those men who fit the rapist's profile. There is no evidence that catharsis is stronger in response to violent pornography than in response to nonviolent pornography. Nonviolent pornography does not tend to increase aggression primarily when arousal is low; indeed, it tends to *decrease* aggression when arousal is low and the emotional response to the pornography is positive.

5. In some samples of preschool children studied, children living with a stepparent or foster parent were much more likely to be fatally abused than were children living with both biological parents. This finding is most consistent with

   d. evolutionary psychology. According to evolutionary psychology, behaviors can be interpreted as attempts to increase the odds of one's genes being passed on to future generations. Research on child abuse shows that parents are more likely to fatally abuse children if they do not share their genes. Although it is possible that stepparents or foster parents experience more negative affect or have more violence in their family background, there is no clear evidence that either would be the case; thus, there is no compelling reason to suspect a strong role of negative affect or of a cycle of family violence.

Catharsis is the reduction of the motive to aggress that is said to result from any imagined, observed, or actual act of aggression, but there is no reason to infer any role of catharsis in this research finding.

6. Brad is more likely than his peers to interpret other people's motives as hostile and to think aggressive thoughts whenever he finds himself in a conflict. He also is more likely to lash out with emotional aggression in such situations. Brad's aggressive behavior is most clearly explained by

    c. **the cognitive neoassociation analysis.** The cognitive neoassociation analysis proposes that unpleasant experiences create negative affect, which in turn stimulates associations connected with anger and fear. Emotional and behavioral outcomes then depend, at least in part, on higher-order cognitive processing. Brad's associations of aggressive thoughts in a number of situations and his tendency to see others as hostile are both likely to promote emotional aggression, according to this perspective. In contrast, Lorenz's theory is instinct-based and has little, if any, direct relevance here. Social learning theory proposes that behavior is learned through the observation of others as well as through the direct experience of rewards and punishments, but there is nothing in this question about such observations or experiences of rewards and punishments. Cultivation is the process by which the mass media construct a version of social reality for the viewing public, but there is no reference to this in the question.

7. According to social learning theory, an effective way to strengthen existing restraints against aggression is to

    d. **demonstrate nonaggressive responses to a provoking situation.** This method teaches a peaceful alternative. But there is nothing in social learning theory that suggests that discouraging displacement would be effective, and encouraging catharsis or modeling punishment should, according to this theory, both increase aggression.

8. The idea that repeated exposure to violent crimes on the local and national television news leads individuals to become overly fearful, distrustful, and more likely to feel threatened is most consistent with the concept of

    a. **cultivation.** Cultivation is the process by which the mass media (particularly television) construct a version of social reality for the viewing public. The version constructed by television news shows is very violent and threatening. Habituation would be evident to the extent that the individuals adapt to such exposure on the news and no longer become aroused by it. Social learning is not implicated because there is no evidence that the individuals learned acts of aggression. And displacement refers to aggressive acts directed at someone other than the source of provocation, so it is not relevant here.

9. John read a magazine containing several pictures of very attractive nude models. John found this to be a very pleasant but not particularly arousing experience. Immediately afterward, John was put in a situation in which he had the opportunity to aggress against another man who had acted toward John in a way that might be considered insulting. Compared to someone who had *not* just seen the pictures, the degree of John's retaliatory aggression against this individual would likely have been

    b. **reduced.** Experiences that produce pleasant affect and low levels of arousal tend to reduce aggression.

10. When Carl thinks of any of the *Lethal Weapon* movies, he imagines violence and mayhem. His thoughts are so strong that he's ready to start a fight at the drop of a hat. For Carl, these movies are most clearly

   b. **an aggression-enhancing situational cue.** Any object or external characteristic that is associated with successful aggression or with the negative affect of pain or unpleasantness can serve as an aggression-enhancing situational cue. For Carl, these movies have some of these associations and make him more likely to be aggressive.

11. Jerry angered Tom, and now Tom has an opportunity to retaliate by aggressing against Jerry. Assume that Jerry could do each of the following just before Tom has the chance to aggress against him. Of these actions, which, according to the research, should be most successful in reducing the degree of aggression that Tom would use against Jerry in retaliation?

   c. **Jerry shows Tom a picture of a kitten who has lost its mother, causing Tom to feel sympathy and empathy for the kitten.** By causing Tom to feel sympathy and empathy, Jerry has created a response in Tom that is incompatible with aggression; by this means, the aggression should be reduced. In contrast, exposure to alcohol or to violent cartoons tends to increase aggression, and giving Tom a punching bag could have any of a number of different effects.

12. When a witness went to the police and told them that she saw Jim leaving the scene of the crime, Jim did not get very upset but instead hired someone to kill her before she could testify in court. Jim's actions illustrate

   b. **instrumental aggression.** Instrumental aggression is inflicting harm in order to obtain something of value. Jim's action is intended to eliminate the witness in order to obtain his freedom. Because the aggression is a means to some end, rather than aggression for its own sake, Jim's actions do not reflect emotional aggression. No information is given about Jim's family background or levels of arousal, so there is no evidence suggesting a cycle of family violence or excitation transfer.

13. According to research by Malamuth, men who fit the rapist's profile report more sexually coercive behavior in the past and more sexually aggressive intentions for the future than do men who do not fit this profile. Men who fit the rapist's profile are also more likely than other men to

   d. **have high levels of arousal in response to violent pornography.** In addition to having relatively high levels of arousal in response to violent pornography, men who fit this profile express attitudes and opinions indicating acceptance of violence toward women. Finally, men who fit this profile are as vulnerable to the weapons effect – in which the mere presence of weapons increases the likelihood of aggression – as anyone else.

14. Whenever people stop Lynda from getting what she wants, she verbally attacks them. But she attacks people only when they have stood in her way. Lynda's behavior is an example of the

   a. **frustration-aggression hypothesis.** The frustration-aggression hypothesis proposes that frustration causes the drive to aggress, and that aggression is the result of frustration. Consistent with this hypothesis, whenever Lynda is frustrated she aggresses, and she aggresses only when frustrated.

15. On the hottest day of the summer, Spike, who is usually not very aggressive, is walking down the street. There is a lot of noise on the street, and the pollution is bad. When Tony sees Spike and comes over to ask him a question, Spike is verbally aggressive to Tony. Spike's aggression is most likely a reaction to

c. **noxious stimuli.** A noxious stimulus is an unpleasant event (such as heat, pollution, or noise). Exposure to noxious stimuli tends to increase people's likelihood of aggressing. The concept of the death instinct concerns the proposal that people have the unconscious desire to return to an original inanimate state; but it cannot explain why Spike would be more aggressive than usual in the situation described in this example. Habituation is the adaptation to something familiar so that psychological and physiological responses are reduced; Spike's reactions indicate that he had not habituated to the noxious stimuli around him. And mitigating information indicates that a person in a particular situation should not be held responsible for hostile actions; this is not relevant in this question.

16. After the home team loses the championship game, many fans of the home team run into the streets and vandalize the neighborhood while yelling, drinking, and fighting. This behavior is *least* likely to reflect

c. **instrumental aggression.** Instrumental aggression is inflicting harm in order to obtain something of value. The fans' behavior in this example is not intended to get them anything of value. Rather, their behavior can be seen as aggressive behavior for its own sake, which is consistent with emotional aggression. It is likely that the fans were aroused by the game, and that this arousal may have enhanced their negative feelings after their team lost, leading to an excitation transfer. In short, the fans were probably frustrated by the loss, and their frustration may have caused their desire to aggress.

17. Freud believed that aggression was the result of

a. **the life instinct deflecting the death instinct outward rather than inward.** Freud proposed the concept of the death instinct – a profound, unconscious desire to escape the tensions of living by becoming still, inanimate, dead. Freud believed that people's life instinct inhibits them from succumbing to their death instinct, and that aggression is the result of the life instinct's deflection of the death instinct so that, rather than harm oneself, an individual harms others. Freud did not propose that people have an instinct that causes them to enjoy inflicting pain on others. And neither the processes of sexual selection nor imitating opposite-sex parents would be relevant to Freud's perspective on aggression.

18. In a bar, Mick aggressed successfully against a man named Walt. A few minutes later, Mick encountered some other men in the bar whom he found to be annoying. According to social learning theory, Mick's motivation to aggress against these other men may have been relatively high because his previous act of aggressing against Walt was likely to

b. **reinforce aggressive actions for Mick.** Because Mick's aggression was successful, aggression was positively reinforced for him. Social learning theory does not propose that aggression reduces arousal, strengthens positive affect, or produces catharsis.

19. When Kentaro asked Florence if he could borrow her class notes for a day, Florence told Kentaro not to bother her and called him annoying. Kentaro was about to make an insulting retort, but did not when he remembered that Florence recently had heard bad news about a loved one back home. Kentaro's decision not to retaliate against Florence's insults best illustrates the

   c. **effects of mitigating information.** Mitigating information indicates that a person in a particular situation should not be held personally responsible for his or her hostile actions. Kentaro learned information suggesting that Florence should not be held responsible for her actions while she was worried about the loved one back home. There is no evidence that affect, rewards and punishments, or gender norms played a role in Kentaro's actions.

20. Which of the following would the social psychological research on aggression suggest is most likely to reduce aggression in society?

   a. **Reducing the prevalence of displays of weapons.** By this means, people's exposure to aggression-enhancing cues would be lessened, thereby reducing the likelihood that they would aggress. Exposing people to violent movies, even those in which the violence is met with stronger violence, is likely to increase, rather than decrease, real-world violence; the successful, justifiable violence used by "the good guys" is likely to reinforce the use of violence as a way to solve problems and succeed. Research suggests that parents who punish their children may serve as models of aggression, and that the children are likely to imitate such models eventually. Finally, responding directly to one's emotional states is likely to cause more, rather than less, aggression; for example, people so responding would be less likely to take into account mitigating information or to be sensitive to norms against aggression.

Answers to Essay Questions: Sample Essays

1. How are men and women similar or different in terms of aggression?

   In virtually all cultures studied in virtually any time period, men are more violent than women. Men, for example, are much more likely to commit, and be the victims of, murder. Males in general (both young boys and adult men) are more likely to engage in overt, physical acts of aggression than females (both young girls and adult women). Even in the toddler years, gender differences can be seen – two-year-old boys are more likely to be interested in violent, scary books than are two-year-old girls. But the gender differences in aggression become less clear when considering measures of non-physical aggression. Although they are less physically aggressive than boys, girls are often more indirectly, or relationally, aggressive than boys, especially from around age eleven until they become young adults. An example of indirect or relational aggression is spreading mean-spirited, false stories about someone in order to get others to dislike this person. In addition, even concerning overt aggression, the gender difference may be more complicated than had been realized previously. When the aggression can be hidden – from others or from themselves – the tendency for males to be more overtly aggressive than females may be reduced or even eliminated. For example, in one study, male participants behaved more aggressively than female participants under ordinary conditions. However, when experimental conditions made participants feel anonymous and deindividuated, female participants were just as aggressive as the males.

2.   Explain what is meant by the weapons effect. Describe an experiment, discussed in the main text, that illustrates the weapons effect.

The weapons effect refers to the tendency for the presence of guns and other weapons associated with aggression to increase aggression. The presence of a gun can serve as an aggression-enhancing situational cue for an angered individual, making the individual more likely to resort to aggression or to engage in greater degrees of aggression. As Berkowitz said, "The finger pulls the trigger, but the trigger may also be pulling the finger." An experiment that illustrates the weapons effect was conducted by Berkowitz and LePage (1967). In this study, male participants were provoked by a confederate, and subsequently were given the opportunity to deliver shocks to the confederate. The participants delivered more shocks to the confederate if a revolver and rifle were present in the room with them than if badminton racquets and shuttlecocks were present. The weapons – the revolver and the rifle – apparently served as aggression-enhancing cues.

3.   A group on campus has asked you to indicate the factors that make brief exposure to nonviolent pornography more or less likely to lead to aggressive behavior. How would you summarize the research findings relevant to this question?

To the extent that the nonviolent pornography elicits a pleasant emotional response and low levels of arousal, aggression should not increase and retaliatory aggression may even be reduced. To the extent that it elicits a negative emotional response and/or high levels of arousal, however, aggression may increase. Male-to-female aggression is particularly likely to increase after exposure to arousing nonviolent pornography if restraints against male-to-female aggression are reduced, as when men are given repeated opportunities to retaliate against a woman who has angered them. Research has found that men who viewed many pornographic images over an extended period of time (e.g., thirty-six pornographic films over six weeks) were more likely than other men to express negative attitudes toward women.

12

Law

LEARNING OBJECTIVES: GUIDELINES FOR STUDY

You should be able to do each of the following by the conclusion of Chapter 12.

1. Identify the three stages of jury selection. Explain the purpose of the voir dire and of peremptory challenges. (*pp. 437–438*)

2. Summarize the extent to which general demographic and personality factors predict how jurors will vote. Describe the process of scientific jury selection. Discuss the arguments made by proponents and opponents of scientific jury selection concerning the ethical issues raised by its use. (*pp. 438–439*)

3. Identify the attitudes that scientific jury selection has identified as predictive of verdicts in cases involving capital punishment. Describe the purpose of death qualification. Explain the controversy surrounding the use of death-qualified juries in determining verdicts. (*pp.439–443*)

4. Describe three approaches used by police to extract confessions from suspects. Differentiate false confessions that result from compliance from those that result from internalization. Identify the conditions under which people are most likely to internalize confessions to crimes they did not commit. Discuss the attributional dilemma that juries face, and the decisions that they make, when confessions obtained deceptively are admitted into evidence during a trial. (*pp. 443–445*)

5. Describe a polygraph, and identify the assumptions underlying its use. Indicate the problems endemic to the use of polygraphs. (*pp. 445–446*)

6. Summarize the acquisition, storage, and retrieval stages of eyewitness testimony. Describe how these stages are susceptible to errors caused by factors such as arousal, the weapon-focus effect, the cross-race identification bias, misinformation, the suggestibility of young children, and the difficulties encountered during line-ups. (*pp. 446–451*)

7. Explain why jurors often cannot distinguish credible from noncredible eyewitnesses. Summarize how experts may help jurors to become more competent judges of eyewitnesses. (*pp. 451–455*)

8. Summarize the general effects of pretrial publicity on perceptions of defendants. Give two reasons why pretrial publicity is potentially dangerous. List and explain three reasons why jurors are often unable or unwilling to follow a judge's plea to disregard inadmissible evidence. Explain why comprehension, timing, and jury nullification are important factors in explaining why judges' instructions often have little impact on jurors. (*pp. 455–459*)

9. List factors that influence the selection of a jury foreperson. Summarize the impact that the foreperson has on the jury. (*pp. 459-460*)

10. Define the three stages of the deliberation process. Discuss the relative importance of deliberations versus initial juror votes in terms of the final verdicts. Explain how the leniency bias produces one exception to this tendency. Describe the informational and normative influences that affect jury deliberation. (*pp. 460-461*)

11. Discuss the effects of jury size and the requirement of unanimity on jury deliberation. (*pp. 461-463*)

12. Explain how defendants are treated after being found guilty in a court of law. Define the sentencing disparity, and why it occurs. Summarize factors that may affect the defendant's experience in prison. Discuss lessons learned from the Stanford Prison Study. (*pp. 463-465*)

13. Differentiate between decision and process control. Identify the effects of process control on perceptions of justice. Contrast the adversarial and inquisitorial models of justice. (*pp. 465-467*)

MAJOR CONCEPTS: THE BIG PICTURE

Below are five basic issues or principles that organize Chapter 12. You should know these issues and principles well.

1. The selection of jurors is an often controversial process. Through the voir dire and peremptory challenges, potential jurors are excluded from serving on the jury. Lawyers often rely on intuition – including implicit personality theories and stereotypes – in trying to select jurors who they believe will be most favorable to their side. Lawyers sometimes hire consultants to help them conduct scientific jury selection. These consultants may determine correlations between demographics and attitudes relevant to a specific trial, and these correlations can be used to guide a lawyers' selection of jurors. Jurors with positive attitudes toward the death penalty are more likely to find a defendant guilty than jurors who are against the death penalty.

2. Once the jury is selected, evidence is presented in court. Underlying the courtroom drama are problems concerning the accuracy of the evidence, the biasing effects of factors extraneous to the evidence, and the ineffectiveness of judges' instructions. Confessions and eyewitness testimony have strong effects on verdicts, but judges and juries often do not reject coerced confessions and are often unable to distinguish credible from noncredible eyewitnesses. Pretrial publicity and inadmissible testimony that leaks into court – both of which juries are instructed to ignore – can bias the jury.

3. Jury deliberations pass through multiple stages. Informational and normative influences may pressure jurors toward conforming to the majority opinion. Despite the deliberation process, the initial majority opinion typically wins, although deliberation produces a bias toward leniency. Deliberation and verdicts are affected both by the size of the jury and whether or not verdicts must be unanimous.

4. Sentencing decisions are usually made by judges, and these are often controversial. A common complaint is that punishments are inconsistent from one judge to the next. A source of this sentencing disparity is that judges receive sentencing recommendations from people who have different views of the goals of sentencing. Once sentenced to prison, convicts – and

their guards – may find themselves becoming dehumanized by their institutional roles in this setting.

5.   Satisfaction with justice depends not only on winning and losing but on the procedures used to achieve the outcome. In general, people are more satisfied with the adversarial model of justice than with the inquisitorial model. More generally, any method that offers participants a voice in the proceedings is more likely to be seen as fair and just than is a method that does not offer this opportunity.

KEY TERM EXERCISE: THE CONCEPTS YOU SHOULD KNOW

Below are all of the key terms that appear in **boldface** in Chapter 12. To help you better understand these concepts, rather than just memorize them, write a definition for each term in your own words. After doing so, look at the next section where you'll find a list of definitions from the textbook for each of the key terms presented in random order. For each of your definitions, find the corresponding textbook definition. Note how your definitions compare with those from the textbook.

Key Terms

1.   weapon-focus effect

2.   inquisitorial model

3.   sentencing disparity

4.   peremptory challenge

5.   leniency bias

6.   scientific jury selection

7.   polygraph

8.   misinformation effect

9.   adversarial model

10.   voir dire

11.   death qualification

12.   jury nullification

13.   cross-race identification bias

Textbook Definitions

a.   The pretrial examination of prospective jurors by the judge or opposing lawyers to uncover signs of bias.
b.   A means by which lawyers can exclude a limited number of prospective jurors without the judge's approval.

c.   A method of selecting juries through surveys that yield correlations between demographics and trial-relevant attitudes.

d.   Inconsistency of sentences for the same offense from one judge to another.

e.   A jury-selection procedure used in capital cases that permits judges to exclude prospective jurors who say they would not vote for the death penalty.

f.   A mechanical instrument that records physiological arousal from multiple channels; it is often used as a lie-detector test.

g.   The tendency for the presence of a weapon to draw attention and impair a witness's ability to identify the culprit.

h.   The tendency for people to have difficulty identifying members of a race other than their own.

i.   The tendency for false postevent information to become integrated into people's memory of an event.

j.   The jury's power to disregard, or "nullify," the law when it conflicts with personal conceptions of justice.

k.   The tendency for jury deliberation to produce a tilt toward acquittal.

l.   A dispute-resolution system in which the prosecution and the defense present opposing sides of the story.

m.   A dispute-resolution system in which a neutral investigator gathers evidence from both sides and presents the findings in court.

ANSWERS FOR KEY TERM EXERCISE

Each of the key terms listed below is followed by the letter of the textbook definition that matches it.

1.	weapon-focus effect	**g**	8.	misinformation effect	**i**
2.	inquisitorial model	**m**	9.	adversarial model	**l**
3.	sentencing disparity	**d**	10.	voir dire	**a**
4.	peremptory challenge	**b**	11.	death qualification	**e**
5.	leniency bias	**k**	12.	jury nullification	**j**
6.	scientific jury selection	**c**	13.	cross-race identification	**h**
7.	polygraph	**f**			

PRACTICE QUIZ: TEST YOUR KNOWLEDGE OF THE CHAPTER

Multiple-Choice Questions

1.   Marie is accused of stealing money from the store where she works. Marie claims she did not steal. The director of security at the store hires a trained examiner to administer a polygraph on her. The examiner would determine that Marie is lying if

a.   Marie's level of arousal is higher than other people's when asked about stealing from the store.

b.   the measures of Marie's conscience indicate that she is trying to suppress some thoughts or memories.

c.   Marie's level of arousal is higher in response to questions about stealing from the store than it is in response to other arousing questions that are not about stealing from the store.

d.   the measures of Marie's eye movements indicate that Marie's eyes keep shifting and not focusing on her examiner.

2. The police arrest Fred for a crime. Earlier that night, during the time that the crime occurred, Fred had been drinking. The police tell him that people often do unusual things when they've been drinking, things they can't always remember doing. The police act very friendly toward Fred, and they advise him to plea-bargain for a lesser charge. This scenario exemplifies

    a. a type of polygraph test.
    b. the leniency bias.
    c. the kind of misleading questions that bias the acquisition process.
    d. tactics used to extract confessions.

3. Research on eyewitness testimony suggests that

    a. there is no reliable method to distinguish accurate from inaccurate eyewitness identifications.
    b. jurors underestimate eyewitness accuracy.
    c. eyewitness confidence does not reliably predict their accuracy.
    d. eyewitness testimony tends to have little persuasive impact on death-qualified juries but considerable persuasive impact on other juries.

4. Expert witnesses who testify in court on the subject of eyewitness evidence tend to

    a. lead jurors to scrutinize the evidence more carefully.
    b. lead jurors to rely on the eyewitness evidence more and on other factors less.
    c. be ignored by jurors.
    d. lead jurors to be biased in favor of the prosecution.

5. The voir dire is one stage of the

    a. jury selection process.
    b. jury deliberation process.
    c. inquisitorial model.
    d. jury nullification process.

6. Jury nullification is one reason why jurors might

    a. exhibit familiarity-induced biases.
    b. exhibit misinformation effects.
    c. disregard judges' instructions.
    d. favor sentencing disparity.

7. Orientation, open conflict, and reconciliation best describe the three stages in

    a. jury nullification.
    b. eyewitness memory.
    c. jury deliberation.
    d. peremptory challenges.

8. In court, a lawyer calls witnesses and introduces evidence suggesting that Anne is guilty of drunk driving. Anne's lawyer then cross-examines witnesses and discredits evidence to suggest that Anne is innocent. This process illustrates

    a. the adversarial model.
    b. the open-conflict stage of deliberations.
    c. peremptory challenges.
    d. the inquisitorial model.

9. Acquisition, storage, and retrieval are the three stages in

    a. the voir dire.
    b. the process by which police attempt to extract confessions from suspects.
    c. adversarial models of resolving disputes.
    d. eyewitness memory.

10. The defense attorney in a trial thought that jurors living in a particular neighborhood would be prejudiced against her client. During the jury selection process, the attorney noted that one of the prospective jurors was from that particular neighborhood. The attorney didn't think that the judge would agree with her that this prospective juror would be biased, but the attorney wanted to exclude this juror anyway. To exclude this person from serving on the jury, the attorney most probably would use

    a. jury nullification.
    b. the adversarial model.
    c. peremptory challenge.
    d. an appeal based on normative influence.

11. According to research, prospective jurors who favor the death penalty are

    a. highly suspicious of police.
    b. cynical about defense lawyers.
    c. tolerant of protecting the accused.
    d. likely to be excluded from verdict trials, but not from sentencing trials.

12. The fact that people divulge information that isn't allowed into trial records is one of the potential dangers of

    a. peremptory challenges.
    b. pretrial publicity.
    c. expert witnesses.
    d. the leniency bias.

13. Research on jury deliberation suggests that verdicts tend to be

   a. determined by whatever the majority of jurors initially believe even before the deliberation, although deliberation tends to produce a bias toward acquittal.
   b. mostly random, and therefore it is virtually impossible to make any generalizations about how most jurors reach their verdicts.
   c. determined largely by the initial opinion of the foreperson.
   d. influenced more by the judge's instructions than by the initial opinions of the jurors, although deliberation tends to produce a bias toward conviction.

14. Research on confessions has found that

   a. under some conditions, suspects will confess to a crime they did not commit, and they will believe their confessions.
   b. suspects may be coerced or tricked into confessing when they had not planned to, but they will confess only if they actually committed the crime.
   c. confessions have less effect on jurors if they see a videotape that focuses on the defendant confessing than if they learn about the confession through testimony.
   d. suspects may be coerced into confessing to a crime they did not commit, but they will not be led to believe that they may have actually committed the crime.

15. Wayne was waiting in line at the bank. Suddenly, he saw three people in the bank pull out guns, go to a few cashiers, demand and receive money, and run out the door. Research suggests that because Wayne saw the guns, he will

   a. be especially able to accurately identify the bank robbers.
   b. be less able to accurately identify the bank robbers.
   c. have very accurate acquisition but less accurate retrieval.
   d. be accurate in identifying the bank robbers if they are of a different race than his.

16. Jenny is a lawyer very familiar with social psychological research. Jenny asks an eyewitness to a car accident to "please estimate the speed of the green car when it contacted the red car." Based on this wording, one can infer that

   a. because she said "speed" rather than "miles per hour," Jenny is hoping to raise the witness's estimate of how fast the green car was going.
   b. because she said "car" rather than a specific make and model of car, Jenny is trying to make the eyewitness look less competent.
   c. because she said "please estimate," Jenny is trying to make the witness feel less pressure to be specific, which should cause the witness to exaggerate the speed of the car.
   d. because she used the word "contacted" rather than "collided" or "smashed," Jenny is trying to lower the witness's estimate of how fast the green car was going.

17. The following people all witnessed a crime. All other things being equal, which one is most likely to *falsely* identify a suspect as the criminal?

    a. A witness who sees five people in a line-up who resemble each other
    b. A witness who is told before observing a line-up that the real criminal might or might not be present
    c. A witness who is brought to a show-up in which the police bring the suspect in alone
    d. A witness who sees the mug shot of the suspect and then sees the suspect and four other people in a line-up

18. Critics of scientific jury selection oppose this process because they claim that it

    a. tends to result in hung juries.
    b. tips the scales of justice in favor of wealthy clients.
    c. biases jurors against the defendant.
    d. produces the leniency bias.

19. During police questioning, Gary confessed to a crime. All other things being equal, in which of the following cases are jurors in Gary's trial most likely to find Gary guilty?

    a. The jurors learn that the police had extracted the confession by threatening Gary with harm if he didn't confess.
    b. The jurors see a videotape that focuses on the coercive interrogation that the police used to extract the confession from Gary.
    c. The jurors learn that the police had extracted the confession by offering Gary favorable treatment.
    d. Gary's confession is ruled inadmissible in a pretrial hearing and it is not introduced in the trial.

20. While witnessing a crime, Rose was highly aroused, saw a weapon, and observed that the criminal was of a different race than hers. The defense lawyer argues that these are all factors that may make her testimony less reliable because each can affect

    a. acquisition.
    b. storage.
    c. retrieval.
    d. informational influence.

Essay Questions

1. Explain scientific jury selection. What are the arguments supporting and opposing the use of this technique?

2. Briefly describe the three stages of eyewitness memory. Describe a bias that might influence the third stage of an eyewitness memory.

3. What are two situational factors that affect which juror is selected as foreperson? Describe the impact that the foreperson typically has on the jury's deliberations.

ANSWERS TO THE PRACTICE QUIZ

Multiple-Choice Questions: Correct Answers and Explanations

1. Marie is accused of stealing money from the store where she works. Marie claims she did not steal. The director of security at the store hires a trained examiner to administer a polygraph on her. The examiner would determine that Marie is lying if

   c. **Marie's level of arousal is higher in response to questions about stealing from the store than it is in response to other arousing questions that are not about stealing from the store.** The polygraph is a mechanical instrument that records physiological arousal from multiple channels; it is often used as a lie-detector test. In theory, the polygraph should reveal that guilty suspects who deny that they are guilty show more arousal when asked crime-relevant questions than when asked other questions that are arousing but not relevant to the crime. The suspect's levels of arousal are not compared with other people's levels because people's baseline levels of arousal are likely to vary dramatically from one person to another. Rather, the suspect's levels of arousal in response to crime-relevant questions are compared to his or her own levels of arousal in response to questions that are arousing but not relevant to the crime. The polygraph is designed to measure levels of arousal; it cannot measure people's conscience to determine whether they are trying to suppress thoughts or memories, and it cannot measure eye movements.

2. The police arrest Fred for a crime. Earlier that night, during the time that the crime occurred, Fred had been drinking. The police tell him that people often do unusual things when they've been drinking, things they can't always remember doing. The police act very friendly toward Fred, and they advise him to plea-bargain for a lesser charge. This scenario exemplifies

   d. **the tactics used to extract confessions.** Police use a wide variety of tactics to get confessions from suspects. Minimizing the offense by offering excuses (i.e., by telling Fred that people do unusual things when drinking) and pretending to befriend the suspect and offer advice are among these tactics. A polygraph is a mechanical instrument that records physiological arousal from multiple channels; it is often used as a lie-detector test. In this example, no mechanical instruments or attempts to measure arousal or deception were used. The leniency bias is the tendency for jury deliberation to produce a tilt toward acquittal; but this is not relevant in this example. The acquisition process is the first stage of human memory, followed by storage and retrieval. Acquisition refers to one's perceptions at the time of the event to be remembered. In this example, the event had already happened, so acquisition is not an issue. In addition, there is no mention of the police asking misleading questions.

3.   Research on eyewitness testimony suggests that

c.   **eyewitness   confidence does not reliably predict their accuracy.** Surprisingly, a witness's confidence is not a good predictor of the accuracy of his or her testimony. Eyewitnesses can become more or less confident as a result of social factors that are unrelated to eyewitness accuracy. Research suggests that it *is* possible to distinguish between accurate and inaccurate eyewitness identifications by asking witnesses to describe how they came to their judgments; they are more likely to be accurate to the extent that they describe their judgments as quick, effortless, and automatic. Jurors tend to   overestimate, not underestimate, eyewitness accuracy. Eyewitness identifications tend to be persuasive and have a great deal of impact; there is no evidence to suggest that its impact is relatively small in death-qualified juries (juries in which prospective jurors who oppose the death penalty are excluded).

4.   Expert witnesses who testify in court on the subject of eyewitness evidence tend to

a.   **lead jurors to scrutinize the evidence more carefully.** The accuracy of eyewitness testimony tends to be overestimated, but the use of experts can prompt jurors to become more skeptical and cause them to scrutinize the evidence more carefully. Thus, these experts typically are *not* ignored. There is no evidence to suggest that expert witnesses lead jurors to rely on the eyewitness evidence more and on other factors less (indeed, the opposite should occur), or that they lead jurors to be biased in favor of the prosecution.

5.   The voir dire is one stage of the

a.   **jury selection process.** The voir dire is the pretrial examination of prospective jurors by the judge or opposing lawyers to uncover signs of bias. This is the third stage of the jury selection process. The first two stages involve identifying potential jurors and selecting a representative sample. The jury deliberation process is the decision-making process juries go through after the testimony has been presented in court. The inquisitorial model is a system of resolving disputes in which a neutral investigator gathers evidence from both sides and then presents the findings in court. Jury nullification refers to the jury's power to disregard, or "nullify," the law when it conflicts with the jurors' personal conceptions of justice.

6.   Jury nullification is one reason why jurors might

c.   **disregard judges' instructions.** Jury nullification refers to the jury's power to disregard, or "nullify," the law when it conflicts with the jurors' personal conceptions of justice. Because juries deliberate in private, they can choose to disregard their judge's instructions. Jury nullification does not explain familiarity-induced biases, misinformation effects, or sentence disparity. Familiarity-induced biases refer to the tendency for witnesses to be more likely to identify someone in a line-up if they had previously seen that person before, such as in a mugshot, but this tendency has nothing to do with juries.

Misinformation effects are also not relevant here; rather, they refer to the finding that eyewitness memory can be altered by exposure to postevent information. Finally, sentencing disparity refers to judges' assignment of different sentences to criminals who have committed similar offenses. As such, it is not a reaction on the part of jurors. Moreover, few jurors would favor such disparity.

7.   Orientation, open conflict, and reconciliation best describe the three stages in

    c.   jury deliberation. After the evidence is presented and the judge gives the jurors instructions and tells them to return with a verdict, the jury deliberates and tries to reach a verdict. The jury deliberation process typically moves through three stages. First, juries begin in a relaxed, orientation period during which they set an agenda, raise questions, and explore the facts. Second, as soon as differences of opinion are revealed, a period of open conflict develops during which jurors debate evidence and dispute interpretations. Third, the jury smooths over the conflicts and affirms its satisfaction with the outcome during the period of reconciliation. Jury nullification refers to the jury's power to disregard, or "nullify," the law when it conflicts with the jurors' personal conceptions of justice, but it does not necessarily proceed through any stages. Orientation, open conflict, and reconciliation are not relevant to eyewitness memory, which involves acquisition, storage, and retrieval. Peremptory challenges are the means by which lawyers can exclude a limited number of prospective jurors without having to state reasons or get the judge's approval, but these challenges do not progress through the stages of orientation, open conflict, and reconciliation.

8.   In court, a lawyer calls witnesses and introduces evidence suggesting that Anne is guilty of drunk driving. Anne's lawyer then cross-examines witnesses and discredits evidence to suggest that Anne is innocent. This process illustrates

    a.   the adversarial model. The adversarial model is a dispute-resolution system in which the prosecution and the defense present opposing sides of the same story; this model is illustrated in Anne's case. The open-conflict stage of deliberations is the second of three stages of jury deliberation, during which jurors debate evidence and dispute interpretations; but the example does not mention the role or behaviors of a jury. Peremptory challenges are the means by which lawyers can exclude a limited number of prospective jurors without having to state reasons or get the judge's approval; this example does not mention anything about the jury selection process. Finally, the inquisitorial model differs from the adversarial model in that it is a system of resolving disputes in which a neutral investigator gathers evidence from both sides and then presents the findings in court.

9.   Acquisition, storage, and retrieval are the three stages in

    d.   eyewitness memory. Eyewitness memory involves the perceptions of an event at the time of occurrence (acquisition), the placing in memory of those perceptions to avoid forgetting (storage), and the recall from memory of those perceptions (retrieval). These are not stages in the voir dire (the pretrial examination of prospective jurors by the judge or opposing lawyers to uncover signs of bias), police tactics to extract a confession (police may try to influence people's memories but acquisition, storage, and retrieval are not three stages in these police interrogations), or adversarial models of resolving disputes (in which the prosecution and the defense oppose each other, and both present one side of the story).

10. The defense attorney in a trial thought that jurors living in a particular neighborhood would be prejudiced against her client. During the jury selection process, the attorney noted that one of the prospective jurors was from that particular neighborhood. The attorney didn't think that the judge would agree with her that this prospective juror would be biased, but the attorney wanted to exclude this juror anyway. To exclude this person from serving on the jury, the attorney most probably would use

c. **peremptory challenge.** A peremptory challenge is a means by which lawyers can exclude a limited number of prospective jurors without the judge's approval; this is what the attorney could use to exclude the prospective juror she feared would be biased, without having to get the judge's approval. Jury nullification refers to the jury's power to disregard, or "nullify," the law when it conflicts with the jurors' personal conceptions of justice, but this is not relevant here. The adversarial model is not a technique used by an attorney to exclude certain people from serving on the jury, but rather is a dispute-resolution system in which the prosecution and the defense present opposing sides of the story. Normative influence produces conformity because a person fears the negative social consequences of appearing deviant, but this influence is not relevant in this question.

11. According to research, prospective jurors who favor the death penalty are

b. **cynical about defense lawyers.** Prospective jurors who favor the death penalty are more prosecution-minded on a host of issues. For example, they are more concerned about crime, more trustful of police, more cynical about defense lawyers, and less tolerant of procedures that protect the accused. They are not likely to be excluded from verdict trials; indeed, because of the death-qualification procedure, prospective jurors who *oppose* the death penalty are more likely to be excluded from verdict trials in cases that might result in the death penalty for the accused.

12. The fact that people divulge information that isn't allowed into trial records is one of the potential dangers of

b. **pretrial publicity.** Pretrial publicity often includes information (such as prior convictions of the defendant) that may not be admissible in court. Hence, to the extent that jurors are exposed to this publicity, it could jeopardize a fair trial. A peremptory challenge is a means by which lawyers can exclude a limited number of prospective jurors without the judge's approval, but there is no danger in this process that is related to the issue raised in the question. There is no reason to assume that expert witnesses are particularly likely to divulge information that isn't allowed into trial records, nor is the leniency bias (the tendency for jury deliberation to produce a tilt toward acquittal) relevant in this example.

13. Research on jury deliberation suggests that verdicts tend to be

a. **determined by whatever the majority of jurors initially believe even before the deliberation, although deliberation tends to produce a bias toward acquittal.** The initial majority opinion is the best predictor of eventual verdicts, although a bias toward leniency does often emerge from deliberation. These research findings suggest that verdicts are not simply random. Forepersons do not exert more than their fair share of influence on the verdict. Judge's instructions often are too complex, come too late, and may rely on details of laws that jurors disagree with – each of these problems contributes to the fact that judge's instructions often do not have that much impact; in addition, the second part of this answer – that deliberation produces a bias toward conviction – is the opposite of the real bias toward leniency.

14.   Research on confessions has found that

a.   **under some conditions, suspects will confess to a crime they did not commit, and they will believe their confessions.** Although rare, suspects may be led to believe that they committed a crime they had not committed under a particular set of conditions. Research has suggested that when people are uncertain about their own actions and are presented with false evidence that points strongly to their guilt, people may come to believe that they are guilty even if they are not guilty. The issue of false confessions is particularly important because confessions often have a very strong effect on verdicts. Showing the jury a videotape that focuses on the defendant confessing *increases* the effect of the confession on the jury's interpretations.

15.   Wayne is waiting in line at the bank. Suddenly, he saw three people in the bank pull out guns, go to a few cashiers, demand and receive money, and run out the door. Research suggests that because Wayne saw the guns, he will

b.   **be less able to accurately identify the bank robbers.** There is a tendency for weapons to draw witnesses' attention and impair their ability to identify the culprit – this phenomenon is known as the weapon-focus effect. When a criminal pulls out a weapon, witnesses are less able to identify the culprit than if no weapon were present. This is probably because the witnesses either are agitated by the sight of the weapon or tend to focus on the weapon and have their attention drawn away from the face(s) of the culprit(s). By interfering with their observation of the event as it occurred, the weapon-focus effect interferes with the acquisition stage of eyewitness memory, which refers to one's perceptions at the time of the event to be remembered. There is no evidence to suggest that observing a weapon makes one more accurate in identifying culprits if they were of a different race; indeed, because of the cross-race identification bias (which refers to the finding that people are better able to identify members of their own race than members of other races), the arousal and distraction caused by the presence of the weapon should probably make witnesses *less* accurate in identifying culprits of a race different from theirs.

16.   Jenny is a lawyer very familiar with social psychological research. Jenny asks an eyewitness to a car accident to "please estimate the speed of the green car when it contacted the red car." Based on this wording, one can infer that

d.   **because she used the word "contacted" rather than "collided" or "smashed," Jenny is trying to lower the witness's estimate of how fast the green car was going.** Research has shown that the wording of a question such as this can affect a witness's response, and may even influence the witness's memory for the event in question. For example, research has found that participants give lower estimates of the speed of a car involved in an accident that they had witnessed if the verb "contacted" is used in the question than if the verb "collided" or "smashed" is used. There is no research evidence to support any of the alternative answers for this example.

17. The following people all witnessed a crime. All other things being equal, which one is most likely to *falsely* identify a suspect as the criminal?

d. **A witness who sees the mug shot of the suspect and then sees the suspect and four other people in a line-up.** When witnesses view a line-up after having looked at mug shots, they are inclined to identify anyone whose photograph they have previously seen. This tendency, known as a familiarity-induced bias, can result in false identifications. The three alternative answers to this question all concern factors that *reduce* the chances of inducing a witness to falsely identify someone as the criminal.

18. Critics of scientific jury selection oppose this process because they claim that it

b. **tips the scales of justice in favor of wealthy clients.** Scientific jury selection is a method of selecting juries through surveys that yield correlations between demographics and trial-relevant attitudes. Because hiring experts to conduct scientific jury selection is expensive, this method favors wealthy clients who can afford the service. Clients without the resources to pay for these services cannot afford to use this selection procedure even though it might benefit them. Scientific jury selection is not typically criticized for the reasons stated in the alternative answers to this question. There is no evidence that scientific jury selection tends to result in hung juries, that it biases jurors against the defendant, or that it produces the leniency bias, which is the tendency for jury deliberation to produce a tilt toward acquittal.

19. During police questioning, Gary confessed to a crime. All other things being equal, in which of the following cases are jurors in Gary's trial most likely to find Gary guilty?

c. **The jurors learn that the police had extracted the confession by offering Gary favorable treatment.** Research suggests that when a defendant is said to have confessed in response to an offer of favorable treatment, jurors may not completely disregard the confession. They may recognize that the confession was involuntary, but they vote guilty anyway. In contrast, if jurors learn that the confession came in response to a threat of harm or punishment, they are much more likely to completely discount the confession and are thus less likely to vote guilty. Seeing a videotape that focuses on the coercive interrogation that the police used on the defendant to extract the confession makes jurors more likely to discount the confession as involuntary, making them less likely to vote guilty. If the defendant's confession is ruled inadmissible in a pretrial hearing and is not introduced in the trial, the confession should have absolutely no impact on the jurors (unless they were exposed to it in pretrial publicity – but this is not suggested in this example), and thus they should be less likely to vote guilty than if they learned of the confession.

20. While witnessing a crime, Rose was highly aroused, saw a weapon, and observed that the criminal was of a different race than hers. The defense lawyer argues that these are all factors that may make her testimony less reliable because each can affect

a. **acquisition.** Acquisition is the first stage of human memory, followed by the stages of storage and retrieval. Acquisition refers to one's perceptions at the time of the event to be remembered. During this stage, information about a crime is gathered. Arousal, the weapon-focus effect (which is the tendency for weapons to draw witness's attention and impair their ability to identify the culprit), and the cross-race identification bias (which refers to the finding that people are better able to identify members of their own race than members of other races) are all factors that can interfere with the acquisition stage. Because these factors have their effects as the witness observes the event, they are most relevant to acquisition rather than to the later stages of storage and retrieval. Informational influence is influence that produces conformity because a person believes others are correct in their judgment; this is relevant to the jury deliberation process, but not to the situation outlined in this example.

Answers to Essay Questions: Sample Essays

1.   Explain scientific jury selection. What are the arguments supporting and opposing the use of this technique?

Scientific jury selection is a method of selecting juries through surveys that yield correlations between demographics and trial-relevant attitudes. During the voir dire, lawyers ask prospective jurors about their backgrounds and then use peremptory challenges to exclude those whose profiles are associated with unfavorable attitudes. Proponents of scientific jury selection argue that picking juries according to survey results is simply a more refined version of what lawyers are permitted to do by intuition. They argue that as long as it is legal for lawyers to use peremptory challenges, there is nothing unethical about using a scientific technique to accomplish what other lawyers try to do using their own intuition, implicit theories, and stereotypes. However, because hiring experts to conduct scientific jury selection is expensive, critics of the use of this technique argue that it favors wealthy clients who can afford it. Clients without the resources to pay for this service are thus essentially discriminated against.

2.   Briefly describe the three stages of eyewitness memory. Describe a bias that might influence the third stage of an eyewitness's memory.

Eyewitness memory is divided into three stages. The first stage is the acquisition stage. Acquisition involves the perceptions of an event at the time of occurrence. The second stage is the storage stage. Storage involves the placing and keeping in memory of those perceptions to avoid forgetting. The third stage is the retrieval stage. Retrieval involves the recall from memory of those perceptions. One kind of bias that can create errors in the retrieval stage is a familiarity-induced bias. When witnesses view a line-up after having looked at mug shots, for example, they are more likely to identify someone in the line-up as the culprit of the crime they had witnessed if they saw this person's photograph among the mug shots than if they did not. When witnesses see someone in a line-up whose face looks familiar, they may confuse the familiarity resulting from exposure to the person's mug shot with that of having witnessed this person at the crime. Thus they are impaired in their ability to accurately retrieve the face of the culprit from memory.

3.   What are two situational factors that affect which juror is selected as foreperson? Describe the impact that the foreperson typically has on the jury's deliberations.

Several factors are related to the selection of a foreperson. People of higher occupational status or with prior experience on a jury are frequently chosen. Men are more likely to be chosen than women. More subtle, situational factors include who speaks first and where people sit. The person who speaks first as the jury is about to begin deliberations is often chosen as foreperson. If the seating arrangements are such that there are particularly salient seats, such as at the head of the table, the people who sit in these seats are more likely to be chosen than are those who sit at other, less salient seats. During the deliberation process, the foreperson calls for votes, acts as a liaison between the judge and jury, and, at the conclusion of the deliberations, announces the verdict in court. The foreperson spends more time than other jurors talking about procedural matters, but less time than the other jurors expressing opinions on the verdict. Forepersons do not exert a disproportionate amount of influence over the jury.

13
Business

LEARNING OBJECTIVES: GUIDELINES FOR STUDY

You should be able to do each of the following by the conclusion of Chapter 13.

1. Define industrial/organizational psychology. Explain the Hawthorne effect and its role in triggering interest in industrial/organizational psychology. (*pp. 471-473*)

2. Describe the traditional employment interview. Cite reasons for which traditional employment interviews can have positive and negative effects on the accuracy of personnel selection. Explain the role of expectations in job interviews. Discuss the effectiveness of alternatives to the traditional job interview, including the use of graphology, polygraphs, integrity tests, structured interviews, and assessment centers. (*pp. 473-478*)

3. Discuss the debate concerning affirmative action in hiring and promotion. Discuss the conditions under which affirmative action should be most and least likely to lead to negative reactions and consequences. (*pp. 478-480*)

4. Define performance appraisals. Differentiate objective from subjective criteria for these appraisals. Explain the potential problems associated with supervisors' evaluations of their subordinates, including the halo effect, the contrast effect, and the restriction of range problem. Describe the problems associated with self-evaluations. (*pp. 480-481*)

5. Explain how the timing of evaluations, the number of evaluators, and the use of training programs can each play a role in improving the accuracy of performance appraisals. Explain the purpose and the three principles of the due process model of performance appraisal. (*pp. 481-483*)

6. Compare and contrast views of leadership that emphasize a trait approach with those that emphasize interactions between the person and situation. Describe the "great person theory" of leadership. Explain Fielder's contingency model of leadership as well as Hollander's transactional model. Explain what is meant by the notion of transformational leaders, and summarize how they differ from transactional leaders. (*pp. 483-488*)

7. Explain what is meant by "glass ceilings" and "glass walls." Describe similarities and differences between women and men in terms of leadership, and discuss reactions to their leadership. Discuss some of the problems faced by racial and ethnic minorities in terms of their chances for advancement in the workplace. (*pp. 488-489*)

8. Summarize the economic factors that affect employee satisfaction. Explain Vroom's expectancy theory, and give examples of how it can be applied successfully. (*pp. 489-490*)

9. Distinguish between intrinsic and extrinsic motivation. Indicate the extent to which employees' perceptions of rewards (as informational or controlling) moderate the effects of these rewards on intrinsic motivation. Summarize equity theory and the effect of equity on worker motivation. Cite reasons for gender differences in equity expectations. (*pp. 490-493*)

10. Explain the role of stock movements in investor strategies. In particular, identify the role of attributions in investor behavior. (*pp. 493-496*)

11. Explain how investors can become entrapped by their initial commitments, and identify factors that can prevent such entrapment from happening. Define the sunk cost principle. (*pp. 496-498*)

MAJOR CONCEPTS: THE BIG PICTURE

Below are five basic issues or principles that organize Chapter 13. You should know these issues and principles well.

1. In business, behavior is influenced not only by economic factors but by social psychology as well. This is evident in all aspects of business, including one of the first steps in the development of a successful business or organization: personnel selection. Most employers use traditional employment interviews in their hiring decisions. Such interviews have mixed effects on these decisions; they reduce the effects of some biases but increase the effects of others. Standardized tests, structured interviews, and assessment centers have been developed as alternatives to the traditional employment interviews. Affirmative action in hiring and promotion can lead to either positive or negative reactions depending on the way it is structured and implemented.

2. The processes by which employees' performances are evaluated and the means by which these evaluations are communicated to the employees can have profound effects on organizations. Performance appraisals are often based on ratings of employees given by their supervisors. Although such ratings have their benefits, they are also vulnerable to several biases. Self-evaluations are sometimes used, but they tend to be self-serving and inflated and may be biased by power and gender differences. New and improved methods of appraisal have been, and continue to be, developed. These new approaches have been designed to improve not only the accuracy of performance appraisals but also their fairness.

3. The work experience in an organization often depends in large part on the quality of leadership in the organization. There are two general approaches to understanding the determinants of good leadership: the trait approach and interactional models. The trait approach to understanding good leadership emphasizes the role of personal traits that characterize people who are good leaders. Interactional models emphasize the interaction of personal and situational factors. Despite recent gains, women and minorities are still underrepresented in positions of leadership and face various obstacles, such as stereotypes and exclusion from social networks.

4. Both economic and social factors influence worker motivation. Various economic incentive programs are used to motivate by reward. The ways in which these rewards are perceived influence whether the rewards enhance or decrease workers' intrinsic motivation. Concerns about equity have significant effects on motivation and performance.

5. Social psychological factors such as social comparison, conformity, and attribution have important effects on economic decision making. For example, investors are influenced by the kinds of attributions they and others make for rising and falling stock prices, and these attributions can in turn affect the stock prices. Individuals and organizations often get psychologically entrapped by initial commitments, leading them to continue with failing courses of action.

KEY TERM EXERCISE: THE CONCEPTS YOU SHOULD KNOW

Below are all of the key terms that appear in **boldface** in Chapter 13. To help you better understand these concepts, rather than just memorize them, write a definition for each term in your own words. After doing so, look at the next section where you'll find a list of definitions from the textbook for each of the key terms presented in random order. For each of your definitions, find the corresponding textbook definition. Note how your definitions compare with those from the textbook.

Key Terms

1. performance appraisal

2. integrity test

3. contingency model of leadership

4. industrial/organizational (I/O) psychology

5. structured interview

6. Hawthorne effect

7. transformational leader

8. assessment center

9. transactional leader

10. escalation effect

11. expectancy theory

12. sunk cost principle

13. normative model of leadership

Textbook Definitions

a. The study of human behavior in business and other organizational settings.
b. The finding that workers who were observed increased their productivity regardless of what actual changes were made in the work setting.
c. Paper-and-pencil questionnaire designed to test a job applicant's honesty and character.
d. Interview in which each job applicant is asked a standard set of questions and evaluated on the same criteria.

e.   Structured setting in which job applicants are exhaustively tested and judged by multiple evaluators.

f.   The process of evaluating an employee's work within the organization.

g.   The theory that leadership effectiveness is determined both by the personal characteristics of leaders and by the control afforded by the situation.

h.   The theory that leadership effectiveness is determined by the amount of feedback and participation that leaders invite from workers.

i.   Leader who gains compliance and support from followers primarily through goal setting and the use of rewards.

j.   Leader who inspires followers to transcend their own needs in the interest of a common cause.

k.   The theory that workers become motivated when they believe that their efforts will produce valued outcomes.

l.   The tendency for investors to remain committed to a losing course of action.

m.   The economic rule of thumb that only future costs and benefits, not past commitments, should be considered in making a decision.

ANSWERS FOR KEY TERM EXERCISE

Each of the key terms listed below is followed by the letter of the textbook definition that matches it.

1.	performance appraisal	f	7.	transformational leader	j
2.	integrity test	c	8.	assessment center	e
3.	contingency model of leadership	g	9.	transactional leader	i
4.	industrial/organizational (I/O) psychology	a	10.	escalation effect	l
			11.	expectancy theory	k
5.	structured interview	d	12.	sunk cost principle	m
6.	Hawthorne effect	b	13.	normative model of leadership	h

PRACTICE QUIZ: TEST YOUR KNOWLEDGE OF THE CHAPTER

Multiple-Choice Questions

1.   The owner of a baseball team has lost more than $15 million of his own money trying to build a team that would win a championship. Not only has the team never won, but the players whose contracts he had purchased are now past their prime. The owner receives an offer from someone who is interested in buying the team at a reduced price. Rather than sell, the owner decides that since he already spent so much on the team, he will continue to put money into it until he can win a championship and justify his expenditures. This reasoning illustrates

a.   expectancy theory.
b.   a failure to apply the contingency model of leadership.
c.   the halo effect.
d.   a violation of the sunk cost principle.

2.   Most evaluations of employee performance are made using

    a.   subjective measures.
    b.   graphology analyses.
    c.   peer-rating processes.
    d.   objective criteria.

3.   Research suggests that when it comes to promoting sound, unbiased hiring, traditional live interviews have

    a.   positive effects.
    b.   negative effects.
    c.   mixed effects.
    d.   effects no different from those of other techniques.

4.   The idea that a leader is effective if he or she listens to followers and fulfills their needs in exchange for expected levels of job performance is most consistent with the

    a.   characterization of a transformational leader.
    b.   contingency model.
    c.   trait approach.
    d.   transactional model.

5.   A major problem with using employees' self-evaluations for performance appraisals is that

    a.   employees tend to overestimate their performance and worth in an organization.
    b.   self-evaluations are more affected by contrast effects than are supervisors' evaluations.
    c.   men tend to be more negative on self-evaluations compared to women.
    d.   people who lack power in the organization tend to be more positive on self-evaluations compared to people with significant power.

6.   A team of researchers varied the pay schedules of some of the employees in a company to see which schedule would lead to the greatest amount of productivity. If the results of this research were consistent with the Hawthorne effect, it would mean that the researchers found that the

    a.   workers who were paid most frequently had the highest levels of satisfaction but the lowest levels of productivity.
    b.   workers who were paid most frequently had the highest levels of productivity.
    c.   extra attention paid to these workers led to an increase in their productivity regardless of changes in their pay schedule.
    d.   extra attention paid to these workers angered them, leading to a drop in their productivity regardless of changes in their pay schedule.

7. An employer wants to hire salespeople who are extroverted rather than introverted. She has all candidates complete a questionnaire that has been designed by personality psychologists to measure a person's degree of extroversion, and she hires the candidates who score highest on this scale. This employer's method of personnel selection illustrates the use of

   a. standardized tests.
   b. integrity tests.
   c. an assessment center.
   d. performance appraisals.

8. As factory supervisor, Harry annually scrutinizes each employee's productivity rate and quality control record. He then gives each employee feedback on his or her job. Harry's behavior is an example of

   a. contingency leadership.
   b. high situational control.
   c. performance appraisal.
   d. an interactional model of leadership.

9. Which of the following statements is an accurate characterization of assessment centers?

   a. They are relatively ineffective.
   b. They involve groups of activities and evaluators.
   c. They provide employees a chance to give feedback to their supervisors.
   d. They are used primarily by transformational leaders.

10. Research suggests that in situations where new employees are told that they were hired for a job because of their sex,

    a. women, but not men, later devalue their own performance, even if they have received positive feedback about their performance.
    b. women later enhance their perceptions of their performance, trying to justify the fact that they were hired.
    c. employees who later receive negative feedback about their performance attribute that feedback to sexism, but employees who later receive positive feedback about their performance believe the feedback.
    d. the employees themselves are unaffected by the information concerning why they were hired, but other candidates who were not hired show great resentment.

11. Xavier is concerned about hiring workers who might steal from the company. Research suggests that Xavier would have the best chance of hiring only honest people if he makes all the job candidates

    a. submit to graphology techniques.
    b. submit to live, unstructured interviews.
    c. turn in self-evaluations.
    d. take integrity tests.

12.   Adequate notice, fair hearing, and a focus on evidence are all components of the

    a.   expectancy theory of worker motivation.
    b.   sunk cost principle of decision making.
    c.   contingency model of leadership.
    d.   due process model of performance appraisal.

13.   Patrick was elected leader of a group. He seemed identical to the other candidates for the leadership role except that he was the tallest. This outcome is most consistent with

    a.   the trait approach to leadership.
    b.   interactional models of leadership.
    c.   the inherently random processes involved in selections of leaders.
    d.   expectancy theory.

14.   Jerry and Dean have shared an office for several years. They do the same work, and Jerry feels that they are equally effective in the organization. One day their boss tells them that they will be getting their own offices. Jerry is initially glad but becomes very upset when he sees that Dean has been given an office that is bigger and in a more desirable location than his. Jerry's performance in his job worsens. This outcome is most consistent with

    a.   intrinsic motivation.
    b.   equity theory.
    c.   the sunk cost principle.
    d.   the Hawthorne effect.

15.   A particular business uses a structured setting for personnel selection in which several job applicants take part in a series of activities – including written tests, activities in which they play the role of workers in various situations, and so on – that are monitored by a group of evaluators. This is an example of

    a.   equity considerations.
    b.   an assessment center.
    c.   an affirmative action policy.
    d.   a structured interview.

16.   While screening candidates for a job, Erica uses a traditional employment interview for Isabella, graphology for Mitchell, a structured interview for Franco, and a polygraph for Ouida. Erica is most likely to be accurate in her assessment of

    a.   Isabella.
    b.   Mitchell.
    c.   Franco.
    d.   Ouida.

17. Tara is intelligent, self-assured, and task-oriented. Her boss, nevertheless, does not recommend Tara for the company's management training program because he thinks she's unsuited to be a manager. This outcome is most consistent with

    a. expectancy theory.
    b. the notion of the glass ceiling.
    c. the restriction of range problem.
    d. the problems of having a transactional leader.

18. Brooke is a department store manager. Her employees are part-time students. To increase sales, Brooke starts a program in which the ten workers with the highest summer sales earn a stipend for college tuition. After she starts this program, Brooke observes that sales increase by 25 percent. This outcome is most consistent with

    a. the contingency model of leadership.
    b. the escalation effect.
    c. expectancy theory.
    d. the halo effect.

19. Research suggests that employees' intrinsic motivation can be enhanced by

    a. the use of high salaries that are clearly better than the salaries of workers in other, related companies.
    b. the use of integrity tests.
    c. the use of performance bonuses that are perceived by workers as informative about the quality of their work.
    d. encouraging employees to focus on the range of economic benefits they are getting in addition to money, such as health insurance.

20. Stephanie instills a sense of purpose in her employees. Lydia is single-mindedly focused on the job. Wanda insists that all of the members of the organization have a say in all decisions. Beverly likes to "rally the troops" and ensure positive relations and energy. In a situation in which leaders have high situational control, the contingency model would predict that the most effective leader would be

    a. Stephanie.
    b. Lydia.
    c. Wanda.
    d. Beverly.

Essay Questions

1. Describe an alternative to the traditional interview that research suggests may be more effective.

2.   Discuss two factors that can boost the accuracy of performance evaluations.

3.   Describe what is meant by transformational leaders. Are such leaders more consistent with the trait approach or with interactional models? Why?

ANSWERS TO THE PRACTICE QUIZ

Multiple-Choice Questions: Correct Answers and Explanations

1.   The owner of a baseball team has lost more than $15 million of his own money trying to build a team that would win a championship. Not only has the team never won, but the players whose contracts he had purchased are now past their prime. The owner receives an offer from someone who is interested in buying the team at a reduced price. Rather than sell, the owner decides that since he already spent so much on the team he will continue to put money into it until he can win a championship and justify his expenditures. This reasoning illustrates

d.   **a violation of the sunk cost principle.** The sunk cost principle is a principle of economics stating that only future benefits and costs, not past commitments, should be considered in making a decision. In this example, the owner of the baseball team is considering his past commitments as he makes his decision, and he decides not to sell the team even though the future costs of owning the team look like they will be higher than the benefits. He is thus in violation of the principle. Expectancy theory proposes that people analyze the benefits and costs of possible courses of action and exert effort when they believe it will produce a desired outcome (monetary or symbolic), but this example is not concerned with the amount of effort that the owner exerts or that he expects his employees to exert. The contingency model of leadership proposes that leadership effectiveness is determined both by the personal characteristics of leaders and by the control afforded by the situation; but this example is not about leadership, and it does not indicate the personal characteristics of the owner or the control afforded by the situation. Finally, the halo effect is a failure to discriminate among distinct aspects of a worker's performance; but it is not relevant in this example.

2.   Most evaluations of employee performance are made using

a.   **subjective measures.** Objective, quantifiable criteria of workers' performances are often unavailable and frequently do not take into account the quality, as opposed to the quantity, of work. Therefore, performance appraisals are usually based on subjective measures – perceptions of employees by their supervisors, coworkers, customers, and so on.

Graphology analyses, which are handwriting analyses used to predict job-relevant traits such as honesty, sales ability, and leadership potential, are rarely used to evaluate worker performance. And peer-evaluations, which are indeed subjective, are not nearly as commonly used as supervisor ratings of subordinates, which are the most common form of subjective evaluations.

3. Research suggests that when it comes to promoting sound, unbiased hiring, traditional live interviews have

    c. **mixed effects.** Research suggests that, on the positive side, live interviews may actually diminish the tendency to make stereotyped judgments. On the negative side, they often lack predictive validity and can be distorted by employers' preconceptions. Such distortions may be less likely to emerge when interviewers use structured questions or when assessment centers rather than traditional interviews are used.

4. The idea that a leader is effective if he or she listens to followers and fulfills their needs in exchange for expected levels of job performance is most consistent with the

    d. **transactional model.** According to the transactional model of leadership, leadership is a two-way street in which there is a mutual influence between a leader and follower. An effective leader sets clear goals for the followers, provides tangible rewards, listens to followers, and fulfills their needs in exchange for an expected level of job performance. The other potential answers to this question all may be considered "top-down" approaches in which the followers are portrayed as passive creatures to be soothed or aroused at management's discretion. Transformational leaders inspire followers to transcend their own needs in the interest of a common cause. The contingency model is the theory that leadership effectiveness is determined both by the personal characteristics of leaders and by the control afforded by the situation; this model would predict that the kind of leader described in this example would be effective only in certain situations (probably those that afford the leader a moderate degree of situational control). The trait approach to understanding leadership is to identify traits that characterize leaders. The idea described in this question emphasizes that effective leadership is determined not only by the personal characteristics of the leader but by the interaction of the leader and the followers; thus, as would not be considered by the trait approach, the kinds of traits that might be found in a good leader in one situation might make for a poor leader in another situation.

5. A major problem with using employees' self-evaluations for performance appraisals is that

    a. **employees tend to overestimate their performance and worth in an organization.** People's tendency to overestimate their performance and worth is a principal reason why self-evaluations often are flawed. The three other potential answers to this question are all opposite to the truth. Contrast effects are more likely to affect supervisors' ratings than self-evaluations; for example, supervisors who first observe a very positive performance by one worker are more likely to judge an average subsequent performance by another worker as less positive, and supervisors who first observe a very negative performance by one worker are more likely to judge an average subsequent performance by another worker as more positive. Men tend to be more boastful on their self-evaluations than women, and people with relatively low power tend to make more modest self-evaluations than people high in power.

6. A team of researchers varied the pay schedules of some of the employees in a company to see which schedule would lead to the greatest amount of productivity. If the results of this research were consistent with the Hawthorne effect, it would mean that the researchers found that the

    c. **extra attention paid to these workers led to an increase in their productivity, regardless of changes in their pay schedule.** The Hawthorne effect refers to the finding that workers who were observed increased their productivity regardless of what actual changes were made in the work setting. This effect is consistent with the outcome illustrated in this selection but inconsistent with the three alternative answers provided.

7. An employer wants to hire salespeople who are extroverted rather than introverted. She has all candidates complete a questionnaire that has been designed by personality psychologists to measure a person's degree of extroversion, and she hires the candidates who score highest on this scale. This employer's method of personnel selection illustrates the use of

    a. **standardized tests.** Many companies today use standardized written tests in their personnel selection process. These tests may be designed to measure (1) various cognitive abilities such as intelligence, (2) personality traits such as extroversion, which was the focus in this question, or (3) a candidate's honesty and character. An integrity test is an example of the third kind of standardized test, but it is not what the employer in this question was trying to measure. An assessment center is a structured setting in which job applicants are exhaustively tested and judged by multiple evaluators, but this employer simply gave the candidates one test. Performance appraisals concern the evaluation of an employee's work within the organization; but this is not relevant here.

8. As factory supervisor, Harry annually scrutinizes each employee's productivity rate and quality control record. He then gives each employee feedback on his or her job. Harry's behavior is an example of

    c. **performance appraisal.** Performance appraisal is the process of evaluating an employee's work within the organization and communicating the results to that person; this is what Harry is described as doing in this example. The contingency model of leadership emphasizes that leadership effectiveness is determined both by the personal characteristics of leaders and by the control afforded by the situation. There is no evidence of such leadership in this example. According to the contingency model of leadership, leaders enjoy high situational control when they have good relations with their staff, a position of power, and a clearly structured task. Although Harry *may* be in such a situation, it is impossible to determine from this question. Interactional models of leadership emphasize the interaction between personal and situational factors. There is no mention of Harry's personal characteristics or of the situational factors in the factory.

9. Which of the following statements is an accurate characterization of assessment centers?

    b. **They involve groups of activities and evaluators.** In an assessment center, a group of applicants takes part in a set of activities (such as written tests and role-playing exercises) that are monitored by a group of evaluators. Assessment centers are said to be more effective than traditional interviews at finding applicants who will succeed in a particular position. They are not designed to provide employees a chance to give feedback to their supervisors. Transformational leaders are leaders who inspire followers to transcend their own needs in the interest of a common cause; there is no evidence that assessment centers are primarily used by these leaders.

10. Research suggests that in situations where new employees are told that they were hired for a job because of their sex,

   a. **women, but not men, later devalue their own performance, even if they have received positive feedback about their performance.** Madeline Heilman and her colleagues came to this conclusion based on a series of studies in which male and female college students were selected as leaders of two-person tasks. This research is consistent with the finding that female business managers who think they were hired through affirmative action are often unhappy with their work.

11. Xavier is concerned about hiring workers who might steal from the company. Research suggests that Xavier would have the best chance of hiring only honest people if he makes all the job candidates

   d. **take integrity tests.** Integrity tests are paper-and-pencil questionnaires designed to test a job applicant's honesty and character. Research has found that these tests are predictive of job performance and counterproductive behaviors such as theft. Using integrity tests would be an improvement over live, unstructured interviews which fail to identify people prone to dishonesty. Research also suggests that graphology, which is handwriting analysis used to predict job-relevant traits such as honesty, sales ability, and leadership potential, is not accurate. Self-evaluations are sometimes used in performance appraisals, but because people often present themselves quite favorably in these self-evaluations, it is unlikely that they could be used to exclude dishonest people.

12. Adequate notice, fair hearing, and a focus on evidence are all components of the

   d. **due process model of performance appraisal.** The due process model is designed to enhance fairness in performance appraisals. According to this model, fairness can be enhanced by such factors as adequate notice, fair hearing, and a focus on evidence of job performance. However, these factors are not components of expectancy theory of worker motivation, the sunk cost principle of decision making, or the contingency model of leadership. Expectancy theory proposes that people analyze the benefits and costs of possible courses of action and exert effort when they believe it will produce a desired outcome (monetary or symbolic). The sunk cost principle is a principle of economics stating that only future benefits and costs, not past commitments, should be considered in making a decision. The contingency model of leadership emphasizes that leadership effectiveness is determined both by the personal characteristics of leaders and by the control afforded by the situation.

13. Patrick was elected leader of a group. He seemed identical to the other candidates for the leadership role except that he was the tallest. This outcome is most consistent with

   a. **the trait approach to leadership.** The trait approach to understanding leadership emphasizes identification of traits that characterize leaders. One characteristic associated with leadership is height. For example, between the years 1900 and 1992, the tallest candidate for U.S. president won an astonishing twenty-one out of twenty-three elections. Research suggests that this finding is not a random coincidence. Interactional models of leadership, in contrast, emphasize the interaction between personal and situational factors. But this example makes no mention of situational factors. Expectancy theory maintains that people analyze the benefits and costs of possible courses of action and exert effort when they believe it will produce a desired outcome (monetary or symbolic). But the example does not concern worker motivation or performance.

14. Jerry and Dean have shared an office for several years. They do the same work, and Jerry feels that they are equally effective in the organization. One day their boss tells them that they will be getting their own offices. Jerry is initially glad but becomes very upset when he sees that Dean has been given an office that is bigger and in a more desirable location than his. Jerry's performance in his job worsens. This outcome is most consistent with

b. **equity theory.** According to equity theory, people want rewards to be equitable, such that the ratio between inputs and outcomes is the same for the self as for others. In this example, which resembles the situation faced by some of the subjects in Greenberg's study of employees in a large insurance firm, Jerry perceives the distribution of offices to be inequitable. Because Jerry believes that he works as hard and is as valuable as Dean, Jerry is not happy when Dean is rewarded more than he is. When people feel undercompensated for their work, as Jerry does, they become more likely to lower their job performance. People are intrinsically motivated when they engage in an activity for the sake of interest, challenge, or sheer enjoyment. If Jerry were very intrinsically motivated, he would not care about his compensation relative to Dean's and he would continue to work hard and perform well. The sunk cost principle is a principle of economics stating that only future benefits and costs, not past commitments, should be considered in making a decision; but this principle is not relevant in this example. The Hawthorne effect refers to the finding that workers who were observed increased their productivity, regardless of what actual changes were made in the work setting. In contrast to the Hawthorne effect, but consistent with equity theory, Jerry's productivity *decreased* after the change.

15. A particular business uses a structured setting for personnel selection in which several job applicants take part in a series of activities – including written tests, activities in which they play the role of workers in various situations, and so on – that are monitored by a group of evaluators. This is an example of

b. **an assessment center.** Assessment centers are used to evaluate candidates for hiring and promotion. In an assessment center, a group of applicants takes part in a series of activities that are monitored by a group of evaluators. Equity considerations concern the perception that the benefits one receives for working are fair. Although considerations of fairness are important for personnel selection as well, there is no direct evidence that such considerations were relevant in the business or setting described in this question. Affirmative action policies give preference in hiring, admissions, and promotion to women and underrepresented minority groups; there is no evidence that such policies are used in the setting described here. Finally, a structured interview is one in which each job applicant is asked a standard set of questions and evaluated on the same criteria. Although structured interviews may be included among the activities evaluated at an assessment center, they are not the only activity.

16. While screening candidates for a job, Erica uses a traditional employment interview for Isabella, graphology for Mitchell, a structured interview for Franco, and a polygraph for Ouida. Erica is most likely to be accurate in her assessment of

c. **Franco.** Structured interviews are interviews in which each job applicant is asked a standard set of questions and evaluated on the same criteria. This standardization prevents interviewers from unwittingly conducting biased interviews that merely confirm their preconceptions. Some research suggests that structured interviews are better than traditional interviews in the selection of qualified workers. Research also suggests that graphology, which is handwriting analysis used to predict job-relevant traits such as honesty, sales ability, and leadership potential, is inaccurate. The polygraph is a mechanical instrument that records physiological arousal from multiple channels; it is often used as a lie-detector test. However, there are ethical and legal problems associated with the use of the polygraph in personnel selection, such as suggesting that people are lying when they are not.

17. Tara is intelligent, self-assured, and task-oriented. Her boss, nevertheless, does not recommend Tara for the company's management training program because he thinks she's unsuited to be a manager. This outcome is most consistent with

    b. **the notion of the glass ceiling.** The glass ceiling refers to a barrier that women and minorities come up against – a barrier so subtle that it's transparent, yet so strong that it keeps them from reaching the top of the hierarchy. Despite the progress that women and minorities have made in entry-level and middle-level positions, they still seem to be blocked by this glass ceiling when seeking positions of leadership. This example is not relevant to expectancy theory, which is the theory that people analyze the benefits and costs of possible courses of action and exert effort when they believe it will produce a desired outcome (monetary or symbolic). The restriction of range problem refers to the failure of people to make adequate distinctions in evaluating workers (e.g., some people may give everyone positive evaluations). But there is no evidence that Tara's boss thinks everyone is unsuited for the job, so this example is not consistent with this problem. Tara's situation is also not the kind of problem that would more likely result from having a transactional leader. The transactional model of leadership emphasizes that an effective leader provides tangible rewards, listens to followers, and fulfills their needs in exchange for an expected level of job performance; but Tara's boss is *not* providing Tara with tangible rewards and is *not* fulfilling her needs, despite Tara's effective job performance.

18. Brooke is a department store manager. Her employees are part-time students. To increase sales, Brooke starts a program in which the ten workers with the highest summer sales earn a stipend for college tuition. After she starts this program, Brooke observes that sales increase by 25 percent. This outcome is most consistent with

    c. **expectancy theory.** Expectancy theory maintains that people analyze the benefits and costs of possible courses of action and exert effort when they believe it will produce a desired outcome (monetary or symbolic). In this example, the part-time students believe that exerting effort might produce a desired outcome, so they have exerted the effort. The contingency model of leadership is the theory that leadership effectiveness is determined both by the personal characteristics of leaders and by the control afforded by the situation, but there is no mention of Brooke's personal characteristics or of situational control. The escalation effect is the tendency for investors to remain committed to a losing course of action, but this is not relevant here. A halo effect is a failure to discriminate among distinct aspects of a worker's performance, but there is no evidence of such an effect here.

19. Research suggests that employees' intrinsic motivation can be enhanced by

    c. **the use of performance bonuses that are perceived by workers as informative about the quality of their work.** People are intrinsically motivated when they engage in an activity for the sake of interest, challenge, or sheer enjoyment. Rewards that have informational value by offering positive feedback about the quality of one's performance can enhance intrinsic motivation. Performance bonuses are an example of such rewards. In contrast to rewards perceived as serving an informational function, those perceived as serving a controlling function (e.g., salary or commission) usually are administered in order to get people to work at all. Such rewards are likely to undermine intrinsic motivation. High salaries and a focus on the range of economic benefits that the employees are getting are likely to be perceived as serving controlling functions; thus they should decrease intrinsic motivation and instead remind employees of their *extrinsic* motivation for doing their job. Integrity tests are paper-and-pencil questionnaires designed to test a job applicant's honesty and character; these do not enhance intrinsic motivation.

20. Stephanie instills a sense of purpose in her employees. Lydia is single-mindedly focused on the job. Wanda insists that all of the members of the organization have a say in all decisions. Beverly likes to "rally the troops" and ensure positive relations and energy. In a situation in which leaders have high situational control, the contingency model would predict that the most effective leader would be

b. Lydia. According to Fiedler's contingency model of leadership, task-oriented leaders (who are single-mindedly focused on the job, as Lydia is) are more effective than relations-oriented leaders (who are more concerned about the feelings of the employees, as Stephanie, Wanda, and Beverly seem to be) in situations in which leaders have high situational control (that is, when leaders have good relations with staff, a position of power, and a clearly structured task). This model also states that task-oriented leaders such as Lydia are more effective than relations-oriented leaders when the leader has low situational control. Relations-oriented leaders are said to perform better in situations that afford a moderate degree of control.

Answers to Essay Questions: Sample Essays

1. Describe an alternative to the traditional interview that research suggests may be more effective.

One approach to improving personnel selection involves the use of structured interviews. In such interviews, each job applicant is asked a standard set of questions and evaluated on the same criteria as those applied to every other job applicant. This standardization prevents interviewers from unwittingly conducting biased interviews that merely confirm their preconceptions. Some research suggests that structured interviews are more effective than traditional interviews in the selection of qualified workers.

2. Discuss two factors that can boost the accuracy of performance evaluations.

One factor concerns the timing of evaluations in relation to the observation of performance. Evaluations are less prone to error when they are made immediately after performance than after a delay. Once memory for the details of the performance begins to fade over time, evaluators are more likely to be affected by stereotypes, halo effects, and other biases. A second factor that can boost the accuracy of performance evaluations is the number of evaluators used. A system that utilizes multiple raters is better than a system that utilizes just one. Because the individual biases or tendencies of multiple raters largely cancel each other out, the average across raters tends to be more accurate than the ratings of any single evaluator. Assessment centers use multiple raters when evaluating candidates for hiring or promotion.

3.   Describe what is meant by transformational leaders. Are such leaders more consistent with the trait approach or with interactional models? Why?

Transformational leaders inspire followers to transcend their own needs in the interest of a common cause, articulate a vision for the future, and are able to mobilize others to share that vision. They are likely to be charismatic, inspirational, intellectually stimulating, and considerate of others. This characterization of good leaders is more consistent with the trait approach than with interactional models. The trait approach to the understanding of effective leadership identifies traits that characterize great leaders – and, indeed, transformational leaders are identified by the traits and characteristics they possess, such as charisma. Interactional models, in contrast, view leadership as an interaction between personal and situational factors. The idea of the transformational leader is not consistent with the interactional approach because this approach would expect similar leaders to rise to the top and lead and inspire others in any situation.

14

Health

LEARNING OBJECTIVES: GUIDELINES FOR STUDY

You should be able to do each of the following by the conclusion of Chapter 14.

1. Define health psychology and stress. Identify what causes stress. Describe and provide examples of the ways in which stress, caused by major crises, major life events, and microstressors of everyday life, affects physical health. Explain the differential effects of negative and positive life events. *(pp. 503-509)*

2. Describe the three stages of the general adaptation syndrome. Elucidate the conditions that encourage movement through all three stages. *(pp. 509-510)*

3. Outline why stress may lead to coronary heart disease, being sure to discuss the role of Type A behavior pattern. *(pp. 510-512)*

4. Explain how the experience of stressful events affects the immune system and the likelihood of experiencing short-term and chronic disease. *(pp. 512-516)*

5. Discuss the concept of learned helplessness. Identify the types of attributions people make for negative events, and the relationship of attributional style to physical and mental health. *(pp. 516-517)*

6. Define hardiness, and explain why it is an adaptive characteristic. Explain why a perception of control is the most important ingredient of hardiness, and how such perceptions are related to self-efficacy. *(pp. 517-518)*

7. Explain the benefits of optimism and positive thinking, and how they can be illustrated using studies of the placebo effect. *(pp. 518-520)*

8. Define the two principal types of coping. Describe problem-focused coping, and explain how an excessive need to control a situation can lead to increased stress. Discuss the relationship between procrastination and stress. *(pp. 520-522)*

9. Describe emotion-focused coping. Explain how distraction, anxiety-reduction techniques, suppression of unwanted thoughts, opening up to others, and a high level of self-awareness affect stress and coping. *(pp. 522-527)*

10. Define proactive coping. Explain the effect that self-complexity and social support have on the manner in which people cope with stress. Differentiate the three models of social support. *(pp. 527-530)*

11. Identify the social psychological components of a successful approach to treatment, and explain why they are effective. Outline factors that promote the adoption of risk-decreasing behaviors. *(pp. 530-535)*

12. Define the factors that affect the pursuit of happiness also known as subjective well-being. Describe when you are most likely to be happy and when you are least likely to be happy. *(pp. 535-537)*

11.   Identify the social psychological components of a successful approach to treatment, and explain why they are effective. Outline factors that promote the adoption of risk-decreasing behaviors. (*pp. 530-535*)

12.   Define the factors that affect the pursuit of happiness also know as subjective well-being. Describe when you are most likely to be happy and when are you least likely to be happy. (*pp. 535-537*)

MAJOR CONCEPTS: THE BIG PICTURE

Below are five basic issues or principles that organize Chapter 14. You should know these issues and principles well.

1.   Theorists have proposed that all change ends up being stressful, but negative events tend to be more stressful than positive events. Simple daily hassles can be an especially important source of stress in our lives, as can major crises like a catastrophe or a war.

2.   Stress can have strong negative effects on the body. Selye proposed a three-stage model called the general adaptation syndrome to describe how the body responds to stress. According to this model people have an initial alarm reaction to stress, followed by a resistance stage, which eventually leads to an exhaustion stage where the body breaks down. Stress, particularly when it is associated with the Type A behavior pattern, has been shown to have strong negative effects on the heart. Stress also affects the immune system by reducing the body's natural defense system. This probably is part of the reason that people under stress are more susceptible to a number of different illnesses.

3.   People may view the same stressful event quite differently. Some may view it as an indication of their incompetence and their general weaknesses, which they believe they cannot overcome. This sort of appraisal, characteristic of learned helplessness, is associated with depression. Others may view the same event as a challenge and as an opportunity for them to take charge of their lives. Such optimism and appraisals of agency are associated with positive health outcomes.

4.   When coping with a negative event, some people will focus on how to overcome the problem whereas others will focus on how to deal with their emotions. People can deal with their emotions by distracting themselves from them or by opening up and expressing them. They can also cope proactively before a stressful event occurs. Self-complexity and social support are two important resources that people can use when they confront stress.

5.   Social psychologists have also examined ways to promote health and have found that social ingredients in a medical intervention can be crucial to its effectiveness. Research on persuasion has also provided important lessons in how to encourage people to engage in behaviors that prevent illness.

KEY TERM EXERCISE: THE CONCEPTS YOU SHOULD KNOW

Following are all of the key terms that appear in **boldface** in Chapter 14. To help you better understand these concepts, rather than just memorize them, write a definition for each term in your own words. After doing so, look at the next section where you'll find a list of definitions from the textbook for each of the key terms presented in random order. For each of your definitions, find the corresponding textbook definition. Note how your definitions compare with those from the textbook.

Key Terms

1. health psychology

2. Type A behavior pattern

3. stress

4. general adaptation syndrome

5. immune system

6. posttraumatic stress disorder (PTSD)

7. self-complexity

8. emotion-focused coping

9. learned helplessness

10. depressive explanatory style

11. placebo effect

12. self-efficacy

13. proactive coping

14. psychoneuroimmunology (PNI)

15. coping

16. problem-focused coping

17. appraisal

18. stressor

19. social support

20. subjective well-being

Textbook Definitions

a. A phenomenon in which experience with an uncontrollable event creates passive behavior toward a subsequent threat to well-being.

b. A condition in which a person experiences enduring physical and psychological symptoms after an extremely stressful event.

c. Cognitive and behavioral efforts to alter a stressful situation.

d. A person's belief that he or she is capable of the specific behavior required to produce a desired outcome in a given situation.

e. The helpful coping resources provided by friends and other people.

f. Anything that causes stress.

g. Up-front efforts to ward off or modify the onset of a stressful event.

h. An unpleasant state of arousal in which people perceive the demands of an event as taxing or exceeding their ability to satisfy or alter those demands.

i. The study of physical health and illness by psychologists from various areas of specialization.

j. A habitual tendency to attribute negative events to causes that are stable, global, and internal.

k. A subfield of psychology that examines the links among psychological factors, brain and nervous system, and the immune system.

l. Efforts to reduce stress.

m. The number of distinct roles or identities people believe they have.

n. A biological surveillance system that detects and destroys "nonself" substances that invade the body.

o. The tendency for an ineffectual drug or treatment to improve a patient's condition because he or she believes in its effectiveness.

p. The process by which people make judgments about the demands of potentially stressful events and their ability to meet those demands.

q. A three-stage process (alarm, resistance, and exhaustion) by which the body responds to stress.

r. Cognitive and behavioral efforts to reduce the distress produced by a stressful situation.

s. A pattern of behavior characterized by extremes of competitive striving for achievement, a sense of time urgency, hostility, and aggression.

t. A term used by social psychologists to describe the pursuit of happiness.

ANSWERS FOR KEY TERM EXERCISE

Each of the key terms listed below is followed by the letter of the textbook definition that matches it.

1.	health psychology	i	11.	placebo effect	o
2.	Type A behavior pattern	s	12.	self-efficacy	d
3.	stress	h	13.	proactive coping	g
4.	general adaptation syndrome	q	14.	psychoneuroimmunology	k
5.	immune system	n	15.	coping	l
6.	posttraumatic stress disorder (PSTD)	b	16.	problem-focused coping	c
7.	self-complexity	m	17.	appraisal	p
8.	emotion-focused coping	r	18.	stressor	f
9.	learned helplessness	a	19.	social support	e
10.	depressive explanatory style	j	20.	subjective well-being	t

PRACTICE QUIZ: TEST YOUR KNOWLEDGE OF THE CHAPTER

Multiple-Choice Questions

1. Gretchen recently lost her job, became engaged to be married, started classes at a junior college, and moved into a new apartment. Which change in Gretchen's life is most likely to produce harmful stress?

    a. Losing her job
    b. Becoming engaged to be married
    c. Starting classes at a junior college
    d. Moving into her own apartment

2. Research suggests that the component of Type A behavior pattern that is most likely to lead to heart disease is

    a. time-consciousness.
    b. hostility.
    c. competitiveness.
    d. a hard-driving attitude.

3. Paul and Ann were recently married. They have since experienced financial crises and disagreements over childrearing. For Paul and Ann, their marriage illustrates the effects of

    a. a life change.
    b. microstressors.
    c. self-enhancement.
    d   learned helplessness.

4. Julio was living near Los Angeles when an earthquake occurred in the area. He is particularly likely to feel stress from the earthquake if he

    a. was distressed before the earthquake.
    b. exhibits a Type A behavior pattern.
    c. has never been in an earthquake before.
    d. is suffering from depression.

5. Stable-unstable, global-specific, and internal-external are all dimensions of attribution in the

    a. reformulated model of learned helplessness.
    b. number of helpers model.
    c. inhibition-confrontation theory.
    d. self-focus model.

6. Having multiple roles, like being a parent, having a high-powered career, and taking care of a parent, is likely to make one

    a. handle stressful situations better.
    b. handle stressful situations worse.
    c. more emotional in stressful situations.
    d. less emotional in stressful situations.

7.   Stress hormones such as adrenaline

    a.   "charge up" the immune system to fight off disease.
    b.   have little effect on the immune system.
    c.   suppress the immune system, thereby lowering the body's resistance to disease.
    d.   cause people to engage in dangerous behaviors that compromise the immune system.

8.   When people confront a trauma head-on and verbally express their experience with it, they are likely to

    a.   become more distressed by the trauma.
    b.   engage in avoidance strategies.
    c.   avoid social support.
    d.   experience emotional relief.

9.   Optimism about one's health outcomes is usually associated with

    a.   better health.
    b.   worse health.
    c.   neither better nor worse health.
    d.   better health for acute illnesses and worse health for chronic illnesses.

10.   Anna is facing a serious bout with cancer. She remains steadfastly optimistic in the face of her diagnosis. Her positive attitude is likely to

    a.   help cure her cancer.
    b.   have a small effect on her immune system.
    c.   make her less likely to follow her doctor's advice.
    d.   cause her cancer to progress more quickly.

11.   Allison's car broke down on the way to work. She checks to see whether there is a bus on this route and whether a coworker who lives nearby can give her a ride. Allison's actions illustrate

    a.   emotion-focused coping.
    b.   problem-focused coping.
    c.   self-focused depression.
    d.   negative affectivity.

12.   Allowing patients to decide on the type of treatment they receive for conditions like alcoholism and obesity is likely to

    a.   increase the effectiveness of the treatment.
    b.   decrease the effectiveness of the treatment.
    c.   neither increase nor decrease the effectiveness of the treatment.
    d.   increase the effectiveness of treatment for obesity, but decrease the effectiveness of treatment for alcoholism.

13. After being at home all week with his children, Charlie feels extremely stressed. To relax, he tries meditating for thirty minutes every night. Charlie's use of meditation illustrates

    a. social support.
    b. emotion-focused coping.
    c. social-clinical interfaces.
    d. negative affectivity.

14. Pete has taken up golf as a hobby. After weeks of practice, he is now confident that he can drive the ball off the tee and keep it in the fairway. Pete's belief is an example of

    a. self-efficacy.
    b. vulnerability factors.
    c. help-seeking.
    d. role enhancement.

15. When Trixy's husband died, her children asked her to live with them, so she returned to her hometown where three of her sisters and many of her friends live. Compared to the average person, Trixy is likely to

    a. cope more effectively with the death of her spouse.
    b. cope less effectively with the death of her spouse.
    c. cope more effectively with the death of her spouse, but less effectively with her family.
    d. cope less effectively with the death of her spouse, but more effectively with her family.

16. The finding that women are less likely to become depressed when they are involved with a spouse or boyfriend is consistent with the _____ model of social support.

    a. number of social contacts
    b. number of helpers
    c. intimacy
    d. perceived availability

17. Research on psychotherapy has shown that one factor that may lead to its effectiveness is

    a. the theoretical orientation of the therapist.
    b. the experience of the therapist.
    c. the amount of schooling the therapist has had.
    d. the hope and positive expectations offered by the therapy.

18. Efforts to fend off stressful situations before they occur are called

    a. emotion-focused coping.
    b. problem-focused coping.
    c. self-efficacy.
    d. proactive coping.

19. Frank decides to develop a program to encourage people to wear seat belts. He decides to show graphic scenes from accidents in which people have died because they were not wearing seat belts. This strategy is likely to be

    a. highly effective.
    b. completely ineffective.
    c. somewhat effective but also to fail in some respects.
    d. effective only for the right audience.

20. Sometimes people want to change their health behaviors but feel they cannot do so. In such cases persuasion should be used in an effort to

    a. arouse fear.
    b. receive advice from credible communicators.
    c. increase self-efficacy.
    d. stress the rewards of the health behavior.

21. A method that social psychologists use to measure subjective well-being of an individual is to

    a. use a questionnaire.
    b. use a lie detector.
    c. ask a friend.
    d. ask a parent.

Essay Questions

1. Explain how change can lead to stress in one's life. Give examples of minor and major events that can cause stress.

2. Compare and contrast problem-focused and emotion-focused coping.

3. Describe how a sense of control over one's life and one's medical treatment can promote health.

ANSWERS TO THE PRACTICE QUIZ

Multiple-Choice Questions: Correct Answers and Explanations

1. Gretchen recently lost her job, became engaged to be married, started classes at a junior college, and moved into a new apartment. Which change in Gretchen's life is most likely to produce harmful stress?

    a. Losing her job Although it was originally proposed that all life changes lead to stress, it is now generally believed that *negative* life changes produce harmful stress. For Gretchen, losing her job is the negative event that she faced that is most likely to produce harmful stress. Becoming engaged, starting classes, and moving into a new apartment are unlikely to produce harmful stress.

2. Research suggests that the component of Type A behavior pattern that is most likely to lead to heart disease is

    b. hostility. Research on Type A behavior pattern has shown that of the various components of this behavior pattern hostility seems to be the most closely linked to heart disease. Time-consciousness, competitiveness, and a hard-driving attitude are components of the Type A behavior pattern, but they have not shown the strong link to heart disease that hostility has.

3. Paul and Ann were recently married. They have since experienced financial crises and disagreements over childrearing. For Paul and Ann, their marriage illustrates the effects of

    b. microstressors. Paul and Ann seem to have many daily hassles or microstressors in their marriage. These somewhat minor daily stressors can accumulate and affect people's health. While Paul and Ann's marriage certainly was a life change for them, their current stressors (financial crises and childrearing) are not so likely to change; and in any case change in and of itself does not produce harmful stress. There is no evidence in this question that Paul and Ann's marriage illustrates the effect of self-enhancement or learned helplessness.

4. Julio was living near Los Angeles when an earthquake occurred in the area. He is particularly likely to feel stress from the earthquake if he

    a. was distressed before the earthquake. As reported in the main text, a study that examined stress levels both before and after an earthquake found that people who were distressed before the earthquake were among those most likely to suffer additional stress from the earthquake. This research emphasizes the effect of major stressors on people's lives. There is no evidence that people with Type A behavior pattern, people who have never experienced an earthquake, or people who are suffering from depression are more likely to feel stress from an earthquake.

5. Stable-unstable, global-specific, and internal-external are all dimensions of attribution in the

    a. reformulated model of learned helplessness. The reformulated model of learned helplessness proposes that people who make internal, stable, global attributions for negative events in their lives are likely to experience depression. When something goes wrong, these people seem to say, "It was my fault, I can't do anything to change it, and it wrecks my whole life." These dimensions of attribution are not included in the number of helpers model, the inhibition-confrontation theory, or the self-focus model.

6. Having multiple roles, like being a parent, having a high-powered career, and taking care of a parent, is likely to make one

    a. **handle stressful situations better.** Having multiple roles actually seems to buffer people from the negative impact of stress. Although people with multiple roles may experience more stress, they are also more adept at handling that stress. There is no evidence that having multiple roles affects the degree to which people are emotional in stressful situations.

7. Stress hormones such as adrenaline

    c. **suppress the immune system, thereby lowering the body's resistance to disease.** Research in psychoneuroimmunology demonstrates that adrenaline and other stress hormones weaken the immune system. They do not "charge it up" and they do have a negative effect. And there is no evidence that adrenaline leads to negative behaviors that weaken the immune system.

8. When people confront a trauma head-on and verbally express their experience with it, they are likely to

    d. **experience emotional relief.** The theory of inhibition and confrontation proposes that when people can put traumatic events into words, they are better able to make sense of them and cope with them. Further, this model proposes that inhibiting thinking about a trauma can lead to more stress. Together, these two points suggest that verbally expressing one's experience with a traumatic event should lead to relief. This model does not suggest that such expression leads to more distress, to the avoidance of social support, or to the use of avoidance strategies.

9. Optimism about one's health outcomes is usually associated with

    a. **better health.** In general, optimism that one's health is going to be good is associated with a positive health outcome. There is considerable debate about why optimism promotes health; its effects on the immune system are small, but optimism is consistently associated with good health. There is no clear evidence, however, that optimism has more of an effect on acute illnesses than on chronic illnesses.

10. Anna is facing a serious bout with cancer. She remains steadfastly optimistic in the face of her diagnosis. Her positive attitude is likely to

    b. **have a small effect on her immune system.** Optimism usually provides a small boost to the immune system, but this effect is unlikely to be the sole reason for the impact of optimism on health. Other ways in which optimism promotes health have yet to be discovered. There is no clear evidence that optimism helps cure cancer, makes people less likely to follow a doctor's advice, or makes people's cancer progress more quickly.

11. Allison's car broke down on the way to work. She checks to see whether there is a bus on this route and whether a coworker who lives nearby can give her a ride. Allison's actions illustrate

   b. **problem-focused coping.** Allison has taken several steps to remedy the problem that is causing her stress. If she is able to catch the bus or hitch a ride, her current situation will be remedied, which should lower her stress. Allison does not seem to be engaging in emotion-focused coping, self-focused depression, or negative affectivity.

12. Allowing patients to decide on the type of treatment they receive for conditions like alcoholism and obesity is likely to

   a. **increase the effectiveness of the treatment.** Generally, when alcoholics or obese people are given the opportunity to choose their own treatment, the treatment is more effective.

13. After being at home all week with his children, Charlie feels extremely stressed. To relax, he tries meditating for thirty minutes every night. Charlie's use of meditation illustrates

   b. **emotion-focused coping.** Charlie is using a strategy, meditation, that removes the harmful emotional effects of stress he is experiencing without eliminating the cause of the stress, staying home with the kids. This type of coping is called emotion-focused coping. Charlie does not seem to be seeking social support from others, and his actions bear little resemblance to social-clinical interfaces or negative affectivity.

14. Pete has taken up golf as a hobby. After weeks of practice, he is now confident that he can drive the ball off the tee and keep it in the fairway. Pete's belief is an example of

   a. **self-efficacy.** Pete's belief that he can hit a good drive is an example of self-efficacy, the belief that one is capable of doing what needs to be done in a specific situation. Vulnerability factors, help-seeking, and role enhancement are concepts that do not address the belief that one can succeed at such a task.

15. When Trixy's husband died, her children asked her to live with them, so she returned to her hometown where three of her sisters and many of her friends live. Compared to the average person, Trixy is likely to

   a. **cope more effectively with the death of her spouse.** Trixy's move to her hometown should provide her with lots of social support from her family and friends, support that should help her to cope more effectively with the death of her spouse. There is no reason to believe that her family will be a stressor with which Trixy will have to cope.

16. The finding that women are less likely to become depressed when they are involved with a spouse or boyfriend is consistent with the _____ model of social support.

   a. **number of social contacts** According to the number of social contacts model of social support, the more contact that people have with others, the more social support they will receive and the better their health outcomes will be. There is a considerable amount of evidence that supports this model. For example, women who are involved in a relationship and have regular contact with their spouse or boyfriend tend to have better health outcomes than women not involved in a relationship. The number of helpers model of social support proposes that it is not the number of social contacts that leads to better health outcomes, but rather the number of contacts with people who can help. The intimacy model of social support suggests that only those contacts with someone whom one can share his or her innermost thoughts are likely to lead to better health outcomes. Finally, the perceived availability model of social support suggests that only those contacts that one believes are available lead to positive health outcomes. These models maintain that only some relationships (i.e., better-quality relationships) lead to better health outcomes (e.g., less depression), and thus all of them are inconsistent with the basic finding that relationships tend to make women less depressed. Nevertheless, these other models represent useful developments in the concept of social support.

17.   Research on psychotherapy has shown that one factor that may lead to its effectiveness is

d.   **the hope and positive expectations offered by the therapy.** Research suggests that a therapist's theoretical orientation, experience, and amount of schooling all bear little relationship to how effective the psychotherapy is. One factor that may make psychotherapy effective, however, is the sense of hope and positive expectations offered by the therapy.

18.   Efforts to fend off stressful situations before they occur are called

d.   **proactive coping.** Proactive coping involves up-front efforts to ward off or modify the onset of stressful situations. Problem-focused coping is an effort to alter a stressful situation, whereas emotion-focused coping is an effort to reduce the distress caused by a stressful situation. Both of these are enacted after the situation occurs. Self-efficacy is the belief that one is capable of performing a specific behavior needed to produce a desired outcome, and is not a method for coping with stressful events.

19.   Frank decides to develop a program to encourage people to wear seat belts. He decides to show graphic scenes from accidents in which people have died because they were not wearing seat belts. This strategy is likely to be

c.   **somewhat effective but also to fail in some respects.** Frank's strategy of showing graphic scenes from accidents is likely to arouse fear and may very well persuade people that they should wear their seat belts. Prevention techniques are usually successful in developing such positive attitudes. However, in order for these positive attitudes to translate into positive action, several further steps need to be initiated. People need good models, supportive norms, and a sense of self-efficacy if their positive attitudes are to be translated into positive actions. Frank's strategy may help somewhat, but because it ignores these later steps it is not likely to be highly effective. Finally, there is no reason to believe that Frank's program will be especially effective with any particular audience.

20.   Sometimes people want to change their health behaviors but feel they cannot do so. In such cases persuasion should be used in an effort to

c.   **increase self-efficacy.** People may want to change their health behavior, have developed a positive attitude toward health outcomes, and have even developed an intention to engage in healthy behavior. However, they think that they cannot follow through on these behaviors. What these people need to develop is a sense of self-efficacy, a sense that they can carry out the positive health behaviors. Arousing their fear and using credible communicators might help to change their attitudes, and stressing the rewards of health behaviors may increase their intentions to engage in these behaviors; but the people described in the question already have positive attitudes and intentions to act, so these modes of persuasion are likely to be ineffective for them.

21. A method that social psychologists use to measure subjective well-being of an individual is to

    a. **use a questionnaire.** To study subjective well-being one must be able to measure it. How do researchers know if someone is happy? Simple: They ask. Better yet, they use questionnaires such as the *Satisfaction with Life Scale*, in which people respond to statements such as "If I could live my life over, I would change almost nothing."

Answers to Essay Questions: Sample Essays

1. Explain how change can lead to stress in one's life. Give examples of minor and major events that can cause stress.

Stress occurs when people perceive that the demands of a situation exceed their ability to meet those demands. Change in people's lives can place a number of demands on them. These demands may result from microstressors or hassles of everyday life, such as child-care duties, work pressure, traffic, inadequate living space, and many other small events that place demands on people's time and energy. Demands may also result from major crises such as divorce, the death of a spouse, or war. Under these conditions people face many new obstacles and tasks to which they are likely to be unaccustomed, thus becoming especially vulnerable to stress.

2. Compare and contrast problem-focused and emotion-focused coping.

When people face a stressful situation, they can cope with it either by trying to change the situation or by dealing with the emotions it gives rise to. Problem-focused coping is an attempt to change the situation that is provoking stress. The advantage of this coping strategy is that if it is effective, the person using it will no longer experience stress. Alternatively, emotion-focused coping is an attempt to relieve the negative emotions that accompany stress without changing the situation that is provoking the stress. The advantage of this strategy is that it may be used to cope with a number of different stressful situations.

3. Describe how a sense of control over one's life and one's medical treatment can promote health.

In general, when people have a sense of control over their lives, especially over the stressful situations they encounter, they experience better health outcomes. This may be true even when the sense of control over the situation and one's ability to handle the situation are illusions. Optimism seems to promote health. Similarly, when people are accurately informed about their medical treatment and choose their own course of treatment, they seem to recover from illnesses more quickly and are better able to end destructive behavior patterns.

Notes

Notes

Notes

Notes

Notes

Notes

Notes

Notes

Notes

Notes

Notes